Global Obligations for the Right to Food

Another World Is Necessary:
Human Rights, Environmental Justice, and Popular Democracy

Series Editors: Judith Blau, Kenneth Gould, and Alberto Moncada

A better world is necessary, but also possible. A point of departure is that neoliberalism is imperiling humans, their societies, and the environments upon which they depend. Yet there are powerful countervailing forces. They include human rights and environmental movements, as well as movements for fair trade, a world parliament, redistribution of land and resources, alternative energy sources, sustainability, and many others. Another development has been the proliferation of forms of popular democracy, including social forums, e-governance, direct democracy, and worker self-management.

Books in this series will go beyond critique to analyze and propose alternatives, particularly focusing on either human rights, environmental justice, collective goods, or popular democracy.

Global Obligations for the Right to Food
Edited by George Kent

Global Obligations for the Right to Food

Edited by
George Kent

ROWMAN & LITTLEFIELD PUBLISHERS, INC.
Lanham • Boulder • New York • Toronto • Plymouth, UK

ROWMAN & LITTLEFIELD PUBLISHERS, INC.

Published in the United States of America
by Rowman & Littlefield Publishers, Inc.
A wholly owned subsidary of The Rowman & Littlefield Publishing Group, Inc.
4501 Forbes Boulevard, Suite 200, Lanham, Maryland 20706
www.rowmanlittlefield.com

Estover Road
Plymouth PL6 7PY
United Kingdom

British Library Cataloguing in Publication Information Available

Library of Congress Cataloging-in-Publication Data:
Global obligation for the right to food / edited by George Kent.
    p. cm.
  Includes index.
  ISBN-13: 978-0-7425-6062-8 (cloth : alk. paper)
  ISBN-10: 0-7425-6062-7 (cloth : alk. paper)
  ISBN-13: 978-0-7425-6063-5 (pbk. : alk. paper)
  ISBN-10: 0-7425-6063-5 (pbk. : alk. paper)
  1. Food relief—International cooperation. 2. Hunger—Prevention—
International cooperation. 3. Social responsibility of business. 4. Food supply. I.
Kent, George.
  HV696.F6G59 2007
  363.8'526—dc22
                                             2007034957

Printed in the United States of America

♾™ The paper used in this publication meets the minimum requirements of
American National Standard for Information Sciences—Permanence of Paper
for Printed Library Materials, ANSI/NISO Z39.48-1992.

Contents

Preface

George Kent

PURPOSE AND STRUCTURE

The purpose of this book is to clarify and strengthen the obligations of the global community in relation to the human right to adequate food. Hopefully this will help to bring about more effective efforts on the part of the global community to end hunger and other major forms of malnutrition. At the conference of the United Nations System Standing Committee on Nutrition (SCN) held in Geneva in March 2006, this became a project of the Task Force on International Dimensions of the Right to Food, of the SCN's Working Group on Nutrition, Ethics and Human Rights.

Chapter 1 explains the importance of addressing global obligations relating to malnutrition in all its forms, and it sets the stage for the subsequent chapters. In chapters 2 through 8, the core of the book, experts examine the issue of global obligations from various perspectives. Chapter 9 then reviews what has been learned from these core chapters and offers reflections on the practical meaning of obligations. Chapter 10 reviews the recommendations that were formulated in the preceding chapters.

TERMINOLOGY

Several issues relating to the choice of words used in this book have significant implications for how we understand and think about them.

Food and Nutrition

Although human rights law speaks about the right to food, the underlying concern is to ensure that people are well nourished. Several chapters make it clear that nutrition depends on many things, and not just food supply. For example, in chapter 5, Arun Gupta discusses the importance of breastfeeding, something that can be greatly improved even with current patterns of food supply. In chapter 6, Michael Latham shows that sharp reductions in infectious diseases, especially intestinal worms, malaria, and measles, would make a major contribution to reducing malnutrition in the world.

As explained in chapter 3, Article 11 of the International Covenant on Economic, Social and Cultural Rights speaks of the human right to adequate food. It does not explicitly speak about a right to adequate nutrition. However, the widely accepted understanding is that the authors of the relevant human rights law intended adequacy in relation to nutrition generally, and not just to food supplies.

Extraterritorial Obligations

Human rights specialists have only recently begun to give serious attention to the issue of extraterritorial obligations, so the terminology relating to it has not yet solidified. The most orthodox term so far is *extraterritorial obligations*. We have at times referred to the *external* obligations of states. While that is uncommon usage, its meaning seems clear. The key point is that states have responsibility for actions taken by themselves and also for actions taken by others (e.g., corporations) outside their borders over which they have actual or potential control. States have external obligations under international law in general and human rights law in particular.

States have a broad variety of moral responsibilities. Some of them are enshrined in the law and thus become legal obligations. References to the extraterritorial or external human rights obligations of states inherently emphasize the roles of states and neglect other actors. This is appropriate. Human rights law is state-centric because it is only states that sign and ratify international human rights agreements. Corporations or other agencies may sometimes be complicit in states' violations of human rights, but such nonstate actors cannot be direct violators of human rights.

Human rights law is mainly about the rights of people and the correlative obligations of states. States are obligated to act to ensure the realization of people's rights, not only by doing no harm, but also by taking positive action. Thus, states must organize themselves in a way that ensures the realization of human rights not only internally but also globally.

There is a need to clarify the roles and responsibilities of agents other than states, such as intergovernmental organizations, international nongovernmental organizations, business enterprises, and other agencies that act internationally. On some issues, the moral responsibilities of nonstate actors may seem clear, but they do not become legal obligations until appropriate legislation is enacted.

As indicated below, we have introduced the term *global community* to highlight one point: that there are some moral responsibilities that rest with the collectivity of all people, and at least some of them should be raised to the level of legal obligations. When we speak about global obligations for the right to food, we are concerned not only with legal obligations as they currently exist but also with legal obligations as we might wish them to be. The codification of these obligations would be based on a broad consensus regarding the underlying moral responsibilities.

Global Community

We use the word *global* rather than *international* community, to suggest that ultimately people, all people, carry the responsibilities relating to human rights. Nation-states and other organizations that act internationally should be viewed as acting (or intended to be acting) on behalf of their constituents, and not as autonomous actors. Even if the current nation-state system of global governance should be transformed into a different sort of administrative structure, the global community of people would continue, represented in other ways.

At times we use the term *global community* and speak about its obligations as if it were a singular thing, but we recognize that it includes many elements: nation-states when they act externally rather than internally; international governmental agencies such as the United Nations and its affiliated bodies such as the Food and Agriculture Organization of the United Nations, the World Food Programme, and the World Bank; international governmental agencies that are not affiliated with the United Nations, such as the World Trade Organization and the International Federation of Red Cross and Red Crescent Societies; international nongovernmental organizations of many different kinds, including religious organizations; international business enterprises (commonly described as transnational or multinational corporations); and others. Each of these parts of the global community may have its own types of obligations relating to the realization of human rights. This could be understood as a kind of global division of responsibilities. While there are many things they *may* do, we are especially interested in whether there are things that some of them *must* do.

It is important to recognize the reality of the global community taken as a whole, and its capacity to carry obligations, just as it is important to recognize the reality of the nation-state as a whole and its capacity to carry obligations. The duties that are then carried out by specific agencies (e.g., the Food and Agriculture Organization of the United Nations, or the U.S. Department of Agriculture) may then be viewed as having been assigned to them by the larger entities (e.g., nation-states, or the global community) that they represent.

From the perspective of democratic governance, both the global community and the nation-state represent—or ought to represent—people. The nation-state represents people under its jurisdiction, while the global community represents all people throughout the world.

Hunger and Malnutrition

When we speak of hunger, we do not use that term to refer to the physiological sensation one feels when lunch is late. Instead, we, like many others, use it as an umbrella term to refer comprehensively to malnutrition in all its forms. There are many varieties of malnutrition, such as protein-energy malnutrition, specific micronutrient deficiencies, wasting, stunting, famine, obesity, and so on. Each has its own distinct definition and indicators. The term *starvation* is often used in the popular press, but it has no established technical meaning among specialists in the field.

Hunger and *malnutrition* are used here as comprehensive umbrella terms to refer to this broad collection of nutrition-related concerns. It is important to recognize that action to address any particular kind of nutrition problem may leave other kinds unaffected.

Terminology is important. The August 12, 2006, issue of the *Economist* reported that India has banished famine. Many readers would understand that to mean that the problem of extreme malnutrition in India has been solved. However, the statement is true only if one understands *famine* in its narrow sense: deaths attributable to sudden-onset collapse of the food system. The reality is that chronic malnutrition in India is widespread and deep. Starvation deaths are frequently reported in India's press, and the country has over 1 million malnourished children. Thus, in the absence of further explanation, the *Economist's* usage was misleading.

Human Right to Adequate Food

The *right to food* is a shortened form of the *human right to adequate food*. We are referring to a right that is explicitly affirmed in international human rights law. Moreover, the right is not to any and all food, but to that which is adequate. Chapter 3 explains the legal foundations for this right.

Obligation, Responsibility, Duty

The term *obligation* is generally used here to refer to binding legal obligations. In contrast, *responsibility* is used to refer to a softer mandate, often a moral one. Some moral responsibilities eventually become enshrined as legal obligations in international human rights law and also in national law.

There is a different usage of these terms in the Draft Articles on the Responsibility of States for Internationally Wrongful Acts, adopted by the International Law Commission in 2001. In that context, *responsibility* refers to the duties of states when there has been a breach of an international legal obligation. Nevertheless, we adopt the perspective established in chapter 3 of this book: "A distinction is made here between *obligations*, which are legally binding, and *responsibilities*, which are not."

Adequacy vs. Highest Attainable Standard

Article 11 of the International Covenant on Economic, Social and Cultural Rights recognizes the right of everyone to an *adequate* standard of living, including adequate food. However, Article 12 recognizes the right to enjoyment of the *highest attainable* standard of physical and mental health. While General Comment 12, on food, makes the meaning of *adequate* reasonably clear, General Comment 14, on health, does not really explain *highest attainable*. This is an anomaly that remains to be resolved.

Violating Human Rights

Normally, states, as parties to international human rights agreements, may be held accountable for violating people's human rights. It is sometimes assumed that states may be held accountable only for violating the human rights of people under their own jurisdiction, but we see no reason why they should not be held accountable for violating the human rights of any people, anywhere.

States may sometimes undermine the ability of other states to meet their human rights obligations, through trade agreements, for example. This should be distinguished from direct violations of human rights. Similarly, nonstate actors such as intergovernmental organizations and business enterprises may at times act in ways that hinder states' ability to meet their human rights obligations. Such nonstate actors may at times act in concert with states in the violation of human rights. We do not yet have suitable language to distinguish such indirect contributions to human rights violations. Perhaps such actors should be described as "accessories" to the violation or as "abusers" of human rights.

Nonstate actors are sometimes charged with directly violating people's human rights. Is that possible? That is, do they have the "legal personality" that would make them capable of such violations? We do not think so, because they are not direct parties to the international human rights agreements. Apart from some exceptional cases, they are not subjects of international human rights law. They may commit abuses or crimes of various kinds, but they are not capable of direct violations of human rights. These issues are addressed in detail in chapter 3.

ELITISM?

Some might object to our project, feeling that we address global malnutrition in a way that is elitist, a top-down approach, when the real work that needs to be done is down at ground level, with the people who are most at risk of malnutrition. Certainly, ours is a high-end approach; we address mainly the high-level decision makers rather than those whose rights are not being realized. However, we see this project as an effort to act on behalf of the rights holders, calling to account the power holders of the world for not having formulated adequate programs for addressing the huge problems of malnutrition. The global community has not been doing what it should be doing. The rhetoric has been good, but the actions have been inadequate. We want to stand up and say that, out loud. We are calling on those at the high end to recognize and to fulfill their moral responsibilities and their legal obligations to ensure the realization of the human right to adequate food for those at ground level. There is work to be done in the capitals of the world as well as in the communities of the world.

Many people advocate community-based development planning. However, it is not a simple matter of choosing between bottom-up and top-down approaches. The poor are not solely responsible for their own condition. They are embedded in situations over which they have little control. Those in the capital cities and those in the communities both have important things to offer, things for which they should take responsibility. The real challenge is to devise appropriate working relationships, with all parties making their best possible contributions to what ought to be a collaborative effort. It is important to figure out the appropriate division of responsibilities and then do the work that is needed at all levels.

This book focuses on the responsibilities of the richer countries and the more powerful organizations and corporations, but the poor have serious responsibilities as well. For example, if they receive assistance of various kinds, they should use it well and be willing to be held accountable for the way it is used. One reason why the rich have not been more generous is that they feel that often their largesse is not well used. Corruption is a very deep problem in many poor countries. Not all of their problems are beyond their own control.

We—all of us together—need to find ways to fix the hunger situation. Simply asking for more assistance from the rich is foolish. The rich rightly complain that in the absence of well-formulated programs, giving more money could amount to tossing it into a bottomless pit. There is a need to find effective methods for achieving real goals. The elimination of smallpox throughout the world is a good example of a finite program that came to a conclusion that has been beneficial to all, at a very reasonable cost. Is there any way to imagine a comparable approach to the elimination of the major forms of malnutrition? Is it possible to get beyond the amelioration of symptoms to actual solutions? Our conclusion is that it may indeed be possible, but only if we work toward it. The world has an obligation to make serious plans for the realization of everyone's human right to adequate food.

ACKNOWLEDGMENT

Many individuals and organizations have contributed to the success of this project. We are especially grateful to the Toda Institute for Global Peace and Policy Research, based in Tokyo and Honolulu, for its financial and moral support. Their assistance allowed most of the chapters' authors to come together for a productive meeting in Vancouver, Canada, in June 2006. The effectiveness of Toda's support for work in the areas of peace and policy is demonstrated by the list of Toda publications included at the end of this volume.

1

Global Obligations

George Kent

In December 2006, the United Nations High Commissioner for Human Rights, Louise Arbour, made the point that not only individual states but also the international community as a whole has a duty to fight poverty:

> But as much as States bear the primary responsibility for their own develop-ment, the international community must also meet the commitments it has made to support the efforts of developing countries. Many rich countries have yet to meet development assistance targets they have accepted, yet they con-tinue to spend ten times more on military budgets. They also spend nearly four times their development assistance budget—an amount almost equal to the to-tal gross national product of African countries—to subsidize their own do-mestic agricultural producers. Indifference and a narrow calculus of national interests by wealthy countries hamper human rights and development just as damagingly as discrimination at the local level. (UN 2006)

Similarly, the challenge of ending hunger and other forms of malnutrition must be addressed at the global level, and not only on a nation-by-nation basis. States have responsibilities for the well-being not only of their own people but also of people outside their jurisdictions. The external responsi-bilities of states with regard to malnutrition are analyzed here in terms of both moral and legal considerations.

While most work on food issues generally, and on the right to food in particular, has centered on the obligations of states to their own people, this book is specifically about clarifying the obligations of the global commu-nity as a whole. It is particularly concerned with the external, rather than in-ternal, obligations of states.

THE GLOBAL FOOD SYSTEM

Problems of malnutrition may arise for many different reasons relating to the food supply, health conditions, and the quality of care, especially for children and the elderly. The food system includes primary production in agriculture and fishing (including aquaculture), processing, transport, marketing and, finally, consumption. Globalization in food and agriculture is characterized by "expansion of foreign private investment in agriculture, food processing, and marketing, to a large extent but not only through transnational corporations and an increasing international trade in food facilitated by the reduction in trade barriers" (FAO 2003). These economic dimensions are linked with political, cultural, and other dimensions of globalization as well. Fast food, for example, is growing rapidly not only as a result of trade and foreign investment, but also because of cultural transmission. In some cases, the significant imports are methods of production and marketing, rather than food itself. Broadly, we can say that food and agriculture issues are global when decisions relating to food and agriculture made in one country have impacts in many other countries. In some cases the linkages are direct, as in the cases of trade and investment. In other cases the linkages are more indirect, as in the globalization of food cultures through the influence of mass media and the tendency toward widespread adoption of particular lifestyles.

The decision-making centers in this globalization process are increasingly concentrated, controlled by small numbers of people, corporations, and organizations. These changes bring benefit to some and harm to others. The benefits result largely from the concentration of power, and the harms result from local people's loss of control over their own life circumstances.

With few exceptions (e.g., Aiken and Lafollette 1995; FAO 2004a; Lang and Heasman 2004), analyses of food and agriculture usually focus on the situations within particular countries. There has always been some recognition of the global connections, in studies of world trade, for example, but little attention has been given to the fact that there is a global food and agriculture system that has its own distinct characteristics and dynamics. Data are published on food production, exports, imports, and consumption, but there are few broad-scale analyses of the role of corporations and foreign direct investment, or of the distribution of economic and nutritional benefits associated with the patterns of production, exports, imports, and consumption. Little is said about patterns of control and the trends in consolidation of control over time. There should be deeper examination of aspects of the global system such as:

- the steady decline of traditional food production, and its consequences;
- the steady concentration in control over production and marketing;
- the net flow of food from poorer countries to richer countries;

- the lack of sustainability of some kinds of production, not only locally but also globally, as illustrated by the rapid depletion of large fish in the world's oceans;
- the role of corporations, and the need for greater transparency in their operations;
- the need to find ways to deal decisively with hunger at the global level; and
- the inadequacy of international assistance in dealing with complex humanitarian emergencies.

The globalization of food and agriculture has both positive and negative characteristics, with impacts that fall differently on different groups of people.

There is a need for better description and explanation of the global food and agriculture system in order to make it more visible and understandable. Beyond that, there is also a need for more attention to its management. To the extent that the global system of food and agriculture has been recognized, it has been examined as if from a distance, as if it were a part of nature, beyond deliberate human control.

As shown later in this chapter, under "Global Strategies," there have been many global summits and declarations on food and agriculture. However, the dominant view always has been that the problems must be addressed by national governments, with little more than an advisory role for the global community. The World Trade Organization's Agreement on Agriculture has taken steps toward addressing agriculture issues from a global perspective, but without giving adequate attention to trade's implications for food security. These initiatives have not fully grasped the need for new institutional arrangements for the global governance of food and agriculture.

Global problems have been neglected partly because of the unspoken premise that national governments are the only legitimate actors. This preoccupation with action at the nation-state level has been due, in part, to the system of international relations that has been in place since the middle of the seventeenth century, a system founded on the principle of state sovereignty. As a result, there is little institutional capacity for decision making and action at the global level. While it makes some sense, in legal terms, for states to be the primary authorities for policy making, this may not match the realities in which the problems take form. Global warming, for example, clearly is a global problem, and not one that can sensibly be addressed on a nation-by-nation basis.

Similarly, nutrition problems don't fit neatly into national boundaries. Consider the typical map of hunger in Africa (cf. Feeding Minds, Fighting Hunger 2006). Does anyone imagine that the problem on the ground really is uniform across particular countries, and then changes abruptly where boundaries are encountered? This sort of map supports the illusion that nations are the appropriate administrative units. Contrast this with maps that show the population density of underweight children per square kilometer (cf. CIESIN 2006; UN Millennium Project 2005a, 47). They make it clear that the patterns of malnutrition span political boundaries, often corresponding to niches in the physical ecology. Fine-grained maps that show that problems span national boundaries help to demonstrate the need for a more comprehensive view of the issues.

Most people's food supplies are based primarily on the resources in their own countries, but there is also some dependence on supplies from outside. The north provides shipments of food aid, and also provides a good deal of food to the south through regular marketing channels. However, on balance, the net flow of food in international trade is from south to north: the poor feed the rich (Kent 1982, 2002).

On the whole the poor feed the rich, both within countries and globally. This is not entirely bad, since the rich do pay for the food they get. However, the terms of trade appear to preclude any real catching up by the poor. The economic gap steadily widens. Surely a global food system that provides much greater advantages to the rich than to the poor entails some sort of moral responsibility on the part of the rich toward the poor.

The pattern is clearly demonstrated with regard to food and other resources when we explore the concept of the ecological footprint (Global Footprint 2006). The rich benefit far more than the poor from agricultural and other resources in countries other than their own. The rich have what some call "ghost acreage" in other parts of the world (Borgstrom 1972, 1973).

The food system is local and also regional and global. This point can be made not only on the basis of material relationships among different regions of the world but also in relationships that are less tangible, connections that are spiritual and compassionate. To illustrate, the *Gaia* and the *Deep Ecology* perspectives hold that in some sense the entire world functions as a single organism. Arguably, this view should apply even where there are no visible material connections such as trade. People—all people—and their physical environment constitute one large whole that in a way has a life of its own. If that is so, then the deprivation of any particular part or subsystem of this larger whole must inevitably affect the larger whole. We cannot risk writing off any of our parts. They are all parts of us.

Globalization in terms of increases in global flows of trade and investments are recent, but presumably our connectedness as human beings to each other and to our environment should always be present.

MORAL RESPONSIBILITIES

Human rights derive from a broad consensus on the moral bases of our behavior toward one another. Some, but not all, of what we recognize as moral responsibilities are elevated to legal obligations through the systematic formulation of international law, particularly human rights law. Thus, before examining the character of legal obligations with regard to human rights, it will be useful to establish a framework for understanding moral responsibilities generally.

We live as social beings who provide support to and draw support from the people around us. We aspire to a measure of self-sufficiency, but we are vulnerable, especially at the beginning of the life cycle and at the end. Consider the example of children, those who are in training for independence. As highly dependent beings, small children need to have others take care of them. Who should be responsible for children? The first line of responsibility is with the parents, of course, but others have a role as well. In asking who is responsible, we are not asking whose fault it is that children suffer so much (who caused the problems) but who should take action to remedy the problems. Many different social agencies may have some role in looking after children. What should be the interrelationships among them? What should be the roles of churches, nongovernmental organizations, businesses, and local and national governments?

Most children have two vigorous advocates from the moment they are born, and even before they are born. Their parents devote enormous resources to serving their interests. These are not sacrifices. The best parents do not support their children out of a sense of obligation or as investments. Rather, they support their children as extensions of themselves, as part of their wholeness.

In many cases, however, that bond is broken or is never created. Fathers disappear. Many mothers disappear as well. In some cities hundreds of children are abandoned each month in the hospitals in which they are born. Bands of children live in the streets by their wits, preyed upon by others. Frequently children end up alone as a result of poverty, disease, warfare, or other sorts of crises. Many children are abandoned because they are physically or mentally handicapped. Some parents become so disabled by drugs or alcohol or disease that they cannot care for their children.

In many cases the failures are not the parents' own fault, but a result of the fact that others have failed to meet their responsibility toward the parents. In many cases parents are willing to work hard and do whatever needs to be done to care for their children, but cannot find the kind of employment opportunities they need to raise their children adequately.

In some cases, others look after children who cannot be cared for by their biological parents. In many cultures children belong not only to their biological parents but also to the community as a whole. The responsibility and the joy of raising children are widely shared. Where communities mistreat children, through neglect or through exploitative child labor and trafficking, for example, the next higher level must step in to correct the situation.

In many places, especially in "developed" nations, community-based care is no longer available because of the collapse of the idea and the practice of community. Many of us live in nice neighborhoods in well-ordered societies, but the sense of community—of love and responsibility and commitment to one another—has vanished. In such cases the remaining hope of the abandoned or orphaned child is the government, the modern substitute for community. People look to government to provide human services that the local community no longer provides.

As children mature, the first priority is to help them become responsible for themselves. So long as they are not mature, however, children ought to get their nurturance from their parents. Failing that, they ought to get it from their relatives. Failing that, they ought to get it from their local communities. Failing that, they ought to get it from the local nongovernmental organizations. Failing that, they should get it from local governments. Failing that, it should come from their national governments. Failing that, they ought to get it from the global community. The responsibility hierarchy is presented in figure 1.1 as a set of nested circles, with the child in the center

Figure 1.1. Rings of Responsibility

of the nest, surrounded, supported, and nurtured by family, community, government, and ultimately, international organizations. This model falls squarely into what has been described as "the metaphor of concentric circles morality" (Lichtenberg 2004, 86).

Those who are closest to the needy individual generally have greatest responsibility. There are sometimes exceptions. For example, there are cases in which central governments provide services to the needy directly, bypassing local government. Often this is based on an agreed division of labor, and an understanding that services are likely to be distributed more equitably if they are funded out of the central treasury. Similarly, some programs, such as immunization, cannot be completely managed locally. Nevertheless, the general pattern is that we expect problems to be handled locally, and reach out to more distant agents only when local remedies are inadequate.

This is straightforward. The thought that should be added is that in cases of failure, agents more distant from the child should not simply substitute for those closer to the child. Instead, those who are more distant should try to work with and strengthen those who are closer, in order to help them become more capable of fulfilling their responsibilities toward children. Although there will be cases in which sanctions are necessary, agencies in the outer rings generally should focus on helping to overcome, rather than punish, failures in the inner rings. To the extent feasible, agencies should try to respond to failures in empowering, positive ways. Apart from exceptionally serious cases, local communities should not take children away from inadequate parents but rather should help them in their parenting role. State governments should not replace local governments, but instead should support local governments in their work with children. The global community should help national governments in their work with children.

Just as national governments ought to be representative of the people that live under their jurisdiction, speaking and acting on their behalf, the international governmental organizations in the outer ring should be understood as representing all people. They represent the global community and act on its behalf.

These ideas mesh nicely with the principle of subsidiarity, which is central to Catholic social thought (Bosnich 1996; Minus 2004) and human rights principles (Carozza 2003). A basic definition is that "subsidiarity is the principle that each social and political group should help smaller or more local ones accomplish their respective ends without, however, arrogating those tasks to itself" (Carozza 2003, 38, note 1).

Governments' responsibilities with regard to ordinary children in ordinary circumstances are limited, as they should be. Families should provide daily care and feeding. However, for children in extreme situations, who are abused or who suffer from extremely poor health or serious malnutrition, governments have a role to play. Where there has been a failure in the inner rings of responsibility and no one else takes care of the problem, government must step in.

The responsibilities of agencies in the outer rings are not limited to situations in which there are failures in the inner rings. As John Tobin put it, one should not say that

> accountability of a State will only arise in circumstances where parents have failed in the performance of their responsibilities with respect to a child's health. On the contrary, it is based on co-operation, interdependence and assistance rather than intervention as a measure of last resort. (Tobin 2006, 285)

All parties have some responsibilities all the time. For example, all parties always have the responsibility to do no harm to children. However, the scope of the responsibilities of parties in the outer rings is increased when there are failures in the inner rings.

There are similar rings of responsibility for others who cannot care for themselves, such as victims of disasters, the physically disabled, and mentally ill. These responsibilities need to be clarified so that the care of those who are unable to care for themselves is not left to chance. Thus this framework may be used in relation to all individuals who need protection and support, and not only children.

Within this framework, the primary responsibility for an individual's nutrition status clearly resides with the individual, but others have responsibilities as well. The responsibilities of others are magnified to the extent that the individual has limited capacity to take care of himself or herself. This may occur because of limitations in the individuals themselves (e.g., immaturity, lack of critical knowledge or skills, physical disabilities), or because of limitations imposed on them, such as inadequate access to land or to decent employment opportunities. In a world in which increasing shares of the food we eat come from great distances and from large corporations, the rings of responsibility extend much further than they have in the past. In an age of globalization of food systems, there are compelling reasons to insist that there are global responsibilities for their impacts (FAO 2004a; Lang and Heasman 2004).

Some people imagine that the responsibilities of the "global north" to the "global south" are to be met through the shipment of large cargoes of food to those who are hungry, but experienced analysts of the global food situation agree that such food shipments are appropriate only for extreme emergency situations. Even in emergencies, it may make more sense to provide other kinds of assistance such as money or livelihood support rather than direct food aid (Humanitarian Policy Group 2006). At times there is more political support in the donor country for aid in the form of food commodities than in the form of money, despite the fact that money might be more beneficial at the receiving end (Barrett and Maxwell 2005).

In some contexts, human rights specialists are concerned with *justiciability*, the question of whether individuals who feel their human rights have been violated can take their cases to appropriate courts to obtain authoritative decisions regarding guilt or innocence and appropriate remedies. (For discussion of justiciability in relation to economic, social and cultural rights, see www.escr-net.org/caselaw.) The remedies may call for punishment of the violator, or compensation to the victim, or some sort of administrative remedy. In some cases there may be a call for conflict management procedures outside the formal judicial system, such as the use of truth and reconciliation commissions. In some cases there may be a call for reparations from the wrongdoers to their victims. In some cases repenting wrongdoers might voluntarily offer reparations or compensation of some kind.

There are many good studies of ways in which particular corporations and countries have acted badly, resulting in harm to nutrition status, health, economic standing, and the environment. There are several nongovernmental watchdog groups (cf. Corporate Accountability Working Group 2007) that call corporations to account for their actions that abuse human rights, and call on the states that host these corporations to control their behavior. However, there is the danger that this focus on specific abuses may not get at underlying structural issues. For example, if we concentrate on abuses we might not address the inherent tendency of free markets to widen gaps between rich and poor. The focus on abuses could in effect license normal business practices that have negative effects.

Approaches that focus on violations emphasize the prevention of wrongdoing. In this book, however, our focus is on right-doing. We want to know how to go beyond the prevention of harm and identify the positive things that ought to be done. Thus, this book does not adopt a violation-centered approach to identifying obligations. Instead, as explained below in "Levels of Obligation," and again in chapter 3, we focus on the distinctions that human rights specialists make among different types or levels of obligations: *respect, protect,* and *fulfill,* with *fulfill* in turn being divided into *facilitate* and *provide.* In this approach, the obligation to act to deal with a human rights problem derives not from having caused it, but from having the capacity to remedy it. As we put it in chapter 9, "generally, if you have the capacity to protect someone from great harm or you can deliver great benefits, and you can do that at small cost or risk to yourself, then you are obligated to do so."

The view taken here is that moral responsibility to the needy of the world should not depend so much on the underlying reasons for their neediness as on the simple fact of their neediness. The duty of the rich of the world to help does not derive so much from their having caused the problems as from the simple fact of their having the capacity to help. Assistance does not have to be guilt driven. Of course, past wrongs should be addressed, but remedies for past wrongs should be distinguished from humanitarian assistance based on responding to needs. For more thorough analyses of the moral foundations of assistance, especially in relation to hunger, see Aiken and Lafollette (1995), Chatterjee (2004), Lucas and Ogletree (1976). Shelton's (1985) analysis of the legal foundations of assistance in relation to the hunger problem is one of the earliest on the subject. Narula (2006) provides a recent analysis of global obligations.

The term *assistance* as used here should not be misunderstood. The obligation to assist does not necessarily imply direct feeding or a charity approach of some sort. In terms of the levels of obligation, a policy of fulfillment in the sense of facilitating is preferable to a policy of fulfillment in the sense of providing. To the extent possible, assistance should be provided in ways that are empowering, not disempowering. Or, as the old adage puts it, it is better to offer a hand up rather than a handout.

The legal obligation to provide assistance to people in need under domestic law is frequently discussed in terms of the *duty to rescue*. When the theme is discussed under international law, as the right to assistance, there is a curious change in perspective that arises. The discussion is mainly about the rights of the donors to have access to the needy so that their goods and services can be delivered without interference (cf. Beigbeder 1991; Sandoz 1992). The argument says needy people have a right to receive assistance if other people offer to provide it. It does not say that the needy have a right to receive certain kinds of assistance, and therefore others have an obligation to provide it. The main concern appears to be with the rights of those who provide the assistance, not the rights of those who need it.

The International Commission on Intervention and State Sovereignty advanced an argument of this sort in 2001 in its report *The Responsibility to Protect*, clarifying guidelines for humanitarian intervention. The approach was highlighted in a UN report on *A More Secure World* in 2004, a UN declaration in 2005, and again in the G8 Summit in 2006. On April 28, 2006, in Resolution 1674, the UN Security Council again made similar claims, asserting the right of the international community to provide protection to people whose human rights were being violated. It acknowledged that at least under some circumstances the international community has a responsibility to provide such protection, but this responsibility has not been spelled out.

The responsibility to protect has been viewed mainly as the duty of governments of the countries on the receiving end of the intervention. The terminology could suggest that the countries that do the intervening have specific obligations to intervene when necessary for humanitarian purposes, but a close reading of the discussions indicates that the international community really is using this approach to assert its right to intervene. The *Guardian* recognized this when it referred to "the UN declaration of a right to protect people from their governments" (Williams 2005). Similarly, the African Union proclaims, in its Constitutive Act, "the right of the Union to intervene in a Member State . . . in respect of grave circumstances, namely war crimes, genocide and crimes against human humanity." It does not speak of a duty to intervene.

The assertion of a *right* to intervene with no counterpart *obligation* to intervene under some circumstances implicitly invites the politicization of intervention decisions. Those who intervene within nations on humanitarian grounds should not be free to choose whom and when they help. Interventions in situations like the genocide in Darfur should not be optional. Along these lines, in October 2006, Václav Havel, Kjell Magne Bondevik, and Elie Wiesel issued a report arguing that because of the widespread malnutrition and other humanitarian problems in North Korea, "the international community now has an obligation to intervene through regional bodies and the United Nations, up to and including the Security Council" (Havel, Bondevik, and Wiesel 2006a, 2006b). There should be recognition of obligations, and not only rights, on the part of those who would intervene.

It is not surprising that the donors and protectors tend to emphasize their rights rather than their obligations. However, one would think that if the powerful are going to claim a right to assist under some conditions, they should also have an obligation to assist under some conditions.

This study is not intended to offer a detailed analysis of the political economy of the global food system. The premise here is that there is some sort of moral responsibility of the global north to the global south with regard to food and nutrition. The nature and extent of that responsibility should be clarified by examining moral principles and international legal obligations under human rights law.

THE HUMAN RIGHT TO ADEQUATE FOOD

There have been many global conferences, summits, and declarations on food security, nutrition, and hunger. Several made passing references to the human right to adequate food, but the World Food Summit of 1996 was the first to set out a process for clarifying and implementing that right. Subsequent international consultations, the publication of General Comment 12 in 1999 (UN ECOSOC 1999), the appointment of a special rapporteur on the Right to Food in 2000, and the sponsorship by the Food and Agriculture Organization of the United Nations (FAO) of a series of case studies all helped to build consensus on the meaning of the right.

There was a follow-up to the World Food Summit of 1996, called the World Food Summit: five years later. It was actually held in 2002 because of the events of September 11, 2001. This summit produced a final declaration that called for the creation of an International Alliance Against Hunger. Paragraph 10 of the declaration also called on the FAO Council to establish "an Intergovernmental Working Group . . . to elaborate . . . a set of voluntary guidelines to support Member States' efforts to achieve the progressive realisation of the right to adequate food in the context of national food security" (FAO 2002).

The Intergovernmental Working Group functioned as a subgroup of FAO's Committee on World Food Security. The FAO Council, the executive governing body of FAO, adopted the group's final text, the *Voluntary Guidelines to*

Support the Progressive Realization of the Right to Adequate Food in the Context of National Food Security, on November 23, 2004 (FAO 2005b). It complements and helps to explain international law relating to the human right to adequate food, showing that there are different ways in which the obligations described in that law could be fulfilled. Human rights law specifies what the parties *must* do, their obligations, while the *Voluntary Guidelines* document talks mainly about what they *could* do to fulfill those obligations. The guidelines are explained more fully in FAO's book, *The Right to Food Guidelines: Information Papers and Case Studies* (FAO 2006).

Thus, a new approach to the hunger problem is emerging, based on the premise that there is a human right to adequate food, and it must be taken seriously. The United Nations System Standing Committee on Nutrition (SCN) and its members have facilitated this new thinking, and several countries have been showing how this right can be recognized and realized.

ROLE OF THE GLOBAL COMMUNITY

Discussion of the human right to adequate food has emphasized the role of that right within nations, in terms of the obligations of states to people living under their jurisdictions. The FAO has asked, "How can the human right to adequate food be implemented at the country level?" but it did not ask how it could be implemented at the global level (FAO 2004b, para. 1). Some analyses have been made of the role of the global community in relation to the right (cf. Eide 2005). The purpose here is to work specifically toward identifying the global obligations that are implied by the human right to adequate food. There is a need for clarity not only about what the global community may do but also about what it must do. What are the obligations of rich countries, and what are the obligations of international agencies with regard to hunger and food insecurity in poor countries? This concern was raised in the concluding chapter of my book on the human right to adequate food (Kent 2005). That chapter may be accessed at http://press.georgetown.edu/pdfs/1589010566_Chpt17.pdf.

The right-to-food guidelines acknowledge, "States have the primary responsibility for their own economic and social development, including the progressive realization of the right to adequate food in the context of national food security" (FAO 2005b, 33). The guidelines then go on to say that national development efforts should be supported by an enabling international environment. The relevant international agencies "are urged to take actions in supporting national development efforts for the progressive realization of the right to adequate food in the context of national food security."

Human rights law and the right-to-food guidelines acknowledge the obligations to cooperate and assist internationally, but as shown in the section on "Progressive Realization" later in this chapter, there is no clear assertion that the cooperation and assistance must achieve any particular level. Section III of the guidelines, on International Measures, Actions and Commitments, includes sections on International Cooperation and Unilateral Measures, Role of the International Community, Technical Cooperation, International Trade, External Debt, Official Development Assistance, International Food Aid, Partnerships with NGOs/CSOs/Private Sector, Promotion and Protection of the Right to Food, and International Reporting. All of these sections focus on things the global community could do, not what it must do.

The State of Food Insecurity in the World 2005 highlighted the importance of governance in hunger reduction (FAO 2005a, 10–11). Similarly, the right-to-food guidelines emphasize good governance in Guideline 1 (FAO 2005b). However, both focus on the quality of governance within countries. Consideration should also be given to the quality of global governance as it relates to the human right to adequate food.

This persistent tendency to look inward rather than outward in describing the obligations of nations with regard to human rights is also illustrated by the fact that the United Nations' Committee on Economic, Social and Cultural Rights has prepared an analysis of "The Domestic Application of the Covenant," but has not yet prepared a complementary analysis of the external obligations of nations in relation to the International Covenant on Economic, Social and Cultural Rights (UN ECOSOC 1998).

The global community as a whole is not precisely defined. Some studies have been done on the responsibilities of international organizations in relation to the human right to adequate food (Kent 1994; Windfuhr 1998), but it should be recognized that the global community is much more than international organizations. It encompasses all actors that act globally, including international governmental organizations, international non-governmental organizations, transnational business enterprises, and nation-states in their external relations. It has no recognized representative with authority to speak for it, and no means for entering into agreements.

The global community should not be viewed as an independent entity with its own will and its own voice. It should be understood as the agent of the collectivity of all people, acting through their states and through other agencies, and subordinate to that collectivity. At present the global community is not explicitly and directly a subject of international law. The view taken here is that it does have implied obligations under international law, obligations that could and should be spelled out more clearly.

The global community is no more amorphous than any single state. States manifest themselves by having their constituent members, their people, form governments that manage a specific population and territory. Similarly, it is up to the collectivity of all people, acting through their states, to form a global government, or at least elements of global governance. This would give the global community the voice and the visibility that it needs to have. It is now primarily the United Nations and its associated agencies that serve these functions. Action is frequently taken in the name of the global community, on matters of security and trade, for example. If the global community can take responsibility for issues relating to security, there is no reason why it cannot take comparable responsibility for issues such as health and nutrition.

EXTRATERRITORIAL OBLIGATIONS

This book, centered on clarifying global obligations relating to the human right to adequate food, fits into a broader movement to clarify global obligations with regard to human rights generally (Barry and Pogge 2006; Clapham 2006; Darrow 2003; Gosselin 2006; International Council on Human Rights Policy 2003; Kuper 2005; Pinstrup-Andersen and Sandøe 2007; Skogly 2006). Much of this work is grounded in the core document of the modern global human rights system, the Universal Declaration of Human Rights, which says in Article 28:

> Everyone is entitled to a social and international order in which the rights and freedoms set forth in this Declaration can be fully realized.

This in turn stands on the United Nations Charter, which says, in Article 55:

> With a view to the creation of conditions of stability and well-being which are necessary for peaceful and friendly relations among nations based on respect for the principle of equal rights and self-determination of peoples, the United Nations shall promote:
>
> a. higher standards of living, full employment, and conditions of economic and social progress and development;
> b. solutions of international economic, social, health, and related problems; and international cultural and educational cooperation; and
> c. universal respect for, and observance of, human rights and fundamental freedoms for all without distinction as to race, sex, language, or religion.

Article 56 of the charter says:

> All Members pledge themselves to take joint and separate action in co-operation with the Organization for the achievement of the purposes set forth in Article 55.

Thus the charter and the declaration clearly acknowledge the responsibility of the global community, taken as a whole, for the realization of human rights. Human rights law already recognizes that some obligations are extraterritorial or, more precisely, extrajurisdictional. For example, there is widespread recognition that gross human rights violations such as genocide, torture, and crimes against humanity are matters of concern for the global community taken as a whole. The creation of the International Criminal Court demonstrates this recognition. The primary obligations of states are internal, but they have external obligations as well.

If everyone is entitled to an international order that will ensure the full realization of all human rights, we must work on envisioning and establishing such an order. Surely it should be an order in which the world as a whole carries not only moral responsibilities but also legal obligations for the realization of those rights. We must begin with the understanding that there are global obligations that are beyond those of states to their own people. Then we can begin to work out their exact content.

PROGRESSIVE REALIZATION

The title of the right-to-food guidelines speaks of *progressive realization*. This evokes Article 2 of the International Covenant on Economic, Social and Cultural Rights (ICESCR), which says:

> Each State Party to the present Covenant undertakes to take steps, individually and through international assistance and co-operation, especially economic and technical, to the maximum of its available resources, with a view to achieving progressively the full realization of the rights recognized in the present Covenant by all appropriate means, including particularly the adoption of legislative measures.

The legal character of the human right to adequate food is examined in chapter 3 of this volume and in several other publications (e.g., Eide 2005; FAO 2005b; Kent 2005; UN ECOSOC 1999). An authoritative account of the meaning of progressive realization with regard to human rights in general may be found in General Comment 3 (UN OHCHR 1990). Assuming a general appreciation of that context, here we focus on the significance of the doctrine of progressive realization for the human right to adequate food.

In saying that each State Party to the ICESCR is to take action "to the maximum of its available resources," the covenant says that expectations of duty bearers must be moderated by an appreciation of their limited capacities. The capacities of poor, weak nations are very limited. Of course, as Article 1 of the ICESCR recognizes, the resources that poor countries have available to them may be expanded through assistance from other countries. General Comment 3, paragraph 13, makes it clear that the phrase, "the maximum of its available resources" refers to "both the resources existing within a State and those available from the international community through international cooperation and assistance."

What are the obligations of the richer countries? Paragraph 14 of General Comment 3 says, "International cooperation for development and thus for the realization of economic, social and cultural rights is an obligation of all States. It is particularly incumbent upon those States which are in a position to assist others in this regard." In practice, the widely accepted understanding has been that richer countries may or may not provide assistance, as they wish. "Maximum available resources" has been taken to refer only to the resources available to the poor country, not to the resources available to the donor countries. The obligation to assist has been seen as soft, with no requirement that the assistance must be raised to any particular level.

Why should the doctrine of progressive realization apply only to poor countries? ICESCR Article 2, quoted above, could be read as meaning that not only poor countries but also rich countries must act to the maximum of their available resources. There is no reason to assume that rights to be realized are only those of one's own country. With this reading, just as the expectations of poor countries are to be calibrated to their capacities, the expectations of donor countries and the global community as a whole also should be calibrated to their capacities.

If the global community's capacity is high, as it is, to what level should it provide assistance to countries in need? The answer was clear in the previously cited Article 28 of the Universal Declaration of Human Rights. If we are serious when we say that "Everyone is entitled to a social and international order in which the rights and freedoms set forth in this Declaration can be fully realized," then the global community is obligated to provide assistance up to the point at which all human rights are fully realized. With regard to food in particular, this means that the global community is obligated to ensure that everyone's human right to adequate food is fully realized.

Of course it is national governments that carry the primary obligation for realization of their own people's human rights. Salil Shetty, the director of the United Nations Millennium Campaign, speaking about the prospects for meeting the Millennium Development Goals by 2015, argued, "any country where the leaders are serious about realizing the goals in the next 10 years can in fact make it happen" (Sandrasagra 2006). Perhaps. In any case, we should explain what is to be done to ensure the realization of the human rights of those people who happen to live in countries whose national governments are either unwilling or unable to do what needs to be done. The global community cannot discharge its obligations simply by pointing to the obligations of national governments.

In many cases, hunger persists because national governments lack the capacity or the will to address the problem. The solution cannot then be based on the assumption that they all do have the capacity and the will.

Discussions of the human right to adequate food generally focus on the correlative obligations of national governments to people under their jurisdictions. However, this approach treats rights and obligations as if they end at the national border. It implies that people of poor countries should have much lower expectations for the realization of their rights than people of rich countries.

The title of the right-to-food guidelines says the document is intended to support the progressive realization of the right to adequate food *in the context of national food security*. Why this emphasis on *national* food security? Food security should be addressed as a global problem, and not only as a series of national problems.

The World Bank says:

> The reason undernutrition and micronutrient malnutrition persist at high levels is not that we do not know how to reduce them, nor that countries have applied best practice, yet failed to succeed. It is that most countries have not invested at a scale large enough to get these tested technologies to those who will benefit from them most. (World Bank 2006b, 37–38)

Consider a possible revision of the last sentence.

> It is that *the world* has not invested at a scale large enough to get these tested technologies to those who will benefit from them most.

This formulation would acknowledge the role and responsibility of the global community taken as a whole, rather than pushing it off to the individual poor countries and allowing the rich countries to stand aside. Many countries do not have the capacity or the will to solve the problems of malnutrition within their jurisdictions. To treat this mainly as a problem of individual countries, and not of the world, is to abandon malnourished people in the weaker countries.

LEVELS OF OBLIGATION

As explained more fully in chapter 3, the obligations of states in relation to the human right to adequate food are distinguished into three main categories: *respect*, *protect*, and *fulfill*. In turn, fulfill is divided into two categories: fulfill in the sense of *facilitate*, and fulfill in the sense of *provide*. Paragraph 15 of General Comment 12 interprets these as follows:

- *respect*—"The obligation to *respect* existing access to adequate food requires States parties not to take any measures that result in preventing such access."
- *protect*—"The obligation to *protect* requires measures by the State to ensure that enterprises or individuals do not deprive individuals of their access to adequate food."

- *fulfill (facilitate)*—"The obligation to *fulfill (facilitate)* means the State must pro-actively engage in activities intended to strengthen people's access to and utilization of resources and means to ensure their livelihood, including food security."
- *fulfill (provide)*—"Finally, whenever an individual or group is unable, for reasons beyond their control, to enjoy the right to adequate food by the means at their disposal, States have the obligation to *fulfill (provide)* that right directly. This obligation also applies for persons who are victims of natural or other disasters." (UN ECOSOC 1999)

To put it simply,

- *Respect* means do no harm to others.
- *Protect* means prevent harm to others by third parties.
- *Facilitate* means help others to meet their own needs.
- *Provide* means meet others' needs when they cannot do that themselves.

All of these categories apply not only to the internal obligations of states but also to their external obligations. Viewed globally, *respect* essentially means that the state's external activities should do no harm to the nutrition status of people in other countries. Thus, exports should not include harmful food products that might violate the right to food of people in other countries. The dumping of subsidized, and thus underpriced, food products that undermine their food producers might be a violation as well. For example, there is considerable evidence that under the North American Free Trade Agreement, the United States has been dumping low-priced corn into Mexico, harming Mexico's small-scale corn producers (Kent 2006). Their income has been reduced to such an extent that their nutrition security has been put at risk.

The obligation to *protect* implies a need to act internationally to protect consumers from harmful practices of food enterprises, and to ensure food safety through systems such as the Codex Alimentarius program operated by the Food and Agriculture Organization of the United Nations and the World Health Organization. International initiatives to control obesity and to control the marketing of food to children fall into this category. States also must act to ensure that international organizations themselves do no harm. To illustrate, there are concerns that the World Bank may have harmed food security through its structural adjustment programs and other policies, that some of the World Trade Organization's policies regarding agriculture may have been harmful, and that the agencies that work on HIV/AIDS may have offered mistaken advice regarding infant feeding in the context of HIV.

Respect and *protect* refer to obligations of states, corporations, international agencies, and others to do no harm to people's nutrition security. States themselves must do no harm, and they must provide protection by ensuring that others that they control or influence do no harm. Thus, these obligations are relatively uncontroversial, at least at the level of principle. However, the obligations to *facilitate* and *provide* place greater emphasis on positive obligations, especially for those who are needy, and thus are more likely to raise difficult debates. This book focuses on the need to clarify the nature and extent of these positive obligations as they apply internationally.

GLOBAL STRATEGIES

Every child knows how to solve the hunger problem. Just give the hungry something to eat! Indeed, if we provide sandwiches for all who are hungry on the first day of 2015, we will have fulfilled the Millennium Development Goal of ending hunger by 2015.

Of course we then have to explain that that is not what we mean. We are really seeking something else, a sustainable answer to the problems of malnutrition in all their forms. This means there must be some changes to the institutional arrangements through which society is governed. However, we have not yet figured out how to do that. We have barely asked the question. We need to state the goal more carefully.

The world's understanding of the issues surrounding hunger is reflected in the major international conferences and agreements that have addressed the issue. Chronologically, these efforts have been recorded in the following documents and conferences, among others:

- The Manifesto of the Special Assembly on Man's Right to Freedom from Hunger, held in Rome in March 1963.
- The first World Food Congress, meeting in Washington, D.C., in June 1963, called for "the formulation of a world plan in quantitative terms."
- The Freedom from Hunger Campaign Conference held at the headquarters of the Food and Agriculture Organization of the United Nations in November 1963 unanimously adopted a declaration "to give whole-hearted support to the Freedom from Hunger Campaign until its final goal is achieved."
- The International Undertaking on World Food Security and the Universal Declaration on the Eradication of Hunger and Malnutrition, issued by the World Food Conference held in Rome in 1974.
- The Plan of Action on World Food Security of 1979.
- The Agenda for Consultations and Possible Action to Deal with Acute and Large-scale Food Shortages of 1981.

- The World Food Security Compact of 1985.
- The Plan of Action for Implementing the World Declaration on the Survival, Protection, and Development of Children, issued by the World Summit for Children held at the United Nations in New York in September 1990, included a major section on reducing children's malnutrition.
- The World Declaration and Plan of Action on Nutrition of the International Conference on Nutrition held in Rome in December 1992.
- The Plan of Action that came out of the World Food Summit of 1996, and its follow-up meeting, World Food Summit: five years later.
- The United Nations System Standing Committee on Nutrition's Strategic Plan of April 2000.
- The World Health Organization's Global Strategy on Infant and Young Child Feeding of 2003 (WHO 2003).
- The *Voluntary Guidelines to Support the Progressive Realization of the Right to Adequate Food in the Context of National Food Security*, adopted by the FAO Council in November 2004 (FAO 2005b).
- The Millennium Development Project's *Halving Hunger: It Can Be Done* (UN Millennium Project 2005a).

The impact of these documents and conferences is not impressive. Then secretary of state Henry Kissinger, addressing the World Food Conference in Rome on November 5, 1974, declared the bold objective that, "within a decade, no child will go hungry, no family will fear for its next day's bread, and no human being's future and capacity will be stunted by malnutrition." At the World Food Assembly held in 1984 in Rome, nongovernmental organizations reminded the world that the promise had not been kept.

In 1996, the World Food Summit adopted the goal of reducing the number of undernourished people by half, to 400 million, by 2015. The subsequent review conference, World Food Summit: five years later, conceded that the world was not on track to reach that target.

Referring to the World Summit for Children held in 1990, the secretary-general of the United Nations reported in 1996:

> Despite the commitments made in 1990, there has been little progress in reducing child malnutrition. In sub-Saharan Africa and South Asia, the number of malnourished children is actually rising. Almost a third of all children under five in developing countries are malnourished, and malnutrition still contributes to more than half the deaths of young children in these countries. (UNICEF 1996)

Ten years later, the secretary-general could give a similar report. Not much has changed, even though commitments supposedly were reaffirmed at the Millennium Development Summit of 2000. What happened? What didn't happen?

The recommendations that have come out of global summits on hunger have shared common weaknesses:

- They generally view hunger as an original state of nature, and not as something that is endlessly recreated by major social forces.
- They often fail to make important distinctions among different types of food insecurity or malnutrition, and often neglect some types.
- They fail to articulate a clear vision of a future world without hunger.
- They focus on short-term, mainly technical interventions and assistance, with little coordination.
- They do not appreciate the need for substantial commitments of resources and long-term strategies.
- There is no arrangement for course corrections on the path to the goal.
- Intergovernmental organizations are viewed mainly as facilitators, not as major actors.
- The focus has been mainly on the formulation of national plans of action, not a comprehensive global plan of action. They do not give adequate attention to the role that the international community must play if hunger is to be sharply reduced.

Are these stories about strategies that failed? Whether one is trying to reach a social goal or trying to build a bridge across a river, a good strategy is one for which there is a serious commitment of resources, a clear management structure, and a program of action that could sensibly be expected to result in achievement of the goal. By this standard, there has not been any serious strategy for achieving sharp reductions in hunger and other forms of malnutrition around the world.

In paragraphs 21 through 28, General Comment 12 is explicit about the need for strategy to ensure implementation of the human right to adequate food. It says:

> The Covenant clearly requires that each State party take whatever steps are necessary to ensure that everyone is free from hunger and as soon as possible can enjoy the right to adequate food. This will require the adoption of a national strategy to ensure food and nutrition security for all, based on human rights principles that define the objectives, and the formulation of policies and corresponding benchmarks. (UN ECOSOC 1999)

This speaks about the obligation for strategizing at the national level. Similarly, the right-to-food guidelines, in Guideline 3, emphasize the need for national-level strategies (FAO 2005b). That obligation should not be limited to the national level. Systematic strategies need to be formulated and implemented at every level if the goal of fulfilling every person's human right to adequate food is to be achieved.

Serious strategies at the global level must be accompanied by serious strategies at the national level. However, in many cases, national strategies are weak or nonexistent, sharing the weaknesses listed above in reference to global planning. Under the Millennium Development Project, many countries made a commitment to halve hunger by 2015, but few are on track to reach the goal. Few are making the course corrections that are needed. Part of the task of the global strategy is to find ways to support and strengthen national-level strategies.

What global strategies have been proposed? If someone asked you how to build a house, you would not tell them simply to collect a bunch of wood, and then do lots of hammering and sawing, and nothing more. You would not walk away without saying where the wood is to come from, who would pay for the hammer and the saw, how the carpenters would be paid, or what sort of hammering and sawing is needed. If the job is to get done, one needs a far more complete answer as to how it is to be done. It is difficult to see how the Millennium Development Project or the Global Strategy for Infant and Young Child Feeding or the Global Strategy on Diet, Physical Activity and Health really constitute strategies. So far, none of the global strategies relating to malnutrition would lead one to confidently expect that the goal would be reached.

Serious strategies for addressing malnutrition would offer more than a few scattered recommendations. They would describe stepwise plans of action designed to reach the goal. There would be clear commitments of money and other resources. There would be a well-identified management body. There would be clear incentives for the actors to do what needs to be done. There would be institutional mechanisms in place to ensure that all actors are held accountable for doing their jobs. Just as the construction of a building or a bridge is only possible with detailed planning and periodic course corrections during the process of working toward the goal, the human right to adequate food can only be fully realized through carefully designed and implemented programs of action.

There are many global commitments that have not been honored. One of the most glaring is the promise made in 1970 at the United Nations General Assembly that donor governments would raise their Official Development Assistance to 0.7 percent of their gross national income by the mid-1970s (UN General Assembly 1970, para. 43). That commitment has been reaffirmed many times, but the reality is that their assistance reached an all-time high of only 0.33 percent in 2005, less than half the target level, three decades after the target date (OECD 2006; United Nations Economic and Social Council 2006, para. 2). There have been many other comparable broken promises.

It has been claimed that the global community made a commitment for the achievement of the Millennium Development Goals by 2015, but how is that manifested? Where is the program of action now? The United Nations Millennium Campaign became nothing more than a small advocacy organization that "supports citizens' efforts to hold their government to account for the Millennium promise" (Millennium Campaign 2006). That is hardly enough. If a town wants a bridge built across a river, it is not going to get it simply by organizing an advocacy campaign for it. This would not signify true commitment. We would believe that those in power really wanted a bridge only if they had someone prepare a detailed plan for building it and laid down the money to cover its costs.

The *Economist* described the Millennium Development Goals as "Ends Without Means" (*Economist* 2004, 72). But the concern is not only about money. The commitment about Official Development Assistance reaching 0.7 percent was not tied to specific action plans. There is a need for money, but there is also a need for real commitments to concrete plans, specific courses of action that are seriously expected to achieve the goals that are set out. Nothing like this has ever been established by any of the summit conferences on food and nutrition. Promises have been made, but over time we find that they have had little substance.

The Millennium Campaign is devoted to exhorting the governments of poor countries to do what needs to be done to assure that the goals are met. Who will hold the global community to account for doing its part in fulfilling the Millennium promise?

MONITORING REPORTS

It appears that the Millennium Development Project is being carefully monitored. The program is reviewed overall by the UN Department of Economic and Social Affairs (2006) as well as an interagency group coordinated by the United Nations Statistics Division, the World Bank (2006a), and the World Economic Forum (2006). With regard to food and nutrition in particular, in relation to Millennium Development Goal 1, we have reports from FAO (2005) and UNICEF (2006). There are also regional reports such as *The Millennium Development Goals: Progress in Asia and the Pacific 2006* (Millennium Development Goals 2006).

The major function of these reports is to track the movement toward the goals, nation by nation. They have little to say about the efforts of the global community. The World Bank's *Global Monitoring Report 2006* discusses global activities in a general way, but does not identify specific global commitments and the degree to which they have been fulfilled (World Bank 2006a). The UN's *Millennium Development Goals Report 2006* acknowledges the meagerness of Official Development Assistance and notes that the number of people going hungry is increasing (UN ECOSOC 2006, 5). The World Economic Forum's *Global Governance Initiative: Annual Report 2006* came to the broad conclusion that both poor countries and rich countries were not acting with the vigor required to fulfill the Millennium Development Goals. Its chapter on poverty and hunger found that while "transitory hunger received attention, chronic hunger remained widespread and persistent" (World Economic Forum 2006, 10).

Both the FAO's *State of Food Security in the World 2005* (FAO 2005a) and UNICEF's *Progress for Children: A Report Card on Nutrition* (UNICEF 2006) showed that little progress was being made, especially in sub-Saharan Africa, toward achieving Millennium Development Goal 1.

The UN Millennium Project Task Force on Hunger published its final report, *Halving Hunger: It Can Be Done*, only in 2005 (UN Millennium Project 2005a). How can one assess progress during the same year that the plan is released, or just a year or two after that?

What is being assessed? Are these reports monitoring the impacts of particular programmatic actions, or are they just monitoring trends that would have been followed regardless of the Millennium Development Project?

These monitoring reports focus mainly on whether nations are on track to achieve the Millennium Development Goals. That is useful. However, they do not give comparable attention to the amount and direction of the effort that is expended, whether by developing countries or by the global community. Thus, this monitoring is not linked to policy in that it does not examine the relationships between efforts and results, input and outputs. There is no consideration of the question: What works and what doesn't work, and why? At least some of the monitoring that is undertaken should be policy oriented in the sense that it would help those responsible for managing the program to redirect their efforts when the monitoring signals indicate that that would be appropriate.

The Millennium Project has been clear about the type and level of financial support that should be provided by the international system to support country-level work toward meeting the Millennium Development Goals (UN Millennium Project 2005b, 36–55). It is unfortunate that the periodic progress reports on the project do not give more attention to the shortcomings in the support provided by the richer countries of the world.

An editorial in *Nature* magazine in March 2007 was unstinting in its criticism of a new report on the Millennium Project:

> This bad situation is made even worse by the pseudoscientific veneer conferred by evaluating progress on the MDGs using 48 quantitative indicators compared with a 1990 baseline. Every year, the UN rolls out reports with slick graphics,

seemingly noting with precise scientific precision progress towards the goals. But the reports mask the fact that the quality of most of the underlying data sets is far from adequate. Moreover, the indicators often combine very different types of data, making aggregation and analysis of the deficient data even more complicated.

There are decent data for just a handful of indicators, such as child mortality, but for most of the 163 developing countries, many indicators do not even have two data points for the period 1990–2006. And few developing countries have any data for around 1990, the baseline year. It is impossible to estimate progress for most of the indicators over less than five years, and sparse poverty data can only be reliably compared over decades. To pretend that progress towards the 2015 goals can be accurately and continually measured is false. . . .

Indeed, the lack of data makes it impossible not only to track progress, but also to assess the effectiveness of measures taken. Has the existence of the MDGs changed pre-existing trends? Are bednets helping to control malaria? Are improvements in Asia down to the MDGs or simply economic growth? Currently, it's impossible to tell. Meanwhile, spurious claims of achievement are promoted. (*Nature* 2007)

A response from the director of the United Nations Statistics Division acknowledged that "only 17 countries have trend data for less than half of the indicators" (Cheung 2007).

Nature missed one central point: There really is no global program of action to be assessed. None of the monitoring reports track the fulfillment of commitments by the global community for one simple reason. There never were any commitments to concrete programs of action at the global level. There never was any global strategy that could seriously be expected to achieve the goal of halving hunger or halving wasting as defined in Millennium Development Goal 1.

The Millennium Project has announced a major transition on its website: "As of Jan 1, 2007, the advisory work formerly carried out by the Millennium Project secretariat team is being continued by an MDG Support team under the United Nations Development Program." The new entity, MDG Support, appears to acknowledge that the prospect for meeting the Millennium Development Goals are slim (UN Development Program 2007). The entire project seems to be slipping away.

The Millennium Development Project has been misleading because it has never had any real global program of action. This is not the story of a failed strategy; it is about the absence of strategy. Despite the lofty global rhetoric of the Millennium Development Project and all the summits and agreements on hunger that preceded it, malnutrition and the other MDG issues have always been treated only as a collection of national issues, not as global problems to be addressed with global programs. There never was a plan of action that could reasonably be expected to succeed.

THE NEED TO CLARIFY GLOBAL OBLIGATIONS

There are no scientific mysteries about how to end hunger in the way there might be with difficult diseases. People need food, education, and decent opportunities to do productive work. The challenge is to devise ways to assure that everyone always has these things.

The human right to adequate food means that there is an obligation to reach the goal of ending hunger and assuring food security for all. These obligations fall primarily on national governments, but they are shared by all of us. There are choices that can be made with regard to means, but there is no choice with regard to the obligation to move decisively toward the goal. Thus, *concrete obligations for assuring realization of the human right to adequate food for all can be identified through the formulation of a concrete strategy for realizing that goal.* Once one knows what steps are required to reach the goal, then there is an obligation to take those steps. If there are several different ways to reach the goal, choices may be made among them, but there is an obligation to choose some path that can realistically be expected to reach the goal.

There have been many global plans for responding to large-scale malnutrition, but they propose only to work around the edges of the problem, not to end it. There is a need for a global strategy and program of action that really could be expected to end malnutrition as a major public policy issue in the world. Not only moral considerations but also a fair interpretation of human rights law and principles require such a strategy and program of action.

The final report of the Millennium Task Force on Hunger says that developed countries should contribute more generously to development in poor countries (UN Millennium Project 2005a). However, like General Comment 3 (UN OHCHR 1990), it does not suggest that they have a legal obligation, or should have a legal obligation, to fund the program to any particular level. Reducing the role of the global community to that of an occasional donor or lender leaves the challenge almost entirely to the separate nations. This amounts to an evasion of responsibility. With their greater capacity, it falls primarily on the developed countries of the world to ensure realization of the *Universal Declaration of Human Rights* Article 28: "Everyone is entitled to a social and international order in which the rights and freedoms set forth in this Declaration can be fully realized."

A child may be born into a poor country, but that child is not born into a poor world. That child has rights claims not only against its own country and its own people; it has claims against the entire world. If human rights are meaningful, they must be seen as universal, and not merely local. Neither rights nor obligations end at national borders. While national governments have primary responsibility for assuring the realization of the human right to adequate food for people under their jurisdiction, all of us are responsible for all of us, in some measure. The task is to work out the nature and the depth of those global obligations.

REFERENCES

Aiken, William, and Hugh Lafollette, eds. 1995. *World Hunger and Morality*. New York: Prentice-Hall.

Barrett, Christopher, and Daniel G. Maxwell. 2005. *Food Aid after Fifty Years: Recasting Its Role (Priorities in Development Economics)*. London: Routledge.

Barry, Christian, and Thomas Pogge. 2006. *Global Institutions and Responsibilities: Achieving Global Justice*. Malden, MA: Blackwell.

Beigbeder, Yves. 1991. *The Role and Status of International Humanitarian Volunteers and Organizations: The Right and Duty to Humanitarian Assistance*. Dordrecht, The Netherlands: Martinus Nijhoff.

Borgstrom, Georg. 1972. "Ecological Aspects of Protein Feeding—the Case of Peru." In *The Careless Technology: Ecology and International Development*, ed. M. Taghi Farvar and John P. Milton. Garden City, NY: Natural History Press. www.iucn.org/themes/ceesp/Publications/SL/CT/Chapter%2041%20-%20The%20Careless%20Technology.pdf.

———. 1973. *Focal Points: A Global Food Strategy*. New York: Macmillan.

Bosnich, David A. 1996. "The Principle of Subsidiarity." *Religion & Liberty* 6 (July and August). www.acton.org/publicat/randl/article.php?id=200.

Carozza, Paolo G. 2003. "Subsidiarity as a Structural Principle of International Human Rights Law." *American Journal of International Law* 97: 38–79. www.asil.org/ajil/carozza.pdf.

Chatterjee, Deen K. 2004. *The Ethics of Assistance: Morality and the Distant Needy*. Cambridge: Cambridge University Press.

Cheung, Paul. 2007. Letter to the editor of *Nature*. Available at http://millennium indicators.un.org/unsd/mdg/Resources/Attach/News/2007/Mar/unsd_commentary_nature%2026-3.pdf.

CIESIN (Center for International Earth Science Information Network). 2006. *Where the Poor Are: An Atlas of Poverty*. Palisades, NY: CIESIN. www.ciesin.columbia.edu/povmap/downloads/maps/atlas/cover_front_matter.pdf.

Clapham, Andrew. 2006. *The Human Rights Obligations of Non-State Actors*. New York: Oxford University Press.

Corporate Accountability Working Group. 2007. Website at www.escr-net.org/working groups/workinggroups_show.htm?doc_id=428672&attrib_id=13664.

Darrow, Mac. 2003. *Between Light and Shadow: The World Bank, the International Monetary Fund and International Human Rights Law*. Portland, OR: Hart.

Economist. 2004. "Economics Focus: Ends without Means." *Economist*, 11 September, 72.

Eide, Asbjørn. 2005. "The Importance of Economic and Social Rights in the Age of Economic Globalisation." In *Food and Human Rights in Development*. Volume 1. *Legal and Institutional Dimensions and Selected Topics*, eds. Wenche Barth Eide and Uwe Kracht, 3–40. Antwerp, Belgium: Intersentia.

FAO (Food and Agriculture Organization of the United Nations). 2002. *Declaration of the World Food Summit: five years later*. Rome: FAO. www.fao.org/DOCREP/ MEETING/005/Y7106E/Y7106E09.htm#TopOfPage.

———. 2003. *Report of the Panel of Eminent Experts on Ethics in Food and Agriculture, Second Session, 18–20 March 2002*. Rome: FAO.

———. 2004a. *Globalization of Food Systems in Developing Countries: Impact on Food Security and Nutrition*. Rome: FAO. www.fao.org/documents/show_cdr.asp?url_file=/ docrep/007/y5736e/y5736e00.htm.

———. 2004b. *Implementing the Right to Adequate Food: The Outcome of Six Case Studies*. Rome: FAO. www.fao.org/DOCREP/MEETING/008/J2475E.HTM.

———. 2005a. *The State of Food Insecurity in the World 2005*. Rome: FAO. www.fao .org/docrep/008/a0200e/a0200e00.htm.

———. 2005b. *Voluntary Guidelines to Support the Progressive Realization of the Right to Adequate Food in the Context of National Food Security*. Rome: FAO. www.fao.org/ docrep/meeting/009/y9825e/y9825e00.htm.

———. 2006. *The Right to Food Guidelines: Information Papers and Case Studies*. Rome: FAO. www.fao.org/docs/eims/upload/214344/RtFG_Eng_draft_03.pdf.

Feeding Minds, Fighting Hunger. 2006. "Map of World Hunger: Proportion of Undernourished People (1998–2000)." www.feedingminds.org/img/map_africa_h.jpg.

Global Footprint Network. 2006. www.footprintnetwork.org/.

Gosselin, Abigail. 2006. "Global Poverty and Responsibility: Identifying the Duty-Bearers of Human Rights." *Human Rights Review* 8 (October–December): 35–52.

Havel, Václav, Kjell Magne Bondevik, and Elie Wiesel. 2006a. "Turn North Korea into a Human Rights Issue." *New York Times*, 30 October. www.nytimes.com/ 2006/10/30/opinion/30havel.html?_r=1&oref=slogin&pagewanted=print.

———. 2006b. *Failure to Protect: A Call for the UN Security Council to Act in North Korea*. Washington, DC: DLA Piper/U.S. Committee for Human Rights in North Korea. www.dlapiper.com/files/upload/North%20Korea%20Report.pdf.

Humanitarian Policy Group. 2006. "Saving Lives Through Livelihoods: Critical Gaps in the Response to the Drought in the Greater Horn of Africa." HPG Briefing Note. May. www.odi.org.uk/hpg/papers/RAPID_HornAfricaBriefing.pdf.

International Council on Human Rights Policy. 2003. *Duties sans Frontières: Human Rights and Global Social Justice*. Geneva: ICHRP. www.ichrp.org/paper_files/108_p _01.pdf.

Kent, George. 1982. "Food Trade: The Poor Feed the Rich." *Food and Nutrition Bulletin* 4 (October): 25–33. www.unu.edu/unupress/food/8F044e/8F044E05.htm #Food%20trade:%20the%20poor%20feed%20the%20rich.

———. 1994. "The Roles of International Organizations in Advancing Nutrition Rights." *Food Policy* 19 (July): 357–66.

———. 2002. "Food Trade and Food Rights." *UN Chronicle* 1. www.un.org/Pubs/ chronicle/2002/issue1/0102p27.html.

———. 2005. *Freedom from Want: The Human Right to Adequate Food*. Washington, DC: Georgetown University Press.

———. 2006. "Trade Successes and Human Rights Failures." *UN Chronicle* XLIII (September–November): 30–32. www.un.org/Pubs/chronicle/2006/issue3/0306 p30.htm.

Kuper, Andrew. 2005. *Global Responsibilities: Who Must Deliver on Human Rights.* New York: Routledge/Taylor and Francis.

Lang, Tim, and Michael Heasman. 2004. *Food Wars: The Global Battle for Mouths, Minds, and Markets.* London: Earthscan.

Lichtenberg, Judith. 2004. "Absence and the Unfond Heart: Why People are Less Giving Than They Might Be." In *The Ethics of Assistance: Morality and the Distant Needy*, ed. Deen K. Chatterjee, 75–97. Cambridge: Cambridge University Press.

Lucas, George R., and Thomas W. Ogletree, eds. 1976. *Lifeboat Ethics: The Moral Dilemmas of World Hunger.* New York: Harper Forum Books.

Millennium Campaign. 2006. *Millennium Campaign: Who's Doing What?* www.mil lenniumcampaign.org/site/pp.asp?c=grKVL2NLE&b=173901.

Millennium Development Goals. 2006. *The Millennium Development Goals: Progress in Asia and the Pacific 2006.* Bangkok: United Nations Economic and Social Commission for Asia and the Pacific, United Nations Development Program, and Asian Development Bank. www.mdgasiapacific.org.

Minus, Jeff. 2004. "UN, EU, World Court, Supreme Court: Subsidiarity, Anyone?" *Catholic Culture*, 22 November. www.catholicculture.org/highlights/highlights .cfm?ID=38.

Narula, Smita. 2006. "The Right to Food: Holding Global Actors Accountable under International Law." *Columbia Journal of Transnational Law* 44: 691–800. www.colum bia.edu/cu/jtl/vol_44_3_files/Narula.pdf.

Nature. 2007. "Millennium Development Holes." *Nature* 446 (22 March): 7134.

OECD (Organization for Economic Cooperation and Development). 2006. "Aid Flows Top USD 100 Billion in 2005." OECD, 4 April. www.oecd.org/docu ment/40/0,2340,en_2649_201185_36418344_1_1_1,00.html.

Pinstrup-Andersen, Per, and Peter Sandøe, eds. 2007. *Ethics, Hunger and Globalization.* Berlin, Germany: Springer.

Sandoz, Yves. 1992. "'Droit' or 'Devoir d'ingerence' and the Right to Assistance: The Issues Involved." *International Review of the Red Cross* 288 (May–June): 215–27.

Sandrasagra, Mithre. 2006. "Development: Nine Years, Eight Goals, No Time to Waste." Inter Press Service News Agency, 15 June. www.ipsnews.net/print.asp?idnews=33583.

Shelton, Dinah. 1985. "The Duty to Assist Famine Victims." *Iowa Law Review* 70: 1309–19.

Skogly, Sigrun. 2006. *Beyond National Borders: States Human Rights Obligations in International Cooperation.* Antwerp, Belgium: Intersentia.

Tobin, John. 2006. "Beyond the Supermarket Shelf: Using a Rights Based Approach to Address Children's Health Needs." *International Journal of Children's Rights* 14: 275–306.

UN (United Nations). 2006. "States and International Community Have a Duty to Fight Poverty, High Commissioner for Human Rights Says." Press release. December 8. Accessible at www.ohchr.org/english/press/newsFrameset-2.htm.

UN Department of Economic and Social Affairs. 2006. *The Millennium Development Goals Report 2006.* New York: DESA. http://mdgs.un.org/unsd/mdg/Resources/Sta tic/Products/Progress2006/MDGReport2006.pdf (see also United Nations Millennium Development Goals Indicators website at http://millenniumindica tors.un.org/unsd/mdg/Default.aspx).

UN Development Program. 2007. "MDG Support: Overview." Available at www
.undp.org/poverty/mdgsupport.htm.

UN ECOSOC (United Nations Economic and Social Council). 1998. *Substantive Issues Arising in the Implementation of the International Covenant on Economic, Social and Cultural Rights.* General Comment 9. The Domestic Application of the Covenant. Geneva: ECOSOC E/C.12/1998/24. www.unhchr.ch/tbs/doc.nsf/(Symbol)/E.C.12 .1998.24,+CESCR+General+comment+9.En?Opendocument.

———. 1999. *Substantive Issues Arising in the Implementation of the International Covenant on Economic, Social and Cultural Rights.* General Comment 12 (Twentieth Session, 1999) The Right to Adequate Food (Art. 11). Geneva: ECOSOC E/C.12/1999/5. www.unhchr.ch/tbs/doc.nsf/MasterFrameView/3d02758c707031d58025677f003b 73b9?Opendocument.

———. 2006. "Review of Trends and Perspectives in Funding for Development Cooperation": Note by the Secretary General. Geneva: ECOSOC E/2006/60. 8 May. http://daccessdds.un.org/doc/UNDOC/GEN/N06/341/56/PDF/N0634156.pdf? OpenElement.

UN General Assembly. 1970. *International Development Strategy for the Second United Nations Development Decade.* UN General Assembly Resolution 2626 (XXV). 24 October. http://daccessdds.un.org/doc/RESOLUTION/GEN/NR0/348/91/IMG/NR034891 .pdf?OpenElement.

UNICEF (United Nations Children's Fund). 1996. "Secretary-General Reports Big Progress for Children." Press Release. New York: UNICEF CF/DOC/PR/1996-24.

———. 2006. *Progress for Children: A Report Card on Nutrition* 4 (May). New York: UNICEF. www.unicef.org/progressforchildren/2006n4/.

UN Millennium Project. 2005a. *Halving Hunger: It Can Be Done.* Task Force on Hunger. London: Earthscan/Millennium Project. www.unmillenniumproject.org/ reports/tf_hunger.htm.

———. 2005b. *Investing in Development: A Practical Plan to Achieve the Millennium Development Goals.* London: Earthscan/Millennium Project. www.unmillenniumpro ject.org/reports/.

UN OHCHR. (United Nations Office of the High Commissioner for Human Rights). 1990. "The Nature of States Parties Obligations." CESCR General Comment 3. Geneva: OHCHR. www.unhchr.ch/tbs/doc.nsf/385c2add1632f4a8c 12565a9004dc311/94bdbaf59b43a424c12563ed0052b664?OpenDocument.

WHO (World Health Organization). 2003. *Global Strategy for Infant and Young Child Feeding.* Geneva: WHO. www.who.int/child-adolescent-health/New_Publications/ NUTRITION/gs_iycf.pdf.

Williams, Ian. 2005. "Annan Has Paid His Dues: The UN Declaration of a Right to Protect People from their Governments Is a Millennial Change." *Guardian,* 20 September. www.guardian.co.uk/comment/story/0,,1573765,00.html.

Windfuhr, Michael. 1998. "Role of International Organizations in the Implementation of the Rights Related to Food and Nutrition." Second Expert Consultation on the Right to Adequate Food as a Human Right. Heidelberg, Germany: FIAN— Foodfirst Informationa & Action Network. www.fao.org/Legal/rtf/Windfuhr.pdf.

World Bank. 2006a. *Global Monitoring Report 2006: Strengthening Mutual Accountability— Aid, Trade, and Governance.* Washington, DC: World Bank. http://web.worldbank.org/ WBSITE/EXTERNAL/EXTDEC/EXTGLOBALMONITOR/EXTGLOBALMONI

TOR2006/0,,menuPK:2186472~pagePK:64218926~piPK:64218953~theSite PK:2186432,00.html.

———. 2006b. *Repositioning Nutrition as Central to Development: A Strategy for Large-Scale Action.* Washington, DC: World Bank. http://web.worldbank.org/WBSITE/ EXTERNAL/TOPICS/EXTHEALTHNUTRITIONANDPOPULATION/EXTNUTRI TION/0,,contentMDK:20613959~menuPK:282591~pagePK:210058~piPK:2100 62~theSitePK:282575,00.html.

World Economic Forum. 2006. *Global Governance Initiative: Annual Report 2006.* Geneva: WEF. www.weforum.org/pdf/Initiatives/GGI_Report06.pdf.

2

Extraterritorial Obligations

A Response to Globalization

Rolf Künnemann and Sandra Ratjen

The right to adequate food as enshrined in the International Bill of Human Rights has been a pioneer in the revitalization of economic, social, and cultural rights since the late 1980s. However, two decades later, in spite of considerable progress with regard to the recognition and protection of these rights, globalization increasingly challenges these achievements. In this context, the right to food could be a pioneer again, thanks to the work of civil society on the extraterritorial obligations of states. These obligations offer concrete perspectives for a human rights response to globalization.

Globalization has a profound impact on food economies, agricultural production models, and in particular on people's access to and control of food productive resources such as land, water, seeds, forests, and fishing grounds. Victims of violations across the world have organized themselves against these threats to their right to adequate food, and the political struggle has articulated itself around the fight for "food sovereignty." Rural people are particularly victimized, but urban poor as well, by a global economic paradigm that values the return on capital invested in food production more than the human rights of the people who produce the food. Indeed, the UN Millennium Project has confirmed that rural people (and among them especially small-farm households) make up the bulk of the 854 million hungry and chronically malnourished worldwide. Even though most governments have clear human rights obligations under international law, they follow a hands-off approach or are pressured by international actors into implementing policies that violate economic, social, and cultural rights such as the human right to adequate food.

Human rights across borders are in urgent need of strengthening, in order to make governments aware of their obligations and hold them accountable.

An important ingredient in any such strategy is to overcome the reductionist view that economic, social, and cultural human rights only imply obligations under international law vis-à-vis persons inside the state's territory. In this context, extraterritorial obligations have received growing attention over the past years.

Linked to this development in international human rights law and debates, international civil society and some social movements have started to organize around economic and social human rights. In the 1980s, FIAN International became the first international human rights organization to specialize in the right to adequate food. Since then, FIAN has been addressing countless violations of this right. Meanwhile numerous other organizations have taken up promotional work on the right to adequate food and related economic and social rights. FIAN's work has always paid close attention to the developments of international human rights law. Since 1992 it has been working together with a growing alliance of organizations for a right to petition the UN against violations of the International Covenant on Economic, Social and Cultural Rights through a new Optional Protocol.

UNIVERSALITY OF RIGHTS IMPLIES
UNIVERSALITY OF OBLIGATIONS

Universality is a basic element of human rights. Universality has been underlined again and again by the community of states, most notably perhaps at the World Conference on Human Rights in Vienna in 1993. In fact, universality is part of the definition of human rights. Human rights are different from citizen's rights. Depending on where a person is born, she may have varying citizens' rights or fundamental rights and freedoms under the state's constitution. However, no matter where she may live, she has the same human rights as everyone else and cannot lose these rights wherever she may be. Human rights are not territorial.

Human rights are sources of states' obligations, and these obligations have been articulated and regulated in international and national human rights law. How is the universality of human rights reflected in states' obligations?

It is sometimes held that human rights only generate obligations for the state in which a particular individual is currently located. This belief lacks both pragmatism and legal foundations. It overlooks that human rights are a joint and universal concern of humanity and that obligations should be attributed as best suited by the case at hand. Very often an exclusive obligation of the territorial state (territorial obligation) will be sufficient, but often cooperation is so crucial that it becomes obligatory. Moreover, there are situations where realization of a person's human rights requires action or inaction by a state abroad.

Territoriality has always been part of the concept of state. Nevertheless, states have always been acting beyond their borders, and not only in times of war. The issue of human rights obligations toward a person outside a state's territory—extraterritorial obligations—reaches far beyond humanitarian law. It deserves a central place in the concept of human rights because it reflects the universality of human rights.

Recognition of the fundamental importance of extraterritorial obligations has reemerged only recently. The first international expert conference on the Extraterritorial Scope of Human Rights Treaties took place in January 2003. Nongovernmental organizations (NGOs) have started to refer to it in their parallel reporting under the human rights covenants (Windfuhr 2001). The UN special rapporteur on the right to adequate food discussed the issue (UN ECOSOC 2005). Several general comments of the UN Committee on Economic, Social and Cultural Rights (CESCR) allude to it.

The term *international obligations* is sometimes used for *extraterritorial obligations*, but *international obligations* is already in use to refer to obligations under international law in general—and therefore lacks precision in this context and can lead to confusion. Extraterritorial obligations are not just any state's obligations under international law or obligations referring to international issues. They emanate from individuals' claims of human rights from foreign states and international institutions, and therefore deserve a precise term of reference.

The recent interest in extraterritorial obligations can be seen as a human rights response to globalization. In recent years, transnational corporations, international trade, food aid, development assistance, and intergovernmental organizations have all expanded their reach. The studies presented in this book testify to the relevance of these actors in the field of economic, social, and cultural human rights. The World Bank has been allowed for decades to deny the relevance of human rights for its work. And transnational corporations have worked hard to shape international law according to their business interests in the context of the World Trade Organization—trying to marginalize international human rights law and environmental law.

States, oblivious of their extraterritorial obligations—or in support of the economic and political interests of national elites—have often gone along, or were pressed into going along, with this agenda. The richer countries tended to see the destruction of human rights standards by "their" transnational corporations as a matter to be dealt with by the victims' states, knowing very well that often these states are not willing or are not in a position to enforce human rights against such foreign actors. The richer countries did not concern themselves with their human rights obligations in such contexts. Globalization of profit-making markets, yes, globalization of human rights obligations, no?

The International Covenant on Economic, Social and Cultural Rights (ICESCR) describes the states parties obligations as something to be undertaken "individually and through international assistance and co-operation." The spirit of this treaty gives a central role to international cooperation in general, and assistance in particular.

Nowhere in the covenant is it said that in order for rights holders to benefit from a state's obligations they have to be within this state's territory. Nevertheless, the covenant has all too often been misunderstood as a mutual agreement of states to fully implement human rights obligations only for persons in their own territories, and as offering only a vague promise of cooperation to assist needy states parties so that those states could implement their obligations toward persons in their territory. Such a reduced view of states' obligations falls short of the universality of human rights and the legal content of the covenant. Moreover it deprives states of the political potential embodied in extraterritorial obligations to regulate some of the most pressing political problems in this age of globalization.

Extraterritorial obligations have been challenged on the grounds that they would create administrative chaos. It is said that states have a hard enough time dealing with obligations toward persons in their own territories and would be unable to deal with obligations toward noncitizens outside their borders. Another conflictive issue is the legal nature of extraterritorial obligations. There is a clear need to address these concerns and to detail the respective human rights obligations toward persons outside one's territory.

Human rights analysis provides the concepts to properly deal with this problem. It is useful here to distinguish between two types of extraterritorial obligations: bilateral and multilateral, the latter referring to state obligations when acting within international organizations (Künnemann 2004).

Some fear the possible weakening of the nation state as a result of overloading it with extraterritorial obligations. It has often been said that the nation-state has been weakened in the context of globalization, sometimes to the extent that it may have problems meeting its human rights obligations. Whether one shares this view or not, there can hardly be any doubt about the need to strengthen the nation-state so that it can better implement and enforce its human rights obligations in a world of globalization. Some intergovernmental institutions, such as the international financial institutions, sometimes act as if they see themselves as being de facto beyond state control. Some transnational corporations try to be not only de facto but even de jure beyond states' human rights control. This agenda is often falsely termed "liberalization." The contradiction between an international deregulation agenda on the one hand and social and ecological standards on the other cannot be denied. The same holds true for the governance problem of intergovernmental organizations. In both contexts, extraterritorial obligations allow the nation-state to assert itself and better meet its purposes.

STRENGTHENING HUMAN RIGHTS IN TIMES OF GLOBALIZATION

There is a growing body of research on the effects of globalization on human rights. How should the international community react to human rights violations that are rooted in the process of globalization? Liberalization and privatization have in many countries effectively reduced the state's ability to protect and fulfill economic, social, and cultural rights. There is an urgent need to address the obligations of states to respect, protect, and fulfill the human rights not only of their own people but also of people outside the state's jurisdiction. Steps have been taken in this direction in the Voluntary Guidelines on the Right to Food (FAO 2006) and also the guidelines on development-based evictions and displacement formulated by the UN special rapporteur on the right to adequate housing.

State obligations toward people in other countries—extraterritorial obligations—need to be further strengthened in international human rights law. The firm establishment, monitoring, and enforcement of extraterritorial obligations require a careful approach. They have to be linked to the growing body of understanding of the scope and limits of national human rights obligations.

While acknowledging that all human rights are interdependent, the discussion here is limited to economic, social, and cultural human rights. There is already a lively international debate on extraterritorial obligations in relation to civil and political human rights (Coomans and Kamminga 2004; Lorenz 2005; Schäfer 2006). Over the last few years, first steps have been taken by international courts to develop international jurisprudence on the extraterritorial application of human rights treaties. However, this jurisprudence is so far limited to civil and political rights, and is highly inconsistent (Cerone 2006).

Civil society has an important role to play in helping to clarify extraterritorial obligations. Civil society organizations active in human rights and development are well positioned to bring the perspective of the victims of human rights violations into the discussion. In 2001, Brot für die Welt, EED (German Church Development Service) and FIAN presented the first civil society report on extraterritorial obligations to the UN Committee on Economic, Social and Cultural Rights (Windfuhr 2001). This report was well received by the committee and by civil society, and academics and the UN special rapporteur on the right to food have referred to it in further defining the normative basis and content of extraterritorial obligations.

THE EXTRATERRITORIAL OBLIGATIONS OF STATES

It might be a political goal of states to take into account human rights when making decisions with international effects, but is it also a legal obligation? There is a need to respond adequately to human rights violations that involve the coresponsibility of a state other than the state of the victim. The understanding that both states carry obligations under international law toward these people is an important precondition to effectively implement human rights.

International human rights law is often understood to address only the relationship between the state that has ratified human rights treaties and the individuals and groups who live in this state. The challenge of globalization lies in analyzing the relationship between the state and individuals and groups who live outside the state's borders. Various terms have been used to describe this relationship in terms of human rights obligations. Besides *extraterritorial obligations*, *international obligations* or *transnational obligations* (Coomans and Kamminga 2004) are used as well. The term *extraterritorial obligation* recognizes the fact that the nature of relationship between the state and people residing outside its territory (which are not citizens of this state) is different from the relationship with its citizens and migrants living within its territory.

Extraterritorial obligations should not be confused with *extraterritoriality* in the sense that the power of a state's laws is extended outside its territory. (The extraterritorial application of national laws might be sensible in some instances for a state to comply with extraterritorial human rights obligations under international law. This however needs a very careful approach.) Rather, people outside a state's territory should be empowered to claim their rights on the basis of international law against a state that has contributed to, or even committed, the human rights violation they are suffering.

THE ROLE OF STATES WITHIN INTERNATIONAL INSTITUTIONS

The negative effects on economic, social, and cultural rights of agreements negotiated in the World Trade Organization (WTO) and of conditionalities imposed by the International Monetary Fund (IMF) and the World Bank have been at the center of the debate on extraterritorial obligations. Much of the debate is concerned with documenting the effects of the policies promoted by WTO, IMF, and World Bank, as well as with establishing direct legal obligations and human rights accountability of these international organizations. In terms of extraterritorial states obligations, the question is, how can states assure that international organizations are accountable? A related question is: What extraterritorial obligations do states have when they negotiate international agreements or vote on funding for large-scale development projects? During the last few years, the UN Committee on Economic, Social and Cultural Rights has encouraged state after state belonging to the international donor community (for example, Austria, Finland, Germany, Ireland, Japan, Norway, and the United Kingdom) "as a member of international financial institutions, in particular the International Monetary Fund and the World Bank, to do all it can to ensure that the policies and decisions of those organizations are in conformity with the obligations of states parties to the Covenant, in particular the obligations contained in articles 2 (1), 11, 15, 22 and 23 concerning international assistance and cooperation" (UN CESCR 2001).

The committee has also, in several general comments, addressed national and extraterritorial obligations of states when acting in international organizations. For example, the general comment on the right to work (Article 6 of the covenant) reads:

> In negotiations with international financial institutions, States parties should ensure protection of the right to work of their population. States parties that are members of international financial institutions, in particular the International Monetary Fund, the World Bank and regional development banks, should pay greater attention to the protection of the right to work in influencing the lending policies, credit agreements, structural adjustment programmes and international measures of these institutions. The strategies, programmes and policies adopted by States parties under structural adjustment programmes should not interfere with their core obligations in relation to the right to work and impact negatively on the right to work of women, young persons and the disadvantaged and marginalized individuals and groups. (UN CESCR 2005)

States parties to the covenant constitute a majority of 83 percent (77 percent in terms of voting power) on the board of the World Bank. Limited influence and a lack of effective control should therefore not be an argument against holding states parties accountable for their decisions in international fora. In its general comment on the right to water, the CESCR has made clear that it is the action of the state party that has to be scrutinized: "States parties should ensure that their actions as members of international organizations take due account of the right to water" (UN CESCR 2003). When voting on a decision affecting extraterritorial obligations in a multilateral context, a state should therefore vote according to its obligations as if the outcome depended on it alone. If the outcome then deviates from the state's vote, the state should still take steps to address the violations implied by the vote of the majority.

FOREIGN INVESTMENT AND TRADE

Foreign investment and trade are important aspects of globalization. There are cases in which the policies of international actors of various types have prevented national governments from fulfilling the economic, social, and cultural rights of their people.

Transnational corporations (TNCs), or multinational corporations (MNCs), are the driving force of globalization. It has even been said that we are approaching times "when corporations rule the world" (Korten 2001). MNCs are hard to regulate by nation-states because they organize their businesses transnationally and because they command a lot of economic power. The domestic and extraterritorial obligations to protect, however, require that states get this regulatory job done.

There are four major arguments why it makes sense to strengthen accountability of MNCs in their home country to effectively address their responsibility for human rights violations in other countries:

> Firstly, the bargaining power of host states—a majority of which are developing and in competition with each other for the investment from MNCs—is significantly less than that of home states throughout the entry and operation of MNCs. . . . Secondly, attaining effective jurisdiction over corporations based overseas is fundamental to the success of any model of extraterritorial regulation. It is easier to reach a subsidiary through the parent rather than vice versa, as it is the parent corporation which exercises control over its subsidiaries and/or affiliate sister concerns. . . . Thirdly, given that a developed legal system and the availability of resources are prerequisite for the operation of extraterritorial regulation, home states, which generally possess these preconditions, are better placed to implement the extraterritorial model. . . . Fourthly, chances of conflict arising out of extraterritoriality are greatly reduced if a home state model is adopted, because the economic, social and legal structures of home states provide that human rights standards are defined at a higher level in these states than they are in host states. (Deva 2004)

Eventually, however, multilateral regulation may be necessary to effectively implement states' extraterritorial obligations to protect the victims of human rights abuses by transnational actors. In the absence of such international legislation, however, the Organization for Economic Cooperation and Development (OECD) *Guidelines for Multinational Enterprises* may be useful for holding companies accountable for human rights abuses (OECD 2007). The instrument's distinctive implementation mechanisms include the operations of National Contact Points (NCPs), which are government offices in both home and host states charged with promoting the guidelines and handling complaints presented against MNCs. However, the OECD guidelines are not binding on the activities of MNCs. Future mechanisms could be developed on the basis of the UN Norms on the Responsibilities of Transnational Corporations and Other Business Enterprises with Regard to Human Rights, adopted by the UN Sub-Commission on Human Rights in 2003 (UN ECOSOC 2003).

INTERGOVERNMENTAL ORGANIZATIONS

In his report to the UN Commission for Human Rights in 2004, the UN special rapporteur on the right to housing reported, "Development-induced displacement has seen an even greater intensification in recent years as a result of processes of economic globalization. In effect, economic liberalization policies and structural adjustment programmes have made the dilemma of development-induced displacement all the more urgent" (UN ECOSOC 2004). These policies and programs have to a large extent been influenced by policy advice and funding from international financial institutions (IFIs).

When human rights are violated in the context of a project financed by a multilateral development bank (MDB) or as a result of policies promoted by this institution, all actors involved are jointly responsible. The major responsibility lies with the victims' state, which fails to respect or protect human rights. However, the MDB and its influential member states, should from the outset avoid any actions that contribute to the violation of human rights. Also, the governing states of the MDB should ensure that the partner state and private companies respect human rights in the implementation of their projects.

Many projects have major implications for the human rights of project-affected persons. This raises at least three sets of questions for states' policy making in the MDBs: First, what kind of development projects and concepts are MDBs promoting? Are such development projects compatible with a human rights approach to development? Second, is it in line with the governing states' extraterritorial obligations to support a government or a private company that has a record of being unable or unwilling to respect human rights? Third, how can victims of human rights violations claim their rights if the national judicial system is not working in the interest of the victims?

The World Bank has only recently recognized that human rights are relevant to its work. It is still far from understanding that the World Bank as an institution is bound by international human rights law, whether directly or through its members, and that it has to assume responsibility for human rights violations in the context of projects funded by the World Bank or of policies promoted by it. States should therefore take a two-track approach to comply with their obligations under the International Covenant on Economic, Social and Cultural Rights and other international human rights treaties when governing the World Bank. On the one hand, states should ensure that their own decisions in multilateral development banks do respect, protect, and contribute to the fulfilment of human rights. On the other hand, they should actively promote the international human rights accountability for multilateral development banks, for example by promoting a reporting procedure for MDBs based on Article 18 of the ICESCR.

FOOD SOVEREIGNTY AND EXTRATERRITORIAL OBLIGATIONS

Social movements such as La Via Campesina, the international coalition of peasants' organizations, have started to develop their own approaches to the human rights violations suffered by their members. In cooperation with

FIAN and others, La Via Campesina addresses the increasing marginalization of peasants and their human rights. This work has gained another dimension with the development of a broad movement struggling for "food sovereignty." Tremendous progress has been achieved within civil society regarding this issue. It is a broad political struggle to gain or regain control over food, agriculture, and nutrition policies by peoples and communities. The substance of the debate has increased with the decision of some states to integrate food sovereignty into their national legislation. These states, such as Mali, Nepal, and Venezuela, are the laboratories of concrete and integrated policy making in favor of food sovereignty. As part of this effort, these states are carrying out consultations with the people who are most affected by hunger and malnutrition, namely rural people and in particular smallholder farming households. Topics for consultation include national decisions on various key aspects of food sovereignty, such as agricultural and rural development models, access to resources, consumer protection, and trade.

As the world's food system is increasingly globalized, so is the systematic marginalization of the world's food producers. Consumers' right to food must not be realized as a result of violations of the human rights of food producers, whether in the same country or other countries. The human right to adequate food, like all human rights, must be understood as having global reach.

EXTRATERRITORIAL OBLIGATIONS ARE NEEDED TO STRENGTHEN THE RIGHTS-BASED APPROACH TO DEVELOPMENT AND ASSISTANCE

As the special rapporteur on the right to food has emphasized, under the ICE-SCR, states have an obligation to support the fulfilment of the right to food in other countries. The international community has often been generous in providing assistance, especially in acute crisis situations. However, some states remain unclear about their general obligation to provide assistance under international law. Civil society has been concerned about the absence of food aid in some situations of great need, and it has also been concerned about aid being provided in ways that have important negative impacts. For example, in some cases food aid might have a short-term positive impact on the food situation of the recipients, at least preventing them from dying of hunger, but in the medium and long term have negative effects on the progressive realization of the right to adequate food. This may occur because the food aid impedes access to markets and resources by small-scale producers, or because it disrupts traditional food consumption patterns. Even in the short term, food aid can be detrimental to human rights and dignity.

In recent years, understanding of the ways in which food aid can be harmful has increased. It is not a secret that food aid, especially tied aid (linked to conditionalities imposed on the recipients) is often a way for the world's largest agricultural states to distribute their surpluses, and it frequently serves geostrategic political or commercial interests.

Food and nutrition rights of the individual recipients of "predatory" food aid are often neglected. Indeed, the provision of food aid can impair consumer protection and food adequacy since if it lasts for some time, the consumption patterns can change, bringing about new nutritional problems. This in turn can deprive local producers of their markets, threatening the right to food of additional groups. Related to this issue, the distribution of genetically modified products in food aid has at times been delivered without prior consent and full information to the recipients.

What can the international community learn from these negative impacts? It has been shown that in many instances, aid in cash is more effective than aid in kind in helping people get out of hunger crises in a sustainable and human rights–compatible way. Furthermore, food that is purchased in the target region can ensure that a much greater quality of food is distributed under international food assistance programs. Human rights analysis of food aid policies has played a crucial role in defining these lessons and best practices. Indeed, the human rights approach can help to guide the design, implementation, and evaluation of food aid policies.

A human rights–based approach should guide the design of all international food aid programs. Human rights should provide both the framework and the goal. This approach should be based on a clear understanding of extraterritorial human rights obligations and the ways in which they address some of the major problems of globalization.

CONCLUSION

When the devastating tsunamis of December 2004 struck the countries bordering the Indian Ocean, the reaction of the community of peoples, and later of the community of states, showed to what extent there is a globalized consciousness of moral responsibility. In the broad development of economic, social, and cultural human rights over the past quarter century, the human right to food has served as a pioneer in many ways. There are good reasons to believe that the right to adequate food will also provide the testing ground for dealing with one of the greatest challenges of today: finding a human rights response to globalization.

On the basis of this analysis, we recommend the following:

- Mainstream the right to adequate food and extraterritorial obligations related to this right within the UN system, especially in the Special Procedures of the Commission on Human Rights and the Working Group on the Right to Development, as well as in the work of the UN special representative on business and human rights.
- Encourage the special representative to tackle especially the issue of the negative impact of the aggressive merchandising strategies of industrial food groups worldwide on food safety and quality, and the nutritional situation of children and adolescents.
- Explore the possibilities to deliver parallel reports to the UN CESCR on the extraterritorial obligations of states concerning the right to food.
- Encourage the United Nations System Standing Committee on Nutrition and the nutrition community in general to actively follow the renegotiation process of the Food Aid Convention, which is supposed to regulate the use of commodities in emergency food assistance (Food Aid Convention 1999; Elliesen 2005).
- Follow the growing debate and work of civil society movements in favor of food sovereignty, and explore synergies between the right to food and extraterritorial obligations.
- Engage in dialogue with states at the national level on a human rights–based approach to development and on state policy coherence.
- Call on intergovernmental organizations involved in operational and advisory work related to food and nutrition to respect, protect, and fulfill the right to food.
- Promote justiciability of the right to food and development of case law, including the adoption of an Optional Protocol to the ICESCR. The existence of such a protocol, providing a complaint mechanism for violations of economic, social, and cultural rights at the international level, would strengthen the understanding of the scope of the right to food and related state obligations.

REFERENCES

Cerone, John. 2006. *Out of Bounds? Considering the Reach of International Human Rights Law.* Center for Human Rights and Global Justice Working Paper Number 5. New York University School of Law. http://test.extrajudicialexecutions.org/docs/WPS_NYU_CHRGJ_Cerone_Final.pdf.

Coomans, Fons, and Menno T. Kamminga, eds. 2004. *Extraterritorial Application of Human Rights Treaties.* Antwerp/Oxford: Intersentia.

Deva, Surya. 2004. "Acting Extraterritorially to Tame Multinational Corporations for Human Rights Violations: Who Should 'Bell the Cat'?" *Melbourne Journal of International Law* 5: 37–65. http://papers.ssrn.com/sol3/papers.cfm?abstract_id=630421.

Elliesen, Tillmann. 2005. "Deciding on the Food Aid Convention's Future," *Development and Cooperation* (February). www.inwent.org/E+Z/content/archive-eng/02-2005/stud_art3.html.

FAO (Food and Agriculture Organization of the United Nations). 2006. *The Right to Food Guidelines: Information Papers and Case Studies*. Rome: FAO. www.fao.org/docs/eims/upload/214344/RtFG_Eng_draft_03.pdf.

Food Aid Convention. 1999. United Nations Treaties. http://untreaty.un.org/ENGLISH/bible/englishinternetbible/partI/chapterXIX/treaty80.asp.

Korten, David. 2001. *When Corporations Rule the World*. 2nd edition. Bloomfield, CT: Kumarian Press.

Künnemann, Rolf. 2004. *The Extraterritorial Scope of the ICESCR*. Heidelberg: FIAN International, EED (German Church Development Service), Brot für die Welt. www.fian.org/live/index.php?option=com_doclight&Itemid=100&task=details&dl_docID=42.

Lorenz, Dirk. 2005. *Der territoriale Anwendungsbereich der Grund—und Menschenrechte. Zugleich ein Beitrag zum Individualschutz in bewaffneten Konflikten*. Berlin: Berliner Wissenschafts-Verlag.

OECD (Organization for Economic Cooperation and Development). 2007. *Guidelines for Multinational Enterprises* website. www.oecd.org/department/0,2688,en_2649_34889_1_1_1_1,00.html.

Schäfer, Bernhard. 2006. *Zum Verhältnis Menschenrechte und humanitäres Völkerrecht. Zugleich ein Beitrag zur extraterritorialen Geltung von Menschenrechtsverträgen*. Potsdam: Deutsches Institut für Menschenrechte.

UN CESCR. (United Nations Committee on Economic, Social and Cultural Rights). 2005. General Comment 18. The Right to Work. Geneva. 7–25 November. UN Doc. E/C.12/GC/18. www.unhchr.ch/tbs/doc.nsf/(Symbol)/E.C.12.GC.18.En?OpenDocument.

———. 2001. Concluding Observations on Germany. 24 September. UN Doc. E/C.12/1/Add.68. www.unhchr.ch/tbs/doc.nsf/(Symbol)/E.C.12.1.Add.68.En?Open document.

———. 2003. General Comment on the Right to Water. 20 January UN Doc. E/C.12/2002/11. www.unhchr.ch/tbs/doc.nsf/385c2add1632f4a8c12565a9004dc311/a5458d1d1bbd713fc1256cc400389e94?OpenDocument&Highlight=0,CESCR.

UN ECOSOC (United Nations Economic and Social Council). 2003. *Norms on the Responsibilities of Transnational Corporations and Other Business Enterprises with Regard to Human Rights*. E/CN.4/Sub.2/2003/12/Rev.2. 26 August. www.unhchr.ch/Huri docda/Huridoca.nsf/0/64155e7e8141b38cc1256d63002c55e8?Opendocument.

———. 2004. *Report of the Special Rapporteur on Adequate Housing as a Component of the Right to an Adequate Standard of Living*, Miloon Kothari. 8 March. UN Doc. E/CN.4/2004/48. www.unhchr.ch/Huridocda/Huridoca.nsf/(Symbol)/E.CN.4.2004.48.En?Opendocument.

———. 2005. *Report of the Special Rapporteur on the Right to Food*, Jean Ziegler. 24 January. UN Doc. E/CN.4/2005/47. http://daccessdds.un.org/doc/UNDOC/GEN/G05/104/24/PDF/G0510424.pdf?OpenElement.

Windfuhr, Michael. 2001. *Parallel Report: Compliance of Germany with Its International Obligations under the ICESCR*. Heidelberg: FIAN International, EED (German Church Development Service), Brot für die Welt. www.fian.org/live/index.php?option=com_doclight&Itemid=100&task=details&dl_docID=82.

3

International Legal Dimensions of the Right to Food

Federica Donati and Margret Vidar

The right to food, like any other human right, carries with it mainly obligations of states toward their own people. However, there are also international dimensions that are increasingly recognized, discussed, and debated. These include obligations of states that are effective outside their territories and toward people not under their jurisdiction, obligations of states as members of intergovernmental organizations, and obligations of intergovernmental organizations as such, as well as the responsibilities of nonstate actors, international nongovernmental organizations (INGOs) and transnational corporations (TNCs).

The discussion is closely linked to the process of globalization and the recognition of increasing interdependence of all countries. The role of the state itself as an institution is also undergoing changes, often entailing limitations of states' ability to make adequate interventions, privatization, and the rising influence of other global actors, in particular corporations. In some cases, the human rights system of state responsibility toward its own people is being called into question and found insufficient in the modern world.

Apart from the obligations that states have toward people living under their own jurisdiction, the international obligations they have relating to human rights could be divided in the following manner:

1. Obligations that states have undertaken vis-à-vis other states with regard to human rights generally. International treaties are set up to be among states. Therefore, they are making a legal commitment to other states to respect human rights. For this reason, human rights treaties often provide for an interstate complaint procedure, for instance Article 41 of the International Covenant on Civil and Political Rights (ICCPR). Thus, if

country A believes country B is violating the rights of the latter's own people, the former may submit a complaint to a designated authority, such as the Human Rights Committee, responsible for the ICCPR.

2. Obligations of states toward other states with regard to the rights of the latter's nationals present in the first country. The protection and enforcement of such obligations are functions normally carried out in practice through embassies and consulates, based on principles of reciprocity, and the principle that it is generally in a state's interest to look after its own. On rare occasions, protection activities may lead to national- or international-level state complaints or court procedures.

3. Obligations toward persons outside their jurisdiction. This is the main focus of the current debate and of this book. The traditional opinion, in line with the principles of states being the primary duty bearers with regard to persons under their jurisdiction, is that states are not, could not, and should not be responsible for individuals or groups outside their jurisdiction. Anything else could lead to chaos and abuse. These notions are increasingly challenged on grounds of international solidarity in an increasingly interconnected world, supported by various treaty provisions on international cooperation.

4. Obligations that states have as they exercise their membership in international organizations. It is indisputable that states have the same human rights obligations whatever the context in which they are working, such as voting in the United Nations General Assembly, the World Bank, the Food and Agriculture Organization (FAO) of the United Nations, and International Monetary Fund (IMF), or World Trade Organization (WTO). However, this principle has been largely ignored to date. Closely linked to this concept is the call issued by the Committee on Economic, Social and Cultural Rights (UN CESCR 1999a) for countries to bear in mind their human rights obligations during bilateral and multilateral trade and other negotiations.

The obligation of states as members of international organizations and as international actors should be distinguished from obligations that intergovernmental bodies may have as such. They all have international legal personality, can enter into contracts, and enjoy certain diplomatic immunities. However, the intergovernmental bodies are not and cannot be parties to human rights treaties, which are the sole domain of states. Despite this, it can be argued that intergovernmental bodies as such and their secretariats have independent human rights obligations, on the basis that human rights are generally universally recognized and that all members of the UN and other intergovernmental organizations have extensive human rights obligations. These issues will all be discussed in the light of the human right to food.

A separate legal question is whether nonstate actors such as corporations and nongovernmental organizations (NGOs) can be held to have independent human rights obligations. There is a minority school of thought that holds this to be so, in light of the failure of both the home states and the states in which they operate to adequately protect human rights and hold third parties to account. This, however, is in opposition to the general principle of human rights law that only states are duty bearers, and physical or legal persons can only breach legislation and rules that a state has established, rather than the human right as such.

TNCs and INGOs are not considered international legal persons, although the latter may be recognized by intergovernmental organizations (IGOs) through various means, such as granting "consultative status" with the Economic and Social Council. Instead, TNCs and INGOs are regulated by the states in which they are headquartered and in which they operate. They may have legal human rights–related obligations as stipulated by national legislation.

A distinction is made here between *obligations*, which are legally binding, and *responsibilities*, which are not. At the international level, states have human rights obligations, IGOs have more limited human rights obligations as well as other legal obligations, but TNCs and INGOs have only responsibilities, for which they cannot be held legally accountable. This distinction is commonly made in human rights discussions. Under general international law, however, the concept of *state responsibility for internationally wrongful acts* is used for describing which acts and under which circumstances a state can be internationally accountable for acts carried out by state agents. In this context, *responsibility* refers to a legal rather than moral responsibility.

Another distinction is sometimes made between direct and indirect obligations in two ways: First, we say that states have direct obligations for acts that are committed by agents of the state, and indirect obligations to prevent acts by nonstate actors. For instance, if the police kill someone unlawfully, then this involves a direct obligation, but if a person not performing any official functions commits murder, then the state has an indirect responsibility to see to it that it does not go unpunished. Second, we say that nonstate actors can sometimes be held indirectly accountable when they are complicit in human rights violations by the state. For instance, if an oil company is exploiting natural resources under a license by government, knowing that in the process peasants have been forcibly evicted without compensation and protesters suffered violence by the police, then that company could bear indirect responsibility.

Most of the discussion in this chapter refers to human rights obligations outside the national jurisdiction of a state. The term "international obligations" includes both obligations to cooperate internationally, which require at least two states, and extraterritorial obligations, some of which a state can implement without reference to other states.

Any act or omission by the state that contravenes international human rights law is a violation in the context of this chapter. Thus defined, acts by nonstate actors that are not in conformity with human rights law are defined as abuses, whereas the failure of the state to control the act or punish it, could constitute a violation of the right.

This chapter will unfold in the following way. First, the meaning of the right to food will be explained. Then the domestic obligations will be listed, so as to give grounding for the discussion about international-level obligations of states and international organizations and the responsibilities of international nongovernmental organizations and transnational corporations.

NORMATIVE CONTENT OF THE RIGHT TO FOOD

Article 11 of the International Covenant on Economic, Social and Cultural Rights (ICESCR) sets out the right to adequate food as part of the right to an adequate standard of living. In addition, it recognizes the fundamental right to be free from hunger. The concept "right to food" in human rights debates may mean the right to adequate food as an umbrella term, the right to adequate food and the right to be free from hunger together, or even the entire body of human rights law that recognizes food and nutrition related rights.

The two paragraphs of Article 11 are closely related. The measures listed in paragraph 2 apply equally to implementation of that paragraph and to the previous one on the right to adequate food. The fundamental right to be free from hunger is often seen as closely related to the right to life, recognized in the International Covenant on Civil and Political Rights (ICCPR). It is also often taken to constitute the absolute minimum for the right to adequate food.

The Committee on Economic, Social and Cultural Rights (CESCR) offered a definition of the right to food in its General Comment 12 (UN CESCR 1999a). The CESCR was established to monitor the implementation of the ICESCR by states parties. *States parties* refers to states that have ratified the treaty under discussion, and thus have accepted their obligations under it. The CESCR issues general comments to explain its interpretations of provisions of the ICESCR, while its reviews of state reports are further means of generating authoritative interpretations of the content of states' obligations under the covenant. The Human Rights Committee and other treaty bodies use similar procedures for the other main human rights treaties. Although general comments are not legally binding, they represent authoritative interpretations and declarations of the law.

According to the CESCR definition, "the right to adequate food is realized when every man, woman and child, alone or in community with others, has physical and economic access at all times to adequate food or means for its procurement" (UN CESCR 1999a, para. 6). The right to food also contains elements related to availability, accessibility, adequacy, and acceptability, as well as sustainability and relationship to other human rights and to human dignity. The adequacy aspect relates both to quantity and quality, in terms of food safety and nutrition value. The acceptability refers to the culture to which an individual belongs as well as individual tastes and choices. Sustainability is mainly a limitation on the production, processing, and consumption patterns related to food, and includes environmental, economic, and social sustainability.

The enjoyment of the right to food should not interfere with the enjoyment of other human rights. Thus, it would be unacceptable to have to sacrifice the right to education of children for their right to food, or to give up civil rights in return for the right to food. Malnutrition is a violation of human dignity according to the Commission on Human Rights (UN CHR 1997, para. 1). Physiologically adequate food procured in ways that deny human dignity cannot fully realize the right to adequate food. For instance being forced to scavenge through rubbish for one's food may fulfill one's nutritional needs, but would fall short of realization of the right to adequate food.

The UN Commission on Human Rights established the mandate of the United Nations special rapporteur on the right to food. The rapporteur is tasked with seeking, receiving, and responding to information on all aspects of the realization of the right to food including the urgent necessity of eradicating hunger, establishing cooperation with governments, IGOs (in particular FAO), and NGOs, on the promotion and effective implementation of the right to food and making appropriate recommendations on the realization thereof, taking into consideration the work already done in this field throughout the UN system and identifying emerging issues related to the right to food worldwide (UN CHR 2000). The special rapporteur also has been mandated to pay attention to the issue of drinking water, taking into account the interdependence of this issue and the right to food (UN CHR 2001, para, 9).

The definition adopted by the UN special rapporteur on the right to food, seeks to capture the essence of the above elements, for the purposes of the mandate, as follows:

> The right to food is the right to have regular, permanent and unobstructed access, either directly or by means of financial purchases, to quantitatively and qualitatively adequate and sufficient food corresponding to the cultural traditions of the people to which the consumer belongs, and which ensures a physical and mental, individual and collective, fulfilling and dignified life free from anxiety. (UN SR 2001, para. 22)

It should be stressed that the recognition of the right to food does not re-place individual responsibility. The right to food does not mean that the state must provide food directly to everyone. Such a direct entitlement can only arise when a individuals are unable, for reasons beyond their control, to pro-vide for themselves. All individuals must respect the right of others to ade-quate food, and the right to food should primarily be fulfilled through indi-viduals' own efforts to feed themselves and their families. Parents bear special obligations to ensure that their children are adequately nourished. Further-more, equal human rights do not imply equal claim to assistance and enti-tlements. This is determined by the individual's own means and situation.

DOMESTIC HUMAN RIGHTS OBLIGATIONS OF STATES

In international law generally, states have responsibilities toward each other, not toward individuals. Human rights law works on similar princi-ples, that is, by ratifying or otherwise acceding to treaties that are binding on states, states undertake the human rights obligations contained in those treaties. The difference is that individuals are the subject of human rights law, not states. Generally speaking, the individuals thus protected are the ones directly under the jurisdiction of the state in question.

Furthermore, as a rule, only states have obligations under international human rights law. Individuals acting in their own capacity, alone or in groups, have moral responsibilities, but generally cannot be accused of vio-lating international human rights law. National legislation is needed to cre-ate individual legal obligations, such as to not sell unsafe food. It should also be noted that businesses, as legal persons, have similar responsibilities. They have independent legal obligations under national law, and the peo-ple who run them have moral responsibilities. Note that the argument should not be turned on its head: Businesses do not have human rights, al-though the human beings involved in running them certainly do.

Obligations to take steps for the realization of economic, social, and cul-tural rights stemming from the ICESCR are legally binding upon those states that have ratified or acceded to the ICESCR. This, however, does not imply that those states that have not yet ratified or acceded to the ICESCR are ex-empt from achieving the realization of these rights. First, those states that have so far only signed the ICESCR, which is the first formal step to express a state's intention to be bound by the ICESCR at a later stage, are under the ob-ligation not to take actions and measures that run contrary to the spirit of the ICESCR. Second, it can be argued that the realization of a minimum thresh-old of economic and social rights and, in relation to the right to food, the re-alization of—at least—freedom from hunger is part of customary interna-tional law that is binding upon all states regardless of whether they have ratified or acceded to the ICESCR. The nature of the right to be free from hunger as customary international law can be argued on the basis of the great number of resolutions, declarations, and commitments calling for an end to hunger that all states have subscribed to, as well as an increasing number of constitutional and judicial interpretations at the domestic level and of the practice whereby most states most of the time do make efforts to achieve freedom from hunger for their people (Narula 2006, 791).

Obligation to Take Steps to the Maximum of Available Resources

Article 2 of the ICESCR outlines the nature of states parties' legal obligations and determines how they must approach the implementation of the substantive rights contained in Articles 6 to 15 of the ICESCR.

The first paragraph of Article 2 of ICESCR says:

> Each State Party to the present Covenant undertakes to take steps, individually and through international assistance and cooperation, especially economic and technical, to the maximum of its available resources, with a view to achieving progressively the full realization of the rights recognized in the present Covenant by all appropriate means, including particularly the adoption of legislative measures.

In its General Comment 3, the CESCR elaborated on the nature of the legal obligations of states parties as set out in Article 2 (UN CESCR 1991). This general comment reaffirms that the principal obligation is to take steps to achieve progressively the full realization of the rights contained in the ICESCR, including the right to adequate food. This imposes an obligation to move as expeditiously as possible toward that goal. Every state is obliged to ensure for everyone under its jurisdiction access to the minimum essential food that ensures their freedom from hunger, understood as food that will maintain an adult and ensure normal growth of children.

Article 2 requires all states parties to begin immediately to take measures toward the full enjoyment by everyone of all the rights in the ICESCR. The "progressive realization" component of Article 2 is often mistakenly taken to imply that states are obligated to assure the realization of some rights only after they have reached a certain level of economic development or even without taking any special measures at all, but relying on private institutions and the market instead. This is not the intent of the clause. Rather, the duty in question obliges all state parties, regardless of their level of national wealth, to move immediately and as quickly as possible toward the realization of economic, social and cultural rights. This clause should never be interpreted as allowing states to defer indefinitely efforts to ensure the enjoyment of the rights laid down in the ICESCR. According to the special rapporteur on the right to food, the concept of "progressive realization" cannot be used to justify persistent injustice and inequality. It requires governments to take immediate steps to continuously improve people's ability to feed themselves and to eliminate hunger (UN SR 2006, para. 26).

There are also many obligations in the ICESCR that require immediate implementation and that cannot be subjected to progressive realization. These obligations require immediate steps, as they mainly entail the duty of state agents to refrain from taking certain actions that could impair the enjoyment of the right in question. This would apply especially to the nondiscrimination provisions and to the obligation of states parties to refrain from actively violating economic, social, and cultural rights or withdrawing legal and other protections relating to those rights. Furthermore, this duty is not subject to the limitation of "maximum of available resources" discussed below. Thus, it requires that existing resources be devoted in the most effective way possible to the realization of the rights enshrined in the ICESCR (UN OHCHR 1991). The prohibition of discrimination as an immediate obligation is particularly important, as many societies are very unequal and thus are obliged to prioritize the allocation of resources to those groups that suffer discrimination in practice or have suffered from previous discrimination.

The provision of Article 2 on devoting the "maximum of its available resources" toward the realization of the right to food can be used both to encourage more resource allocation or as an excuse not to take action because of lack of resources. As recognized in the Limburg Principles on the Implementation of the International Covenant on Economic, Social and Cultural Rights, however, the requirement of using the maximum of its available resources obliges states parties to ensure minimum subsistence rights for everyone, regardless of the level of economic development in a given country. Furthermore, the principles stipulate that in determining whether adequate measures have been taken for the realization of the rights recognized in the ICESCR, attention should be paid to equitable and effective use of and access to the available resources (Limburg Group 1987).

The CESCR is also of the view that a minimum core obligation to ensure the satisfaction of, at the very least, minimum essential levels of each of the rights contained in the ICESCR is incumbent upon every state party (UN CESCR 1991). The establishment of this minimum core obligation has as a corollary that a state party cannot, under any circumstances, justify its noncompliance with it. This is understood to be of a non-derogable nature, that is, there are no exceptions that could justify the absence of a minimum essential level of economic, social, and cultural rights.

The term "available resources" applies both to domestic resources and to any international economic or technical assistance or cooperation available to a state party. In the use of available resources, due priority should be given to the realization of rights recognized in the ICESCR, considering the need to assure to everyone the satisfaction of subsistence requirements as well as the provision of essential services.

There is a strong presumption that retrogressive measures that push back the level of realization of economic, social, and cultural rights are not permitted under the ICESCR. Any deliberately retrogressive measure would require the most careful consideration and would need to be fully justified by reference to the totality of the rights provided for in the ICESCR and in the context of the full use of the maximum available resources (UN CESCR 1990, para. 9). In addition, Article 5 of the ICESCR prohibits the lessening of standards of respect for human rights once achieved. Thus governments may not adopt policies that lead to deterioration in access to food that fulfils the standards of adequacy, accessibility, availability, acceptability, and sustainability.

The adoption of legislative measures mentioned in Article 2 will, in many cases, be indispensable if economic, social, and cultural rights are to be made real, but laws alone are not a sufficient response at the national level. Administrative, judicial, policy, institutional, financial, and educational measures and many other steps will be required by governments in order to ensure these rights to all. The specific measures depend on the situation, and the state has a considerable margin of discretion in determining what measures are appropriate in a given circumstance. However, CESCR affirms that it has the authority to determine whether a particular measure is appropriate (UN CESCR 1990, para. 4).

If we apply these general concepts of legal obligations to the right to food, it becomes clear that the obligations of states to act to ensure their people's realization of the right to food, like other economic, social, and cultural rights, are limited by the provisions that the realization may be achieved progressively, and may be limited by the maximum of available resources. This means that a poor country is not expected immediately to ensure the same level of assistance for food that a rich country can afford. However, even the poorest country is bound to ensure the highest level of realization of the rights that its resources will permit and, at the very least, a basic minimum level of the right to food.

Obligations to Respect, Protect, and Fulfill

In its General Comment 12 (UN CESCR 1999a) the CESCR introduced an analysis based on three types or levels of obligations to the right to food: the obligations to respect, to protect, and to fulfill. In turn, the obligation to fulfill incorporates both an obligation to facilitate and an obligation to provide.

The FAO Council adopted in November 2004 the *Voluntary Guidelines on the Progressive Realization of the Right to Adequate Food in the Context of National Food Security* (FAO 2005), also known as the right-to-food guidelines. The guidelines build on existing international law, in particular the ICESCR and General Comment 12, but focus on practical recommendations for actions that can be taken at the national level to fulfill the right to adequate

food. The Right to Food Guidelines build on the CESCR levels of obligations as follows:

> States Parties to the [ICESCR] have the obligation to respect, promote and pro-
> tect and to take appropriate steps to achieve progressively the full realization
> of the right to adequate food. States Parties should respect existing access to ad-
> equate food by not taking any measures that result in preventing such access,
> and should protect the right of everyone to adequate food by taking steps so
> that enterprises and individuals do not deprive individuals of their access to
> adequate food. States Parties should promote policies intended to contribute
> to the progressive realization of people's right to adequate food by proactively
> engaging in activities intended to strengthen people's access to and utilization
> of resources and means to ensure their livelihood, including food security.
> States Parties should, to the extent that resources permit, establish and main-
> tain safety nets or other assistance to protect those who are unable to provide
> for themselves. (FAO 2005, para. I.17)

This shows the understanding of the negotiators of the right-to-food
guidelines that the progressive realization element is primarily relevant for
obligations to fulfill, or in the words of the guidelines, to "promote appropriate policies." The qualification of available resources is primarily relevant
for the obligation to provide, or, in the words of the guidelines, to establish
safety nets and other assistance "to the extent that resources permit."

The obligation to *respect* the right to adequate food requires states parties
not to take any measures that result in reducing existing access to food. This
obligation means that governments should not arbitrarily take away people's access to food or make it difficult for them to gain access to food. The
obligation to respect the right to food is effectively a negative obligation, as
it entails limits on the exercise of state power that might threaten people's
existing access to food. Violations of the obligation to respect would occur,
for example, if the government arbitrarily evicted or displaced people from
their land, especially if the land constituted their main means of feeding
themselves. Another example is if the government took away social security
provisions without making sure that vulnerable people had alternative ways
to feed themselves, or if the government knowingly introduced toxic substances into the food chain, as the right to food entails access to food that
is "free from adverse substances." In situations of armed conflict, it would
mean that government troops must not destroy productive resources and
must not block, delay, or divert relief food supplies intended for the civil-
ian populations (UN SR, 2006, para. 22).

The obligation to protect the right to food requires measures by the state to
ensure that enterprises or individuals do not deprive individuals of their access to adequate food. This obligation means that the government must pass
and enforce laws to prevent powerful people or organizations from violating

the right to food. The obligation to protect requires states to regulate nonstate actors, including corporations that may threaten other people's right to food. The government must also establish bodies to investigate and provide effective remedies, including access to justice, if that right is violated. The government would also fail to protect the right to food if it took no action when a company polluted a community's water supply (UN SR 2006, para. 23).

In order to *protect* the right to food, the government might also have to take action if people were denied access to food on the basis of gender, race, or other forms of discrimination. It might also have to introduce laws to protect consumers against harmful food products or against unsustainable means of production. That could include the introduction of labeling on foods or legislation on the use of pesticides or genetically engineered food (UN SR 2006, para. 23).

The obligation to *fulfill* is a positive obligation, requiring direct action, through appropriate policies and programs to fulfill the right to food of those who are not able to realize it for themselves. First and foremost, then, states must actively seek to identify vulnerable groups and individuals, as mentioned in Guidelines 13 and 14 of the right-to-food guidelines (FAO 2005).

The obligation to *fulfill (facilitate)* means the state must proactively engage in activities intended to strengthen people's access to and utilization of resources and means to ensure their livelihood, including food security. The exact measures to be taken depend on the situation in the particular country. Article 11, paragraph 2, of the ICESCR gives some guidance, as it specifies production, harvesting, conservation, processing, retailing, and consumption of food. Further examples could include land reform and other measures to improve access to natural resources, such as recommended in Guideline 8 of the right-to-food guidelines (FAO 2005). Measures to improve employment prospects, through training, equipment, and credit in rural and urban areas are also facilitating measures. Logic dictates that under the obligation to facilitate come also measures to facilitate the enjoyment of the right itself, through information about rights and entitlements and creation of recourse mechanisms, that is, institutions and mechanisms to which individuals can turn in the event their rights are violated, such as ombudspersons and human rights commissions in addition to the courts.

Finally, whenever individuals or groups are unable, for reasons beyond their control, to realize their right to adequate food by the means at their disposal, states have the obligation to *fulfill (provide)* means for the realization of that right directly. This obligation also applies for persons who are victims of natural or other disasters and as a result are no longer able to procure food for themselves. This obligation means that the government must take positive actions to identify vulnerable groups, to establish emergency response plans, and to take action to ensure that people are provided for in such circumstances. The form of provision depends on the situation of the country. Some states have comprehensive social security provisions providing for cash payment that cover food and other basics; others have food stamps, school feeding programs, subsidized foods, or direct distribution of free food. For many, international food aid is indispensable for coping. At the very least, such provisions must ensure freedom from hunger.

A state would violate the obligation to provide if it let people starve when they were in desperate need and had no way of helping themselves. Therefore the obligation to provide may entail also that a state must ask for international humanitarian aid, if it is itself unable to provide assistance. States that, through neglect or misplaced national pride, make no such appeals or deliberately delay such appeals are violating their obligation. The question of whether anyone has the obligation to respond to appeals for assistance will be addressed below, in the section on Intergovernmental Obligations.

The legal, administrative, policy, institutional, and budgetary measures aimed at respecting, protecting, and fulfilling the right to adequate food can be either of an immediate or a progressive nature. Generally, obligations to *respect* the right to food are more likely to be immediate and those to *fulfill* it are more likely to be progressive. Obligations to protect may be progressive as well, as establishing legal and institutional frameworks can take some time, whereas instructing the police force to act can be done immediately.

In support of the obligation to always respect, protect, and fulfill a minimum essential level of economic and social rights, the Human Rights Committee in *Womah Mukong v. Cameroon*, in a case concerning food for prisoners, stated:

> Certain minimum standards regarding the conditions of detention must be observed regardless of a State party's level of development. These include . . . provision of food of nutritional value adequate for health and strength. It should be noted that these are minimum requirements which the Committee considers should always be observed, even if economic or budgetary considerations may make compliance with these obligations difficult. Failure to meet these requirements would constitute a breach of the right to be free from torture and cruel, inhumane and degrading treatment. (UN HRC 1991, para. 9.3)

This case is a clear illustration that states have the obligation to provide food directly to those groups that for certain reasons do not have access to means to provide food for themselves. In the particular case of prisoners, if states do not meet this obligation for whatever reason, including economic and budgetary constraints, it will not only violate prisoners' right to food but also their right to be free from torture and cruel, inhumane, and degrading treatment.

INTERNATIONAL HUMAN RIGHTS OBLIGATIONS OF STATES

Under international human rights law, the primary duty bearer is the state and the primary rights holder is the individual. Indeed, the primary relationship in human rights law is between the state and the individuals under its jurisdiction. These domestic obligations were explained above. However, states are not always able to protect their people from the impacts of decisions taken in other countries, given the current context of globalization and strong international interdependence. In such a globalized, interconnected world, the actions taken by one state may have negative impacts on the right to food of individuals living in other states. International trade in agriculture is a case in point. For example, it can be argued that subsidies to farmers in developed countries have negative impacts on farmers and the right to food in developing countries if food products are "dumped" on developing countries (UN SR 2006, para. 28).

As mentioned in the introduction to this chapter, this principle of international human rights law, that states are the primary duty bearers with regard to persons under their jurisdiction, could logically entail that a state is not, could not, and should not be responsible for individuals or groups outside their jurisdiction. Anything else could lead to chaos and abuse. However, one might also argue the contrary: if states recognize that the *primary* responsibility is that of the national state, as in the right-to-food guidelines (FAO 2005, para. III.2), then this also opens the door to the recognition of *secondary* responsibility by others, including other states.

For civil and political rights the presumption is against extraterritoriality. Thus Article 2, paragraph 1 of the ICCPR commits each state party to "respect and to ensure to all individuals within its territory and subject to its jurisdiction the rights recognized in the present Covenant." In turn, this thinking is transferred to economic, social, and cultural rights, even though the relevant treaty provisions are quite different (Skogly and Gibney 2002).

However, it is increasingly held among experts in economic, social, and cultural rights that states do have obligations to at least respect and even protect and fulfill the right to food in other countries. The protection would entail extending the regulation of all agents under the state's jurisdiction—such as transnational corporations and international nongovernmental organizations incorporated or headquartered in the country—to prevent them from abusing human rights of individuals in other countries. In chapter 1 of this book, George Kent maintains that no human being should suffer hunger and malnutrition in a world that has the capacity to assure that everyone is fed adequately. Supporting the notion of obligations to fulfill are human rights treaty provisions on international cooperation. International cooperation is also considered a general principle of international law.

From both a moral and a practical point of view, all countries should ensure that their policies do not contribute to human rights violations in other countries. Indeed, as such actions would not fall in any way under the sovereignty of other states, there could be few arguments against an obligation to respect the right to food in other countries. This should also be seen as a minimum requirement, or minimum content, of international cooperation.

Poorer and less powerful states may be unable to take the legislative and administrative steps needed to protect their own people from the activities of third parties, whether within or outside the state. A poor state may also be tempted not to regulate corporate and individual conduct that infringes on other individuals' right to food. If it did, it might lose foreign currency earnings or suffer other economic losses. Other countries may suffer from such high levels of corruption as to make them both unwilling and unable to take action. In the light of such realities, the human rights of individuals in one country are affected by actions of individuals and especially corporations operating internationally and with headquarters in another country. It would thus be logical to demand that the headquarters country should take responsibility for regulating that corporation

Lack of capacity to respect, protect, and fulfill the right to food is a frequent result of a state's poverty. This gap could be filled by international assistance. There is a generally accepted obligation to request international assistance. There is also a strong case for the recognition of an obligation to provide international assistance. Yet, there has always been a strong resistance from donor states to recognize any legally binding and meaningful obligations to assist (Cotula and Vidar 2002, 22).

Scholarly understanding of human rights obligations has deepened considerably since the adoption of ICESCR. In particular, appreciation of the negative and positive obligations implied is much stronger than it was in 1966 when the ICESCR was adopted by the United Nations General Assembly. Therefore, we will refer as much to the current authoritative interpretations of these provisions in general as to the specific wording of Articles 2, 11, and 23 of ICESCR.

Extraterritorial Obligations

The term *extraterritoriality* generally refers to effects of a state's action on people living under the jurisdiction of other states, that is, outside the territory of the first state. This concept differs from the one on the obligation to cooperate under Articles 55 and 56 of the Charter of the United Nations (UN Charter) or Articles 2, 11, and 23 of the ICESCR, discussed in the following section.

Several international and regional monitoring bodies have already affirmed that human rights obligations cannot simply stop at territorial borders. The European Court of Human Rights, for example, ruled in *Loizidou v. Turkey* that the "responsibility of Contracting Parties can be involved because of acts of their authorities, whether performed within or outside national boundaries, which produce effects outside their own territory" (European Court of Human Rights 1998, para. 52).

According to Article 2:1 of the International Covenant on Civil and Political Rights (ICCPR), obligations are binding only on states parties. However the Human Rights Committee, the body established to monitor the implementation of the ICCPR, said that the positive obligations on state parties to ensure ICCPR rights will only be fully discharged if individuals are protected by the state, not just against acts committed by agents of the state, but also against acts committed by private persons or entities. There may be circumstances in which a failure to ensure ICCPR rights would be considered violations of those rights by state parties if they permit or fail to take appropriate measures or to exercise due diligence to prevent, punish, investigate, or redress the harm caused by such acts by private persons or entities. Thus, the subjects of the state, such as corporations, do not commit human rights violations themselves, but the state itself may violate human rights when it fails to control those subjects.

In the case of privatization of some public services, the obligation to protect human rights, including the right to food, is very important in so far as states have to ensure that socioeconomic rights are consistently protected once private actors take over such services. States have to "ensure that privatization does not constitute a threat to the availability, accessibility, acceptability and quality" of the services delivered (De Feyter and Gomez Isa 2005, 21). Thus states have to exert due diligence in monitoring the operation of services by private bodies (Maastricht Group 1997). This obligation of due diligence obliges states to implement a regulatory scheme to prevent any abuse by third parties. According to the CESCR, for this regulatory system to be effective it must include independent monitoring, genuine public participation, and imposition of penalties for noncompliance (UN CESCR 2002).

It is generally accepted that as regards the international crimes of genocide, war crimes, crimes against humanity, torture, and forced disappearances, states are obliged to establish jurisdiction over such crimes even extraterritorially, that is, wherever they are committed and whichever the nationality of the perpetrators or the victims, insofar as those accused are found on their national territory. Although international criminal law on this issue had in mind only natural persons and not legal persons, such as corporations, it could be argued that international law does not prohibit the extension of extraterritorial jurisdiction to legal persons (De Schutter 2006, 17).

State responsibility in international law is usually conceived of as direct, as when the state is the cause of the breach through one of its agents. This can be subdivided into negative or positive obligations, as when a breach is attributable to either an act of omission (failure to perform a positive obligation) or an act of commission (action that violates a negative obligation). However, state obligations may also be indirect, whereby state agents are not the immediate agent of harm but an indirect or secondary agent of harm. In the *Velasquez-Rodrigues v. Honduras* case, the Inter-American Court of Human Rights found that a state is responsible for human rights violations if it fails in its duty to prevent human rights violations by third parties and to investigate, prosecute, and punish those directly responsible for the acts. This judgment made it clear that state responsibility extends to protection against violence by private individuals and to state compensation, even when the act of violation was not performed by state officials or performed by others on behalf of the state (Inter-American Court of Human Rights 1988). In this context, the responsibility for indirect violations corresponds to the obligation to protect human rights.

The argument of sovereignty could be raised against extraterritoriality: Why should and how could a state, the sending state, try to regulate behavior of any person or corporation once they are under the jurisdiction of another, the receiving state? Furthermore, such regulations would only affect the behavior of foreign entities in a country, not that of a state's own national entities, as the latter would only have to obey national law, but the former would also have to obey such special regulations. This could be considered unfair. However, the proposal is not that states are obliged to extend the entire legal system of a country to all operations of "their" companies and INGOs abroad, only the universally recognized human rights, including the right to food. Olivier De Schutter lists the principle of universality as a distinct justification for extending the jurisdiction of a state (De Schutter 2006, 11). This principle of universality means that all human beings everywhere should enjoy all human rights; extended protection can achieve that goal. For the right to food, standards on food safety, labeling, and other marketing practices are particularly relevant, such as those found in the *International Code of Marketing of Breast-milk Substitutes* (WHO 1981). A recent example of negotiated expression of an obligation to protect is in the right-to-food guidelines, which stipulate that international food aid should conform to internationally recognized food safety standards (FAO 2005, para. II.15.2).

The notion that the ICESCR implies extraterritorial obligations of states parties is not yet universally accepted. However there are strong advocates for this theory, such as academics and UN experts, including the UN special rapporteur on the right to food. This chapter holds that extraterritorial obligations of states parties is part of an emerging body of opinions and interpretations that may develop into a recognized standard of international human rights law. It is certain that there are obligations concerning the right to food outside a country's borders; it is just not clear exactly what they are. This book aims at contributing to clarifying these obligations, or at least to highlighting the questions and the urgent need for answers.

Obligation to Cooperate Internationally

Under Articles 55 and 56 of the UN Charter, all UN member states pledge to take joint and separate action for the achievements of the goals of the United Nations, which include both the achievement of higher standards of living and of universal respect for and observance of human rights and fundamental freedoms. It has been convincingly argued that the Universal Declaration of Human Rights (UDHR) constitutes the clarification of the human rights and fundamental freedoms referred to in the UN Charter. The right to an adequate standard of living including adequate food is recognized in Article 25 of the UDHR. In addition, Article 28 of the UDHR refers to the international environment.

The application of Articles 55 and 56, however, has always been balanced against the principle of sovereign equality of all states recognized in Article 2:1 of the UN Charter, and the principle of nonintervention in matters "essentially within the domestic jurisdiction of any state," stipulated in Article 2:7 of the UN Charter. The latter provision hindered the discussion of human rights situations in the early years of the UN Commission on Human Rights, but this yielded to the notion that human rights everywhere were of concern to the United Nations and its members. The principle of sovereign equality is in stark contrast to the fact that states are not equal in reality. Some states are powerful, others much less so. In the globalized world, other actors are also becoming more powerful than at least some states. These "nonstate actors" will be discussed later in this chapter.

Article 11 of the ICESCR on the right to an adequate standard of living including the right to adequate food has specific provisions on international cooperation:

1. . . . The States Parties will take appropriate steps to ensure the realization of this right, recognizing to this effect the essential importance of international co-operation based on free consent.
2. The States Parties to the present Covenant, recognizing the fundamental right of everyone to be free from hunger, shall take, individually and through international co-operation, the measures, including specific programmes, which are needed.

From these provisions it would seem that an obligation to cooperate in general is recognized, but that it should also be based on free consent, so that no state can be compelled to cooperate with another state. This would seem to work both ways, in the sense that a country cannot be forced to accept an offer of technical or other assistance from another, nor can a country be compelled to assist a particular state. Philip Alston holds that the "free consent" stipulation does not affect the obligation itself, only how this cooperation should be carried out (Alston 1984, 41). Cooperation is also foreseen through special mechanisms and institutions such as the United Nations and its Specialized Agencies, in Article 22, ICESCR.

Article 23 of ICESCR enumerates some specific ways of international co-operation, namely that they include (but are not limited to) further international conventions and recommendations, technical assistance, technical and regional meetings, and studies. This is, of course, quite limited, but could touch upon the obligations to respect, protect, and fulfill (facilitate and provide).

In General Comment 12, CESCR referred to the spirit of Article 56 of the UN Charter; the specific provisions contained in Articles 2:1, 11, and 23 of ICESCR; and the Rome Declaration of the World Food Summit (FAO 1997). It said that states parties should recognize the essential role of international cooperation and comply with their commitment to take joint and separate action to achieve the full realization of the right to adequate food (UN CESCR 1999a, para. 36).

2.1. Level of Cooperation

It would seem that states could argue, not altogether unreasonably, that the obligation to cooperate is fulfilled through membership in and cooperation through such international organizations, and that there are no bilateral obligations to cooperate.

Even if the obligation to cooperate is understood as more than membership in an international body, the ICESCR does not define any particular level of cooperation. In theory then, each state party that participates in any bilateral cooperation at all could claim its obligations are fulfilled under the ICESCR. This lacunae is, however, filled to some extent by later commitments in various declarations that generally prescribe that 0.7 percent of the gross domestic product of richer countries should be devoted to international development.

Development cooperation, already undertaken by wealthier countries, could also help to create an enabling environment. In the Monterrey Consensus (UN 2002) adopted by the International Conference on Financing for Development, developed states reaffirmed the goal to provide 0.7 percent of gross national product for development assistance to developing countries, and 0.15 to 0.20 percent to least developed countries. George Kent points out in chapter 1 that the 0.7 percent goal originated in a General Assembly resolution in 1970 and has remained a distant goal for most countries ever since.

This oft-repeated commitment suggests one plausible standard for the extent to which richer states would have an obligation to cooperate with poorer ones under the UN Charter. After a dip in the 1990s, Official Development Assistance increased in real terms and as a percentage of GNP in the mid-2000s. However, most donor countries are still far from the goal (OECD 2006). Of course, the 0.7 per cent GNP goal refers to all development assistance, not particularly to food security, let alone the right to food. The World Summit on Social Development endorsed the "20/20 Initiative," or a commitment of allocating 20 percent of official development assistance and 20 percent of national budgets to priority basic social programs (UN 1995, para. 88. c). This commitment has not been implemented. None of the FAO declarations and summits or the right-to-food guidelines provide for any specific cooperation goals.

Finally, it could be argued that the provision of Article 2, concerning the obligation to devote the "maximum of its available resources" applies not only to the primary duty bearer, but also to states with regard to international cooperation. If this holds, then one could argue both that more of total development assistance should be devoted to economic, social, and cultural rights, and that the total development resources should be increased. The exhortation by Kent in chapter 1, that development assistance should be increased until either the right to food is realized or that resources have been exhausted, suggests such an interpretation of "progressive realization" and "maximum of available resources" in Article 2 of ICESCR.

Again, however, this notion remains the field of *de lege ferenda*, or the law as it should be rather than the law as it is, *de lege lata*. The general commitments are only to be found in soft-law instruments, and countries generally do not treat the commitments as legal obligations but as goals that they would hope to meet one day. The provisions of the ICESCR are also not concrete enough to hold states to them. Therefore, working toward a new agreement of states to commit specific levels and types of resources to the right to food globally would be a positive undertaking, even if it were only in a soft-law instrument. The lack of specificity currently makes it near impossible to demand more and better international cooperation for the realization of the right to food as a matter of law. In the meantime, the moral argument remains strong.

General Comment 12 holds that states have a joint and individual responsibility to cooperate in providing disaster relief and humanitarian assistance in times of emergency, including assistance to refugees and internally displaced persons. Each state should contribute to this task in accordance with its ability. Priority in food aid should be given to the most vulnerable populations. Food aid should, as far as possible, be provided in ways that do not adversely affect local producers and local markets, and should be organized in ways that facilitate the return to self-reliance of the beneficiaries for food, through production or procurement. Such aid should be based on the needs of the intended beneficiaries. Products included in international food trade or aid programs must be safe and culturally acceptable to the recipient population (UN CESCR 1999a, paras. 38–39). These issues relate both to the obligation to provide and the obligation to respect.

2.2. Accountability for the Obligation to Cooperate

In four of its general comments (on the right to food, education, health, and water), the CESCR has included specific sections outlining the international obligations of states with regard to these particular rights (UN CESCR 1999a, 1999b, 2000a, 2002). In addition, in its discussions with states parties to the ICESCR of their reports, the CESCR has moved from simply recognizing that international cooperation is an obligation of all states to requiring states to comply with their international obligation to cooperate and take joint action for the realization of economic, social, and cultural rights. For example, the CESCR recommended to Belgium that it should raise its budget for development cooperation in order to meet the 0.7 percent target as set by the donor community (UN CESCR 2000b, para. 30). It also encouraged the Belgian government, as a member of international organizations, in particular the International Monetary Fund and the World Bank, to make all efforts to ensure that the policies and decisions of those organizations are in conformity with the obligations stipulated in the ICESCR and particularly the obligation of international assistance and cooperation (UN CESCR 2000b, para. 31).

In the case of Norway, the committee requested the government to provide disaggregated information on funds allocated to different sectors in the areas of economic, social, and cultural rights (UN CESCR 2005, para. 25). In examining the implementation of ICESCR in Italy, it expressed concern that the level of development assistance at that time, at 0.33 percent of gross domestic product, fell short of the United Nations target of 0.7 percent (UN CESCR 2004, para. 15). Although the CESCR may not be willing to set its own targets in terms of official development assistance, it may still play an important role in scrutinizing whether states live up to the various commitments they have made in international forums.

2.3. Prohibition of the Use of Food as an Instrument of Political or Economic Pressure

Often repeated in UN resolutions on the right to food is that "food should not be used as an instrument of political or economic pressure" and the reaffirmation of "the importance of international cooperation and solidarity" as well as "the necessity of refraining from unilateral measures that are not in accordance with international law" (UN CHR 2000, preambular para. 8 and UN General Assembly 2006b, preambular para. 8).

While international cooperation is mentioned in these resolutions, the main stress is on two acts that are seen as unlawful. This implies that the obligation to cooperate has a minimum content of an obligation to respect. The principle banning the use of food as an instrument of political pressure is the first part and refers to acts such as making food aid conditional on economic or political issues, setting up blockades hindering food supplies reaching another country, and the imposition of sanctions that affect food supplies of the population. The second act of unilateral measures not in accordance with international law is more of a reiteration and a reminder of the principle in the first part. The first principle thus has a broader application, as it would apply to measures otherwise lawful. For instance the Security Council has the authority to legally impose sanctions and blockades. However, these sanctions and blockades may never include withholding food. Unilateral measures, however, are generally allowed, as the only limit is that they must be in accordance with international law.

General Comment 12 holds specifically that states parties should refrain at all times from food embargoes or similar measures that endanger conditions for food production and access to food in other countries. Food should never be used as an instrument of political and economic pressure (UN CESCR 1999a, para. 37). This is a clearly negative obligation, an obligation to respect the right to food in other countries.

The right-to-food guidelines strongly urge states to avoid and refrain from unlawful unilateral measures that impede the full achievement of economic and social development by the population and hinder their progressive realization of the right to adequate food (FAO 2005, para. III.3). This language makes it clear that at stake is the right to food of individuals in countries other than the one applying the measures. Previously, the principles had been firmly brought into the realm of the right to food by their very placement in the right to food resolutions, whether or not World Food Summit participants originally intended this. It is interesting that these provisions are always juxtaposed with provisions about international cooperation, which is a clear indication that the minimum content of an obligation to cooperate internationally would be to refrain from violating the right with actions that have negative consequences in other countries.

Interventions to Protect Individuals from Their Own State

The global community has seen the emergence of a new international concept on the responsibility of the international community to protect individuals against their own state, which may ultimately become a new rule of customary law. Language embodying this norm was adopted by the world's heads of state meeting at the UN's sixtieth anniversary summit in 2005 (UN General Assembly 2005). It was reaffirmed the following year by the UN Security Council concerning genocide, war crimes, ethnic cleansing, and crimes against humanity (UN Security Council 2006). This norm could allow, or even eventually be taken to oblige, states to intervene in other states, even using armed force under Chapter VII of the UN Charter. The secretary-general also acknowledged that the global community has a responsibility to protect and that respect for national sovereignty could no longer be used as an excuse for inaction in the face of genocide, war crimes, ethnic cleansing, and crimes against humanity (UN 2006). However, as Kent pointed out in chapter 1, under the responsibility-to-protect umbrella, some people, such as Evans, actually emphasize the right to intervene and do not plainly acknowledge any corresponding obligation to intervene (Evans 2006).

It is reasonable to argue that this responsibility could include protection from violations of the right to food committed by the home state itself, particularly when these take the form of gross, systematic, and large-scale hunger situations, falling under genocide, crimes against humanity, or war crimes.

International Obligations to Respect, Protect, and Fulfill

According to the special rapporteur on the right to food, states should respect, protect, and support the fulfillment of the right to food of people living in other territories, to fully comply with their obligations under the right to food (UN SR 2006, para. 34). This differs somewhat from General Comment 12, which holds that states should "take steps to respect the enjoyment of the right to food in other countries, to protect that right, to facilitate access to food and to provide the necessary aid when required" (UN CESCR 1999a, para. 36), but is reasonable in light of the primary obligations of the state, under the jurisdiction of which people live. This analytical framework of obligations (to respect, protect, and support fulfillment) thus takes elements both of the obligation to cooperate and the notion of extraterritorial obligations described above.

4.1. Obligation to Respect

The obligation to respect is a minimum obligation that requires states to ensure that their policies and practices do not lead to violations of the right to food in other countries. This obligation does not require any resources to be provided; it is simply the principle to do no harm. States should refrain at all times from implementing policies with foreseeable negative effects on the right to food of people living in other countries. For example, food and water should never be used to exert political or economic pressure, and states should refrain at all times from food embargoes or similar measures that endanger conditions for food production and access to food in other countries or prevent the supply of water, as well as goods and services essential for securing the right to water (UN SR 2006, para. 35).

Policies such as export subsidies for agriculture may also have negative effects when production is exported to agrarian-based developing countries.

It is clear that such policies can have a negative impact on the right to food of people living in those countries since their livelihoods may be destroyed and they may not be able to purchase food, even if the food is cheaper. In Mexico, for example, it is estimated that up to 15 million Mexican farmers and their families, many from indigenous communities, may lose their livelihoods as a result of the North American Free Trade Agreement and competition with subsidized United States maize. This obligation also implies that states should refrain from making decisions within the WTO, the IMF, or the World Bank that could lead to violations of the right to food in other countries (UN SR 2006, para. 35).

General Comment 12 exhorts states parties to "ensure that the right to adequate food is given due attention, whenever relevant, in international agreements, and to consider the development of further international legal instruments to that end" (UN CESCR 1999a, para. 36).

4.2. Obligation to Protect

The obligation to protect requires states to ensure that their own citizens and companies, as well as other parties subject to their jurisdiction, including transnational corporations and international nongovernmental organizations, do not violate the right to food in other countries. This puts an obligation on the state to regulate its corporations and nonstate actors in order to protect the inhabitants of other countries. With the increasing monopoly control by transnational corporations over all components of the food distribution chain, from production, trade, and processing to marketing and retailing of food, and control over the majority of water concessions worldwide, it is becoming more difficult for less powerful national governments to regulate transnational corporations working within their territory to respect human rights, making it essential that the often more powerful "home" states engage in adequate regulation. In water privatization, for example, steps should be taken by "home" states to ensure that the policies and activities of transnational corporations respect the right to water of all people in the countries in which they are working (UN SR 2006, paras. 35–52).

The call for states to regulate their corporations and the impact that their operations may have on people under the jurisdiction of a different state is also supported by the special representative of the secretary-general on the issue of human rights and transnational corporations and other business enterprises. He indicated in his 2006 report that "there are no inherent conceptual barriers to states deciding to hold corporations directly responsible . . . either by extraterritorial application of domestic law to the operations of their own firms or by establishing some form of international jurisdiction" (UN Special Representative 2006, para. 65).

It would make sense to recognize the changing nature of the global-ized world and accept that the obligation to protect operates extraterri-torially. However, this is as of now in the field of *de lege ferenda*. As to whether national governments are *allowed* to protect the right to food of persons in other countries from abuses by TNCs incorporated in their own country, Olivier De Schutter has demonstrated that they *may* make provisions in their legislation to protect universal human rights every-where with regard to their own nationals, including legal persons (De Schutter 2006, 24).

4.3. Obligation to Support the Fulfillment

The obligation to support the fulfillment of the right to food requires states, depending on the availability of resources, to cooperate in facilitating the realization of the right to food in other countries. Developing states that do not possess the necessary resources for the full realization of the right to food should actively seek international assistance, and wealthier states have a responsibility to respond. This notion is strongly supported by most of the relevant provisions of ICESCR, but the provisions of Article 11 on interna-tional cooperation are, on the other hand, qualified by the words "based on free consent." Therefore, it is safer to say that there is a "responsibility" to re-spond rather than an "obligation," which would be legally binding.

Measures to facilitate extraterritorially the fulfillment of the right to food might not necessarily require providing significant material resources or in-ternational assistance. It might be sufficient if countries cooperated to pro-vide an enabling environment—one in which people are able to realize their right to food by their own efforts—in all countries. As Article 28 of the Universal Declaration of Human Rights states, "Everyone is entitled to a so-cial and international order in which the rights and freedoms set forth in this Declaration can be fully realized." For example, equitable trade rules and a fairer intellectual property rights regime could facilitate the domestic realization of the right to food in many countries. The right-to-food guide-lines also recognize the importance of the international community in helping or hindering the realization of the right to food and devote their third and last section to international measures, actions, and commitments, including on trade (FAO 2005).

Obligations of States as Members of Intergovernmental Organizations

It was noted above that the obligation to cooperate is fulfilled to some extent by membership in international organizations. However, the deci-sions made by states within these organizations, in particular the interna-tional financial institutions, can have far reaching effects on the enjoyment of the right to food around the world.

According to Smita Narula, IGOs are the sum of their parts and the parts consist of member states that are not supposed to leave their human rights obligations at the door when entering these corridors of power (Narula 2006, 742). The Maastricht Guidelines also provide that states parties' duty to protect extends to their participation in international organizations, where they act collectively. Member states should use their influence to ensure that violations do not result from the programs and policies of the organizations of which they are members (Maastricht Group 1997, para. 19). Narula quotes the World Bank's Senior Counsel who stated that, as governments are the owners of IGOs, multilateral financial institutions must be careful to ensure that if the treaties that member states have ratified are implicated in their projects, these treaties are appropriately taken into account in project design and finance (Narula 2006, 742).

Fons Coomans has concluded that states have international obligations to respect human rights *de lege lata*, the law as it is (Coomans 2004, 199). This means, inter alia, that when states are exercising their membership rights in IGOs they must avoid any action that could thwart the enjoyment of the right to food by individuals in any country in the world affected by that decision.

INTERGOVERNMENTAL ORGANIZATIONS

IGOs are essentially multistate actors. This may constitute the basis for subjecting them to the requirements of international human rights law through the member states that have ratified human rights instruments (Kent 2005, 32–33).

The notion that intergovernmental organizations as such have independent human rights obligations is not widely accepted. Yet, this is increasingly argued and quite convincingly so (Skogly and Gibney 2002).

As mentioned earlier in this chapter, only states are parties to human rights treaties, so IGOs cannot be directly bound by them. However, IGOs do have legal personalities and are bound to follow any provisions in international law aimed at them specifically. They are also bound by agreements that they have themselves entered into as well as by customary law and "general principles of law recognized by civilized nations," as stated in Article 38 of the Statute of the International Court of Justice, which defines the sources of international law. To the extent that human rights principles are general principles of international law, which we hold to be the case for the core content of the right to food, then this is binding for them as well. However, this is not to say that the obligations of IGOs are the same as that of states. Any possible obligations must be considered within the scope of the mandate and authority of the organization in question. As they are composed of states without being states themselves, IGOs should be considered a category in between state and nonstate actors.

Under Article 55 of the UN Charter, the goals of the United Nations include both the achievement of higher standards of living and universal respect for and observance of human rights and fundamental freedoms. The United Nations and its specialized agencies and funds therefore have an explicit link to human rights that other IGOs do not have.

Still, there are strong arguments for recognizing that all IGOs have an obligation to *respect* human rights. This is supported by the special nature of IGOs as being composed of states and governed by a community of states and the fact that IGOs are subjects of international law. While they are not parties to human rights treaties, human rights principles form part of the UN Charter, customary law, and general principles of law, all of which are binding to some extent on IGOs. This obligation to respect we regard as a full-fledged obligation, not just a responsibility.

Another issue is that there are no effective recourse mechanisms to hold IGOs to account. Even though Article 96 of the UN Charter and Article 65 of the Statute of the International Court of Justice allow their governing bodies to seek the Court's advisory opinion, this could only be done if the majority of member states agree. This does not mean that effective recourse mechanisms could not be established. UN agencies submit to the UN Administrative Tribunal and the specialized agencies to an International Labor Organization (ILO) Administrative Tribunal for adjudication of personnel cases brought against them (Bouayad-Agha and Hernández 2002). The World Bank has established an Inspection Panel where groups and individuals can bring complaints about the bank's projects on social and environmental grounds (Clark 2002). The obvious way, then, to establish accountability for IGOs would be for member states to establish independent panels or even special tribunals that have the mandate to receive complaints about human rights violations and order appropriate redress, restitution, compensation, or assurances of nonrepetition as the case may be.

ICESCR specifically foresees a role for UN specialized agencies. Article 22 states that matters arising out of the ICESCR and its implementation can be referred to relevant specialized agencies involved in relevant technical assistance for consideration of international measures for further realization.

In General Comment 2, CESCR considered the implications of Article 22. It stated, first, that UN agencies should respect all human rights. Those involved in promoting economic, social, and cultural rights, for instance, should strive to ensure that their activities are fully consistent with civil and political rights as well. Agencies should scrupulously avoid involvement in projects that, for instance, involved the use of forced labor or large-scale evictions or displacement, or were discriminatory. Indeed, agencies should promote all human rights in all their activities. CESCR also pointed out that development activities did not always contribute to economic, social, and cultural rights, as development projects had often been found to be ill conceived and even counterproductive in human rights terms.

General Comment 2 made the following specific recommendations to development agencies:

- Consider the requirement of a "human rights impact statement" in connection with major development projects.
- Institute human rights training for all UN agency personnel.
- Consider economic, social, and cultural rights at every stage in development projects, from initial needs assessment to final evaluation (UN CESCR 1990).

The 2006 General Assembly resolution on the right to food requested "all relevant international organizations, including the World Bank and the International Monetary Fund, to promote policies and projects that have a positive impact on the right to food, to ensure that partners respect the right to food in the implementation of common projects, to support strategies of Member States aimed at the fulfillment of the right to food and to avoid any actions that could have a negative impact on the realization of the right to food" (UN General Assembly 2006c, para. 16).

Following the secretary-general's call for integration of human rights into development and peacekeeping activities of the United Nations (UN Secretary-General 1997, para. 196), much work has been undertaken within different parts of the United Nations on a human rights–based approach to development, culminating in a Common Understanding adopted by member agencies (UN 2003). Specifically on food and nutrition, the UN System Standing Committee on Nutrition (SCN) adopted a human rights–based Strategic Framework in 2006 that aims to mainstream human rights into the work of the SCN (UN SCN 2006).

The UN's Common Understanding and the SCN's Strategic Framework did not discuss possible direct obligations of the UN agencies themselves; they only considered how the UN agencies could support the states in fulfilling their obligations as the direct duty bearers. However, this consideration indicates the recognition of some responsibility and role for the UN agencies themselves in helping to assure the realization of human rights.

Agencies with Food-Related Mandates

The realization of the right to food is part of the mandate and raison d'être of FAO. This means that FAO has legally binding obligations related to the right to food. The preamble of the constitution of FAO states its purpose as:

- raising levels of nutrition and standards of living of the peoples under their respective jurisdictions
- securing improvements in the efficiency of the production and distribution of all food and agricultural products

- bettering the condition of rural populations
- and thus contributing toward an expanding world economy and ensuring humanity's freedom from hunger

The last words are directly related to the wording of paragraph 2 of Article 11 of ICESCR, which recognizes the fundamental right to be free from hunger. This is no coincidence: FAO's director-general proposed the wording of Article 11:2, and FAO's constitution was amended in 1965, by adding the last sentence above, at the time agreement had been reached on the final text of the ICESCR (Moore and Vidar 1999).

Similarly, the World Health Organization (WHO) has a mandate to work for the "highest attainable standard of health," which is the same wording as in Article 12 of ICESCR. Nutrition is seen as part of health in this context. The mission statement of the United Nations Children's Fund (UNICEF) states that UNICEF is guided by the Convention on the Rights of the Child, which includes child nutrition (UNICEF 1996). However, this may not imply legally binding human rights obligations in the same sense that states have legally binding human rights obligations.

The above-mentioned organizations have direct legal obligations with regard to food, agriculture, and fisheries (FAO) and nutrition (UNICEF and WHO). While their mandates are not linked to human rights treaties specifically, the World Food Programme (WFP) was established for international food aid and the International Fund for Agriculture Development (IFAD) to provide international funding for agriculture and rural development and thus have legal obligations to fulfill those mandates. Furthermore, the United Nations Development Programme (UNDP) and the World Bank routinely support programs aimed at improving food security. All these agencies are part of the United Nations family and thus have a strong link with human rights.

While we maintain that FAO, WHO, UNICEF, and to a lesser extent other relevant UN family organizations have direct and legally binding right-to-food obligations, by the nature of UN organizations, these obligations cannot be the same as those for states. Furthermore, having legal obligations to fulfill a mandate is not the same as having *human rights* obligations that they could be held accountable for. Rather, they have obligations to fulfill their mandates and to contribute within their mandates to the realization of the right to food, and to support efforts of states as the primary duty bearers. In terms of the respect-protect-fulfill trichotomy, they could have an obligation to respect and to support the fulfillment of the right to food.

Some distinction should perhaps be made between the governing bodies of IGOs, which are composed of states, and the secretariats, which implement the decisions of IGOs. In practice, however, this is difficult to do. But it is important to bear in mind that the individual states participating in decision making within the governing bodies do have human rights obligations that remain legally binding on them. Experience from the World Bank would seem to indicate that implementation of the board's policy decisions is not always smooth (Clark 2002, 212), so there is an additional reason to have internal mechanisms to ensure recourse in case established norms are not followed. At the same time, the precise human rights obligations should be spelled out in appropriate form.

International Financial Institutions

Much of the academic debate about obligations of IGOs concerns international financial institutions and their obligations to respect human rights, including the right to food. It is argued that structural adjustment programs and other forms of cooperation promoted by the World Bank, IMF, and other international and regional financial institutions should respect the right to food and other human rights and strive to contribute to creating an enabling environment for the realization of, in particular, economic, social, and cultural rights.

This debate stems from the fact that the financial IGOs have been imposing "structural adjustment" conditions on borrowing countries that require them to rapidly liberalize their economies. Various research studies have shown that these requirements cause at least short-term hardships for the poorest people in less developed countries. These conditions have had a negative impact on the enjoyment of human rights (Abouharb and Cingranelli 2006). For example, an evaluation of a land credit program in Brazil financed by the World Bank claims that 46 percent of the families who have participated in this program have not been able to produce adequate food for their consumption from the land they till, and that 47 percent of these families have not been able to pay back the credit for purchasing the land with what they have produced. In addition, it appears that the beneficiary families had little or no influence in key decisions, like the selection of plots to be bought or in the bargaining process for purchasing the land (Medonça 2006). Other studies show that structural adjustment programs in various countries contributed to drops in the production of basic food crops and subsequent food shortages, thus affecting the right of access to sufficient and adequate food of the local population (Narula 2006).

Some studies claim that impoverished countries still face an unacceptably high and rising number of conditions in order to gain access to World Bank and IMF development finance. On average, poor countries face as many as sixty-seven conditions per World Bank loan. Many of these conditions relate to privatization reforms (Eurodad 2006). It could be argued that this is not in line with the essential role of international cooperation in the realization of economic, social, and cultural rights, including the right to food as provided for by the ICESCR and interpreted by the CESCR.

General Comment 2 holds that even when structural adjustment programs are unavoidable and when they entail austerity measures that affect
economic opportunities and social entitlements, endeavors to protect the
most basic economic, social, and cultural rights become more, rather than
less, urgent. In this regard the CESCR made it clear that the relevant United
Nations agencies should make a particular effort to ensure that such protection is, to the maximum extent possible, built into programs and policies designed to promote structural adjustment (UN CESCR 1990). The
General Assembly resolution discussed above also singles out the World
Bank and the International Monetary Fund in its call on IGOs to respect
and support the realization of the right to food (UN General Assembly
2006c, para. 16).

Funding Constraints of UN Agencies

Unlike its individual members, the UN cannot play political favorites or
exclude any of its member countries from assistance. However, the regular
program funds of UN agencies are very limited and pale completely next to
the amount of bilateral assistance that flows to poorer countries as well as
the tied funds provided voluntarily by national governments to UN humanitarian relief bodies such as the WFP and the UN High Commissioner for
Refugees. Too often, the humanitarian arms of the UN issue appeals that go
unanswered by donors. For this there seems to be no legal recourse at present, although there is some movement toward providing more untied funding that staff of the UN agencies can allocate solely on the basis of need.

There have been some developments in the field of humanitarian assistance to try to separate politics from the people in need, through the application of the principles of impartiality, neutrality, and so on. Yet, institutions that have been set up to respond to emergencies, such as the WFP or
the Red Cross and Red Crescent societies, do not yet have funding that is
untied. They must raise funds emergency by emergency, and thus be at the
mercy of the "CNN factor" and international politics.

States have taken some joint action to improve "predictable and timely
response to humanitarian emergencies, with the objectives of promoting
early action and response to reduce loss of life, enhancing response to time-
critical requirements and strengthening core elements of humanitarian response in underfunded crises, based on demonstrable needs" and upgraded
the Central Emergency Response Fund (CERF) to include voluntary contributions (UN General Assembly 2006a, para. 15). A fully funded CERF of
$500 million would, however, have composed a mere 4 percent of the 2006
total humanitarian funding (UN OCHA 2006, slide 23). Oxfam suggested the
fund should be increased to $1 billion to ensure quicker and more equitable
emergency assistance (Oxfam 2006, 26). Should CERF be fully funded at all

times, and especially if increased, it has the potential to play an important role in addressing the lacunae in state obligations discussed above. It would not, however, create new obligations or strengthen international obligations with regard to the right to food.

We conclude that IGOs have an obligation to respect the right to food and to support the fulfillment of this right within the scope of their respective mandates. When IGOs work on food and nutrition issues, they should do that in conformity with human rights law, especially with regard to the right to food. However, in order to operationalize these obligations and make them really meaningful, it is necessary for the relevant governing bodies to adopt relevant standards and to establish mechanisms that can provide redress in case of violations.

NONSTATE ACTORS

This section will analyze issues related to the responsibility of nonstate actors with regard to human rights including the right to food. In the broader group of nonstate actors, the section will mainly examine transnational corporations (TNCs), but also briefly consider human rights responsibilities of international nongovernmental organizations (INGOs).

In this era of globalization, private actors, particularly large private transnational corporations have come to hold power greater than that of many states. Yet "the global reach of TNCs is not matched by a coherent global system of accountability," as stated by a report of the UN secretary-general on the impact of the activities and working methods of transnational corporations (UN Secretary-General 1996). Despite wielding greater power than ever before, transnational corporations avoid being held accountable with regard to human rights.

It has been argued that the global trading system has outstripped the ability of multilateral institutions to respond effectively to the economic dimensions of human rights abuse, and there remains a climate of impunity surrounding economic activities that promote or sustain human rights abuse and a resulting lack of regulatory clarity as to what might constitute real liabilities in such situations (Ramasastry and Thompson 2006).

In general, there are two ways to make corporations respect human rights: one is indirect, the other direct. Corporations can be held to account under national law by governments that have a duty to protect their people and people living in other countries against negative impacts on the right to food of third parties. From this perspective, governments are responsible for regulating and preventing the activities of corporations that are inconsistent with human rights. This is the indirect method discussed above in "International Human Rights Obligations of States."

The CESCR has indicated that states parties have the obligation to protect the enjoyment of economic, social, and cultural rights. This includes protecting people from interference by third parties such as corporations in the realization of their right to food (UN CESCR 1999a, para. 15). However, the CESCR then added:

> While only States are parties to the Covenant and are thus ultimately accountable for compliance with it, all members of society—individuals, families, local communities, non-governmental organizations, civil society organizations, as well as the private business sector—have responsibilities in the realization of the right to adequate food. (UN CESCR 1999a, para. 20)

The CESCR did not go as far as stating that third parties have or should have direct, legally binding human rights obligations. Instead it said they had human rights responsibilities and that the "private business sector—national and transnational—should pursue its activities within the framework of a code of conduct conducive to respect of the right to adequate food, agreed upon jointly with the Government and civil society" (UN CESCR 1999a, para. 20). This should be seen as an addition to the human rights obligations of states to legislate the conduct of third parties under their jurisdiction, not a replacement of that obligation.

International human rights law has thus introduced an element of responsibility of nonstate actors into the edifice of international public law, but further instruments would have to be developed to create direct and enforceable obligations of nonstate actors. This would be quite possible as an extension of the legitimate powers of states. Under international law, the state has the right and the duty to regulate acts carried out by private parties. Human rights law is still largely state-centric (Stokke 2002). States, as the creators of international law, have the power to change this should they so decide, through the adoption of new treaties and the establishment of appropriate institutional mechanisms, such as those that Mike Brady discusses in chapter 4 of this book.

The argument for a direct way of attributing human rights responsibilities to TNCs is based on the notion that "every organ of society" in the Universal Declaration of Human Rights encompasses private enterprises as well. One commentator states:

> The Universal Declaration is not only addressed to governments. It is a common standard for all people and all nations, for every individual including juridical persons. Every individual and every organ of society excludes no one, no company, no market, no cyberspace. The Universal Declaration applies to them all. (Henkin 1999, 25)

This view is valid in the sense that the UDHR constitutes common values and standards of humanity, and constitutes a powerful moral and ethical argument. However, this would hardly suffice to impart legal obligations. The common view is not that the UDHR establishes customary law, but that many of its substantive provisions articulate it. The reference to "every organ of society" is unlikely to be one of those that constitute customary law. The responsibilities are therefore of a moral, rather than legal, nature.

The Commission on Human Rights has requested all states and private actors to take fully into account the need to promote the effective realization of the right to food and to cooperate fully in the fulfillment of the mandate of the special rapporteur on the right to food (UN CHR 2004). These resolutions are nonbinding on states and have only minimum power of persuasion on nonstate actors.

At present there are no mechanisms for holding TNCs accountable at the international level. Instead, much attention has been given to ways in which TNCs could hold themselves accountable through the development of voluntary instruments such as appropriate policies and codes of conduct. Numerous codes of conduct have been developed at the international level to strengthen human rights accountability, such as the OECD Guidelines for Multinational Enterprises (OECD 2000). However, a strong and coherent system of accountability that fully outlines TNCs' obligations has, until now, been missing at the international level.

A new set of instruments has been proposed to fill this gap: the Norms on the Responsibilities of Transnational Corporations and Other Business Enterprises with Regard to Human Rights, adopted by then Sub-Commission on the Promotion and Protection of Human Rights in 2003. The Sub-Commission was composed of experts, so the body had only the authority to propose new standards to its parent body, which is now the Human Rights Council. The proposed Norms state that "within their respective spheres of activity and influence, transnational corporations and other business enterprises have the obligation to promote, secure the fulfillment of, respect, ensure respect for and protect human rights recognized in international as well as national law" (UN SCPPHR 2003, para. 1).

The concept of complicity in the context of corporate responsibility refers to situations where the corporation knowingly assists in an illegal act as well as where it benefits from the abuses committed by others. The concept helps lawyers and human rights organizations to bridge the state-nonstate divide and apply international human rights law to nonstate actors such as corporations. Although complicity in war crimes or genocide has been given a specific legal meaning in particular trials, thinking about complicity more generally forces everyone to consider how their actions affect the lives of others around the world (Clapham 2006).

The special representative of the secretary-general on the issue of human rights and transnational corporations and other business enterprises has suggested that it may be desirable in some circumstances for corporations to become direct bearers of international human rights obligations, especially where host governments cannot or will not enforce their human rights obligations (UN Special Representative 2006, para. 65). But these are not propositions about established law or *de lege lata*; they are policy preferences about what the law should become and that requires state action before the proposals take effect. They are statements *de lege ferenda*, which it would be highly desirable for states to act on. Mike Brady explores concrete ways forward in chapter 4.

International nongovernmental organizations (INGOs) are increasing their scope, activities, and influence. They deliver much of the international humanitarian assistance on behalf of governments, IGOs, and on their own account. Many are involved in various forms of development work. INGOs have a strong voice in most UN forums, for instance through consultative status with ECOSOC and liaison status with FAO. INGOs have been instrumental in the development of human rights law and its application. But are they themselves bound by international human rights law?

Many INGOs have incorporated human rights into their mission statements and have even set standards for themselves to ensure that their activities conform to human rights norms (Sphere Project 2004). However, there is no specific external mechanism that can hold them to account. At the moment the only recourse is through national instances, mainly in the country of operation. The lack of an international mechanism, however, is less serious than for TNCs, as INGOs are rarely in a position to dictate to governments or obtain impunity by economic clout.

As INGOs are nonstate actors, they do not have international human rights obligations. They have no human rights obligations to provide food, cash, or services to individuals or communities. However they are responsible for respecting human rights in their work and should, when working on food security and nutrition issues, ensure that their work is in conformity with international right-to-food standards.

CONCLUSION

States have right-to-food obligations primarily for individuals within their own territory and under their jurisdiction. However, states also have right-to-food obligations at the international level and extraterritorially. They must respect the right to food in their unilateral, bilateral, and multilateral activities; we consider this to be *de lege lata*.

It would be desirable to strengthen the sense of obligation by states themselves even to respect the right to food of people in other countries. While deliberate measures such as blockades, sanctions, and other ways of using food as a tool for economic and political pressure seem to clearly constitute violations of the right to food, more indirect consequences of state action are still disputed. For instance, unfair trading rules, trade barriers, dumping of foodstuffs, and other trade related practices may have far-reaching consequences for the realization of people's right to sufficient, nutritious, safe, and culturally acceptable food, yet such actions are not yet undisputable violations of the right to food.

In theory, human rights obligations may be regarded as UN Charter rules and therefore of higher rank than other sources of international law, but there is little evidence that bodies such as those involved in settling trade disputes would be willing to make rulings on this basis without explicit provisions in the trade agreements themselves. Therefore, the best way of enforcing and firmly establishing an obligation to respect the right to food in trade contexts would be to amend the trade agreements to instruct and empower trade dispute mechanisms to take such obligations into account.

States do not have as clear an obligation to *protect* the right to food of people outside their home jurisdictions, although the support for this is growing. In any case, they are *allowed* to do so and in many cases it would be highly desirable for them to take appropriate legislative action.

Certainly states that are members of the UN or parties to the ICESCR have an obligation to cooperate in the realization of the right to food. In terms of the analytical framework of respect, protect, and fulfill, this duty to cooperate covers the dimensions to always *respect* the right to food and to *facilitate* and to *provide* the right to food, in as much as they are in a position to do so.

There is certainly a general obligation on those states that are in a position to assist others to do so, which amounts to an obligation to fulfill. What is sorely missing is a specific obligation on any country to cooperate with any other specific country on the basis of objective standards of realization of human rights. Presently, the targeting of assistance to particular countries depends on political considerations above all. The level and nature of cooperation also is largely undefined, and few countries have reached international goals and commitments in this regard.

States also have right-to-food obligations in governing bodies of intergovernmental organizations. Notions of direct human rights obligations for the organizations as such are growing, but cannot be said to be indisputable at this stage. In particular, new standards and accountability mechanisms have to be established to make the obligations effective. The obligations are to respect and to support the fulfillment of the right to food globally.

The United Nations and other intergovernmental agencies must be provided with adequate funding to respond to requests for assistance according to need rather than according to political considerations. This could be accomplished even without overall increase in resources, as presently most development assistance is bilateral rather than multilateral. This would certainly take a long, uphill battle to accomplish.

Nonstate actors do not have human rights obligations, only moral responsibilities, and thus cannot be said to violate human rights. They can commit *abuses*. However, states can violate the right to food by not controlling the actions of nonstate actors operating under their jurisdiction. The trend is to extend those obligations to protect across national borders, but remains to a large extent *de lege ferenda*. The search is on for alternative mechanisms that can strengthen the direct accountability of nonstate actors, for instance through the notion of complicity in human rights violations.

Following the above analysis, one can discern a general movement toward greater recognition of general and specific obligations of states to cooperate for the furtherance of human rights everywhere. At least a general obligation of those states that are in a position to do so to provide technical and material assistance to other states is already widely acknowledged. This lays the groundwork for future standard setting in relevant intergovernmental forums to establish clearer obligations.

There is an urgent need to strengthen compliance with those aspects of the global dimensions of the right to food *de lege lata*, and to embark on further standard setting for those dimensions found to be *de lege ferenda*.

In furtherance of the above conclusions, we submit the following recommendations:

- Relevant international forums should be tasked with negotiating extraterritorial and international state obligations to provide firmer content to the obligation to cooperate internationally in the realization of the right to food under the ICESCR, including the obligations to respect, protect, and fulfill.
- Substantive human rights provisions should be adopted and recourse mechanisms should be established in all relevant IGOs, including the UN, its specialized agencies, and the WTO to enable complaints of violations of the right to food to be addressed by an independent body and adequate redress provided in case a violation is found.
- The rules of the WTO should be amended so that dispute settlement mechanisms are obliged to take the human right to food into account in the settlement of trade disputes.
- States should recognize human rights law as having higher status than other rules of international law.
- The existing human rights mechanisms, including treaty bodies such as the CESCR and the special procedures of the Human Rights Council like the special rapporteur on the right to food, should increasingly scrutinize states parties' obligations to cooperate in realizing the right to food at the global level; the special representative of the secretary-general on the issue of human rights and transnational corporations and other business enterprises should pay particular attention to questions

of production, processing, and marketing of food in his mandate with a view to further clarify TNC responsibilities with regard to the right to adequate food and the right to the highest attainable standard of health.

• Academics and scholars should continue to research and clarify what obligations IGOs and TNCs should have and how they could be held to account for nonfulfillment of these obligations.

• The United Nations System Standing Committee on Nutrition should promote implementation of existing international obligations to respect, protect, and fulfill the right to food and support further standard setting to clarify obligations that remain unclear and develop international law further in the ways identified as desirable.

REFERENCES

Abouharb, M. Rodwan, and David L. Cingranelli. 2006. "The Human Rights Effects of World Bank Structural Adjustment, 1981–2000," in *International Studies Quarterly* (2006) 50, 233–62. www.unc.edu/~lmosley/cingranelliabouharb.pdf.

Alston, Philip. 1984. "International Law and the Human Right to Food." In Philip Alston and Katarina Tomasevski (eds.), *The Right to Food*. The Hague: Nijhoff.

Bouayad-Agha, Faith, and Homero L. Hernández. 2002. "Reform of the Administration of Justice in the United Nations System: Options for Higher Recourse Instances." United Nations Joint Inspection Unit. UN Document JIU/REP/2002/5, June 2002.

Clapham, Andrew. 2006. *Human Rights Obligations of Non-State Actors*. New York: Oxford University Press.

Clark, Dana L. 2002. "The World Bank and Human Rights: The Need for Greater Accountability." *Harvard Human Rights Journal* 15 (Spring 2002): 205–26. www.law.harvard.edu/students/orgs/hrj/iss15/clark.shtml.

Coomans, Fons. 2004. "Some Remarks on the Extraterritorial Application of the International Covenant on Economic, Social and Cultural Rights." In Fons Coomans and Menno T. Kamminga (eds.), *Extraterritorial Application of Human Rights Treaties*. Antwerp-Oxford: Intersentia.

Cotula, Lorenzo, and Margret Vidar. 2002. "The Right to Adequate Food in Emergencies." FAO Legislative Study 77. Rome: FAO. www.fao.org/docrep/005/Y4430E/y4430e00.htm#Contents.

De Feyter, Koen, and Felipe Gomez Isa. 2005. "Globalisation, Privatisation and Human Rights." In Koen De Feyter and Felipe Gomez Isa (eds.), *Privatisation and Human Rights in the Age of Globalisation*. Antwerp: Intersentia.

De Schutter, Olivier. 2006. *Extraterritorial Jurisdiction as a Tool for Improving Human Rights Accountability of Transnational Corporations*. Report for the special representative to the UN secretary-general on the issue of human rights and transnational corporations and other enterprises. December. www.policyinnovations.org/ideas/policy_library/data/01420.

Eurodad (European Network on Debt and Development). 2006. *World Bank and IMF Conditionality: A Development Injustice.* Report June 2006. www.eurodad.org/articles/default.aspx?id=711.

European Court of Human Rights. 1998. *Loizidou v. Turkey* (Article 50). Case 15318/89 [1998] ECHR 60 (28 July 1998). Strasbourg.

Evans, Gareth. 2006. "The Responsibility to Protect: Unfinished Business." In *G8 Summit 2006: Issues and Instruments,* 17 July. www.crisisgroup.org/home/index.cfm?id=4269&l=1.

FAO (Food and Agriculture Organization of the United Nations). 1997. Rome Declaration of the World Food Summit. In *Report of the World Food Summit, Part One, Appendix.* Rome: FAO. www.fao.org/DOCREP/003/W3613E/W3613E00.HTM.

———. 2005. *Voluntary Guidelines to Support the Progressive Realization of the Right to Adequate Food in the Context of National Food Security.* Rome: FAO. www.fao.org/righttofood.

Henkin, Louis. 1999. Keynote Address: "The Universal Declaration at 50 and the Challenge of Global Markets." Quoted in EarthRights International, "The International Law Standard for Corporate Aiding and Abetting Liability." Paper presented to the UN special representative to the secretary-general on human rights and transnational corporations and other business enterprises, July 2006. www.corporate-responsibility.org/module_images/EarthRightsInt_Aiding_Abetting_LiabilityJuly06.pdf.

Inter-American Court of Human Rights. 1988. *Velasquez-Rodrigues v. Honduras.* Judgment of 29 July 1988, Inter-Am Ct. H.R. (Ser. C) No. 4 (1988).

Kent, George. 2005. "The Human Rights Obligations of Intergovernmental Organizations." *UN Chronicle* 42, no. 3 (September–November): 32–33. www.un.org/Pubs/chronicle/2005/issue3/0305p32.html.

Limburg Group. 1987. *Limburg Principles on the Implementation of the International Covenant on Economic, Social and Cultural Rights.* 1987. Reproduced in UN document . E/CN.4/1987/17, Annex.

Maastricht Group. 1997. *Maastricht Guidelines on Violations of Economic, Social and Cultural Rights.* www1.umn.edu/humanrts/instree/Maastrichtguidelines_.html.

Medonça, Maria Luisa. 2006. "Avaliacao Dos Programas De Credito Fundiario Do Banco Mundial No Brasil." MST, 23 August. www.mst.org.br/mst/pagina.php?cd=1886.

Moore, Gerald, and Margret Vidar. 1999. "FAO and the Right to Adequate Food." In *Notes et Documents* 56, nouvelle série (septembre–décembre 1999), Institut International Jacques Maritain, Centre International d'Etudes et de Recherches.

Narula, Smita, 2006. "The Right to Food: Holding Global Actors Accountable under International Law." *Columbia Journal of Transnational Law* 44: 691–800.

OECD (Organization for Economic Cooperation and Development). 2000. *The OECD Guidelines for Multinational Enterprises.* Paris: OECD. www.oecd.org/dataoecd/56/36/1922428.pdf.

———. 2006. "Aid Flows Top USD 100 Billion in 2005." 4 April. www.oecd.org/document/40/0,2340,en_2649_201185_36418344_1_1_1_1,00.html.

Oxfam. 2006. "Causing Hunger: An Overview of the Food Crisis in Africa." Oxfam briefing paper 91. July 2006. www.oxfam.org.uk/what_we_do/issues/conflict_disasters/downloads/bp91_hunger.pdf.

Ramasastry, Anita, and Robert C. Thompson. 2006. *Commerce, Crime and Conflict: Legal Remedies for Private Sector Liability for Grave Breaches of International Law: A Survey of Sixteen Countries*. Fafo report 536, issued under Fafo project New Security Programme. Economic Agendas and Civil Wars. www.fafo.no/pub/rapp/536/536.pdf.

Skogly, Sigrun I., and Mark Gibney. 2002. "Transnational Human Rights Obligations." *Human Rights Quarterly* 24 (3): 781–98.

Sphere Project. 2004. *The Sphere Handbook: Humanitarian Charter and Minimum Standards in Disaster Response*. Revised edition. Geneva: Sphere Project. www.sphere project.org/content/view/27/84/lang,English/.

Stokke, H. 2002. "What Is Left of State Responsibility? Turning State Obligations into State Responsibility in the Field of Economic, Social and Cultural Rights." In M. Scheinin and M. Suksi (eds.), *Human Rights in Development Yearbook 2002*, pp. 37–70. Leiden, Netherlands: Brill.

UN (United Nations). 1995. *Report of the World Summit for Social Development* (Copenhagen, 6–12 March 1995). UN document A/CONF.166/9, 19 April 1995.

———. 2002. *Monterrey Consensus*, adopted by the International Conference on Financing for Development. UN document A/Conf/198/3.

———. 2003. *The Human Rights Based Approach to Development Cooperation: Towards a Common Understanding among UN Agencies*. www.unescobkk.org/fileadmin/user _upload/appeal/human_rights/UN_Common_understanding_RBA.pdf.

———. 2006. Press Release: "Secretary-General Urges Human Rights Activists to Fill Leadership Vacuum," UN document SG/SM/10788, HR/4909, OBV/601. 8 December 2006.

UN CESCR (United Nations Committee on Economic, Social and Cultural Rights). 1990. General Comment 2, "International Technical Assistance Measures" (Article 22). UN document E/1990/23. www.ohchr.org/english/bodies/cescr/comments .htm.

———. 1991. General Comment 3, "The Nature of States Parties Obligations" (Article 2, par.1). UN document E/1991/23. www.ohchr.org/english/bodies/cescr/com ments.htm.

———. 1999a. General Comment 12, "The Right to Adequate Food" (Article 11). UN document E/C.12/1999/5. www.ohchr.org/english/bodies/cescr/comments .htm.

———. 1999b. General Comment 13, "The Right to Education" (Article 13). UN document E/C.12/1999/10. www.ohchr.org/english/bodies/cescr/comments.htm.

———. 2000a. General Comment 14, "The Right to the Highest Attainable Standard of Health" (Article 12). UN document E/C.12/2000/4. www.ohchr.org/english/ bodies/cescr/comments.htm.

———. 2000b. "Concluding Observations: Belgium." UN document E/C.12/1/Add.54, 1 December. www.unhchr.ch/tbs/doc.nsf/(Symbol)/E.C.12.1.Add.54.En?Opendocu ment.

———. 2002. General Comment 15, "The Right to Water" (Articles 11 and 12). UN document E/C.12/2002/11. www.ohchr.org/english/bodies/cescr/comments .htm.

———. 2004. "Concluding Observations of the CESCR: Italy." UN document E/C.12/1/Add.103, 14 December. www.unhchr.ch/tbs/doc.nsf/(Symbol)/E.C.12.1 .Add.103.En?Opendocument.

———. 2005. "Concluding Observations of CESCR: Norway." UN document E/C.12/1/Add.109, 23 June. www.unhchr.ch/tbs/doc.nsf/(Symbol)/E.C.12.1.Add .109.En?Opendocument.

UN CHR (United Nations Commission on Human Rights). 1997. *The Right to Food.* Resolution 1997/8, UN document E/CN.4/RES/1997/8. 3 April. www.unhchr.ch/ Huridocda/Huridoca.nsf/TestFrame/849a952371e7386ec125662d0050e638?Op endocument.

———. 2000. *The Right to Food.* Resolution 2000/10, UN document.E/CN.4/RES/ 200/10. www.unhchr.ch/huridocda/huridoca.nsf/(Symbol)/E.CN.4.RES.2000.10 .En?Opendocument.

———. 2001. *The Right to Food.* Resolution 2001/25, UN document E/CN.4/RES/2001/ 25, 20 April. http://ap.ohchr.org/documents/E/CHR/resolutions/E-CN_4-RES-2001-25.doc.

———. 2004. *The Right to Food.* Resolution 2004/19, UN document E/CN.4/RES/ 2004/19. In *Commission on Human Rights: Report on the 60th Session.* 15 March–23 April 2004.

UN General Assembly. 2000. *United Nations Millennium Declaration.* Resolution 55/2, adopted 8 September, UN document A/RES/55/2. www.un.org/millennium/ declaration/ares552e.htm.

———. 2005. *2005 World Summit Outcome.* Resolution 60/1, adopted 16 September, UN document A/RES/60/1. 24 October. www.un.org/Depts/dhl/resguide/r60.htm.

———. 2006a. *Strengthening of the Coordination of Emergency Humanitarian Assistance of the United Nations.* Resolution 60/124, UN document A/RES/60/124. 8 March.

———. 2006b. *The Right to Food.* Resolution 60/165, UN document A/RES/60/165. 2 March 2006. www.un.org/Depts/dhl/resguide/r60.htm.

———. 2006c. *The Right to Food.* Resolution 61/163, adopted 19 December.

UN HRC (United Nations Human Rights Committee). 1991. Communication No. 458/1991, *Womah Mukong v. Cameroon.* UN document CCPR/C/51/D/458/1991. www1.umn.edu/humanrts/undocs/html/458–1991.html.

———. 2004. General Comment 31, "Nature of the General Legal Obligation on States Parties to the Covenant" (on Civil and Political Rights). UN document CCPR/C/21/Rev.1/Add.13. http://ohchr.org/english/bodies/hrc/comments.htm.

UNICEF (United Nations Children's Fund). 1996. "UNICEF Mission Statement" (Decision 1996/1). In *Report of the Executive Board of the United Nations Children's Fund on the Work of Its First Regular Session of 1996, 21–25 January 1996, to the Economic and Social Council.* UN document E/ICEF/1996/12 (Part I), E/1996/32 (Part I), 26 March.

UN OCHA (United Nations Office for the Coordination of Humanitarian Affairs). 2006. "Humanitarian Reform: Building a Stronger, More Predictable Humanitarian Response System" (powerpoint presentation), undated. www.reliefweb.int/ humanitarianreform/Generic%20Reform%20Presentation%2022%20Dec%.

UN OHCHR (United Nations Office of the High Commissioner for Human Rights). 1991. Fact Sheet No. 16 (Rev.1). Geneva: The Committee on Economic, Social and Cultural Rights. Geneva. www.unhchr.ch/html/menu6/2/fs16.htm.

UN SCN (United Nations System Standing Committee on Nutrition). 2006. *Strategic Framework.* Adopted by the 33rd Session of SCN, March. www.unsystem.org/ scn/Publications/strategic_framework200604.pdf.

UN SCPPHR (United Nations Sub-Commission on the Promotion and Protection of Human Rights). 2003. *Norms on the Responsibilities of Transnational Corporations and Other Business Enterprises with Regard to Human Rights.* Resolution 2003/16, UN document E/CN.4/Sub.2/2003/12/Rev.2.

UN Secretary-General. 1996. *Report of the Secretary-General on the Impact of the Activities and Working Methods of Transnational Corporations,* UN document E/CN.4/Sub.2/1996/12.

———. 1997. *Renewing the United Nations: A Programme for Reform.* Report of the Secretary-General, UN document A/51/950, 14 July.

UN Security Council. 2006. *Protection of Civilians in Armed Conflict.* Resolution 1674, UN document S/RES/1674. 28 April. www.womenwarpeace.org/issues/res1674.pdf.

UN Special Representative. 2006. *Interim Report of the Special Representative of the Secretary-General on the Issue of Human Rights and Transnational Corporations and other Business Enterprises.* Mr. John Ruggie, to the Commission on Human Rights. UN document E/CN.4/2006/97, 22 February.

UN SR (Special Rapporteur on the Right to Food). 2001. *Preliminary Report of the Special Rapporteur of the Commission on Human Rights on the Right to Food.* Jean Ziegler, submitted to the General Assembly. UN document A/56/210, 23 July. www.unhchr.ch/Huridocda/Huridoca.nsf/0/569b727953a8c72bc1256ace0050d7d4/$FILE/N0146552.pdf.

———. 2004. *Report of the Special Rapporteur on the Right to Food.* Mr. Jean Ziegler to the Commission on Human Rights. UN document E/CN.4/2004/10, 9 February.

———. 2005. *Report of the Special Rapporteur on the Right to Food.* Mr. Jean Ziegler, to the Commission on Human Rights. UN document E/CN.4/2005/47. 24 January.

———. 2006. *Report of the Special Rapporteur on the Right to Food to the Commission on Human Rights.* UN document E/CN.4/2006/44. 16 March.

WHO (World Health Organization). 1981. *International Code of Marketing of Breast-milk Substitutes.* Adopted on 21 May. www.who.int/nutrition/publications/code_english.pdf.

4

Holding Corporations Accountable for the Right to Food

Mike Brady

Baby Milk Action

Cambridge, United Kingdom

> Nestlé's fundamental purpose is to meet the needs of its customers and consumers for quality food products that offer value for money. By doing this successfully, we generate long term, sustainable economic results and development for all those with a stake in the business. With factories located in more than 80 countries, and with Nestlé companies in virtually every country in the world, the effects of our business development are felt by economies around the globe.
>
> Nestlé Sustainability Review (Nestlé 2006a)

As food transnational corporations become increasingly powerful, governments have a responsibility to ensure that their business activities do not have a negative impact on the right to food. Regulation takes place in general at a national level in the country where the corporation is operating. There is some scope in certain countries to hold a corporation accountable for its impact elsewhere. What is currently lacking is a global regulatory system capable of holding transnational corporations to account through new or reformed international institutions. This chapter argues that national governments collectively have a human rights obligation to put such a system in place.

While acknowledging the positive contribution of business, this chapter explores how the power of food transnational corporations has grown to the point that it is necessary for nation-states to take collective action as the global community to hold them to account and why initiatives such as the United Nations Global Compact are inherently unable to do so. It examines efforts by UN bodies, governments, and regional authorities, such as the European Parliament, to introduce regulations to protect the right to food and the current lack of progress. In examining how progress could be made, the chapter discusses how relevant standards should be set, arguing this should be through UN bodies with a health remit in consultation with relevant parties, not as a negotiation with business interests where the right to food is traded off against financial concerns. The International Code of Marketing of Breast-milk Substitutes and subsequent relevant resolutions of the World Health Assembly (WHA) provide a useful model as to how to develop standards. How such standards should be monitored is explored with reference to present monitoring systems at international and national levels and with imaginative ideas presented as to how the global community could introduce monitoring systems that would be effective. Monitoring in itself is insufficient to ensure compliance, and the chapter examines how the global community could enforce standards. Given the growth of transnational corporations and the challenges faced by single nations in holding them to account, the chapter considers whether a new form of corporation needs to be introduced. This could take the form of the globally incorporated company, where transnationals above a certain turnover and territorial extent are required to register with a global body and abide by and report on certain terms of reference. The chapter closes with conclusions and recommendations for action in the immediate and longer term to hold corporations accountable in relation to the right to food.

THE POWER OF FOOD TRANSNATIONAL CORPORATIONS

Trade has played a role in food security since time immemorial. However, corporations have driven international trade to a new level. Fifty-one of the world's largest economies are not nation-states but transnational corporations (TNCs) if we compare gross domestic product and turnover (Anderson and Cavanagh 2000). Transnationals have evolved beyond operating in multiple nations and trading goods to transcending frontiers. The same company name and brands appear across the world. While there are varying degrees of autonomy of national operations, usually the central headquarters of each TNC standardizes management approaches and production techniques. Increasingly trade is not between companies based in different countries, but is in the form of internal transactions between parts of the same corporation. In the U.S. economy, intrafirm trade amounts to 40 percent of total trade (Clausing 2001). In this chapter, the self-proclaimed "world's largest food company," Swiss-based Nestlé, will be the focus of much of the discussion. The World Health Assembly's International Code of Marketing of Breast-milk Substitutes will be used as an example of a standard by which corporations such as Nestlé, the company with the largest share of the baby food market, are required to abide.

Transnationals are growing at a staggering pace, many faster than the world economy, as they take over and merge with other companies. Nestlé has a long-term annual growth target of 5–6 percent growth, organically and through acquisitions, meaning it will more than double its turnover every twelve to fifteen years (Nestlé 2006b). It boasts that there is not a single country on the planet where its products are not sold. Cargill, the largest privately owned corporation in the United States, with global sales of $71.1 billion (Cargill 2005), controls 45 percent of the global grain trade, operating in sixty-one countries. A small number of companies hold massive power in the food supply chain, enabling them to force down prices paid to suppliers, while maintaining or increasing prices charged to consumers. This is an issue for farmers not only in developing countries, but also in industrialized countries. For example, in the UK the average annual net farm income for cereal farmers fell sharply from a peak in 1995–1996 (average £44,700) to £3,300 in 2001–2002. The power of the supermarket sector keeps downward pressure on prices paid to farmers. Retailing giants such as Wal-Mart, Carrefour, and Tesco are increasingly active in emerging markets, usually entering through acquisitions of national chains (Vorley 2003).

Industrialization in the food industry has greatly increased the production of food calories at the expense of food quality. Food availability is no longer limited to seasonal fare, as foods are transported and processed. Consumption of starchy staples has decreased, and fat consumption has increased. Consequently over the past 200 years average individual consumption of fat in Western society has increased fivefold and of refined sugars fifteenfold (Lang and Heasman 2004, 132). The impact of junk food on children is particularly significant. If a child drinks one sugar-sweetened soft drink of 120 kcals per day for ten years this would turn into 50 kg of excess growth (Lang and Heasman 2004, 66). Unsurprisingly there has been a rise in obesity, which is not limited to industrialized countries. The International Association for the Study of Obesity has estimated that 1.7 billion people are overweight or obese (Lang and Heasman 2004, 49). This includes 10 percent of the world's children, rising to over 30 percent in many industrialized countries (Dalmeny, Hanna, and Lobstein 2003, 2). Chronic heart disease accounts for 30 percent of all global deaths and poor diet is a contributing factor. As diets westernize, the non-communicable diseases follow. A study in East Africa reported that autopsies found no cases of chronic heart disease in the 1930s, but by the 1960s it was a major health problem (Trowell, cited in Lang 2004, 80). Type 2 diabetes is also showing significant increase, with 150 million sufferers in 1997, expected to double to 300 million in 2025, with the greatest number of new cases in China and India.

Cultural change is complex, but a key aspect of the change in diet is the promotional activities of the food industry. For every US$1 spent by the World Health Organization on trying to improve the nutrition of the world's population, US$500 is spent by the food industry on promoting processed foods (Lang and Millston 2002). By 2001, the world food-industry advertising budget was estimated at US$40 billion, a figure greater than the Gross Domestic Product of 70 percent of the world's nations (Dalmeny, Hanna, and Lobstein 2003, 5). Nestlé spends 7 percent of turnover on marketing and public relations. UBS Warburg reported in 2002 that an estimated 46 percent of Nestlé's income comes from what it describes as "less healthy" foods and would be at risk if regulations restricting promotion or marketing of such foods was introduced. Its study suggested that 18 percent of a company's value could be lost by a fall of just 3 percent in sales, such is the importance of confidence in image (cited in the *Guardian* 2002).

With transnational corporations playing an increasing role in food supply chains and becoming increasingly powerful in influencing dietary habits and food policy, nation-states have less ability to balance that power. Collective action on defining food standards at the international level is developing, as will be discussed, but the regulatory systems to monitor these and corporate impact on the right to food more generally is lacking. Only through cooperating as the global community of nation-states will it be possible to ensure checks and balances are put in place to protect the right to nutritionally adequate food.

OVERSIGHT BY THE GLOBAL
COMMUNITY IS PRESENTLY INADEQUATE

In 2002 the World Health Assembly introduced its *Global Strategy on Diet, Physical Activity and Health*, which states:

> Unhealthy diets and physical inactivity are thus among the leading causes of the major noncommunicable diseases, including cardiovascular disease, type 2 diabetes and certain types of cancer, and contribute substantially to the global burden of disease, death and disability. . . . Factors that increase the risks of noncommunicable disease include elevated consumption of energy-dense, nutrient-poor foods that are high in fat, sugar and salt; reduced levels of physical activity at home, at school, at work and for recreation and transport; and use of tobacco. . . . Of particular concern are unhealthy diets, inadequate physical activity and energy imbalances in children and adolescents. . . . Exclusive breastfeeding for six months and appropriate complementary feeding con-

tribute to optimal physical growth and mental development. . . . Governments have a central role, in cooperation with other stakeholders, to create an environment that empowers and encourages behaviour changes by individuals, families and communities, to make positive, life-enhancing decisions on healthy diets and patterns of physical activity. (WHA 2004, 4–5)

The strategy calls for action in improving food quality and labeling of processed foods and ensuring marketing does not exploit children's inexperience or credulity or encourage unhealthy dietary practices. This was vigorously opposed by elements of the food industry, as reported in the *Observer* newspaper when it obtained internal documents showing the UK sugar industry was planning to offer large sums of money to the World Health Organization in an attempt to overturn its failure to gain a non-governmental organization (NGO) status:

> The sugar industry is planning to offer substantial sums of sponsorship money to the World Health Organisation as part of a secret attempt to influence the body's attempts to combat obesity worldwide.
> The Observer has obtained a confidential briefing document outlining the sugar producers' new strategy for getting into the key meetings held in the WHO's Geneva headquarters.
> The document was written by the British head of the World Sugar Research Organisation, which is wholly funded by sugar producers. It reveals the body's intention to offer a large amount of funding in order to be granted non-governmental organisation (NGO) status—something it has so far been denied. . . .
> Earlier this year, the WHO produced its Global Strategy on Diet, Physical Activity and Health, in the face of lobbying from food manufacturers and, in particular, countries with strong sugar interests. The industry managed to ensure that the strategy did not refer to an expert report, known as 916, which recommended that no more than 10 per cent of an adult's daily calorific intake should come from added sugar. (Revill 2004)

In its 2006 review of progress in implementing the Global Strategy, WHO stated:

> Some food and non-alcoholic beverage manufacturers, food-service providers, and retailers are making changes to their products and services in keeping with the Strategy's recommendations. Even though these initiatives are commendable, they remain isolated and their impact on public health remains limited. Small and medium-sized enterprises, in general, have failed to be engaged in the global effort. Therefore, much additional work is needed to secure industry-wide actions to improve the quality of their food and drink products, the information available to consumers, and the way in which products are marketed. (WHO 2006a, para. A2)

The pursuit of initiatives seeking the voluntary support of industry is sometimes preferred by policy makers as being noncontroversial, unlike regulatory routes, and so, theoretically, more likely to prompt change. Many corporations actively promote "partnerships" with government and UN bodies. As Richter has analyzed, what is meant by "partnerships" may vary greatly, from commercial contracts, to sponsorship, to industry initiatives seeking government and UN endorsement (Richter 2002).

An example of a partnership endorsed by sections of the global community is the Global Alliance for Improved Nutrition (GAIN), which has received large sums from the Bill and Melinda Gates Foundation; U.S. Agency for International Development (USAID); and Canadian International Development Agency (CIDA). GAIN has the goal to "end vitamin and mineral deficiencies through the fortification of staple foods and condiments," and it claims that "only the private sector has the products, the technology, the management and marketing skills to improve nutritional status through fortification of foods" (GAIN 2006). Addressing micronutrient deficiencies through processed foods, rather than, for example, education on nutrition, is attractive to the private sector as it creates the possibility of new products that can be marketed with health claims. This is particularly welcome for companies whose processed foods are otherwise seen as unhealthy due to high levels of salt, sugar, and fat. GAIN acknowledges it needs wider support for this strategy to succeed: "To do this it needs the support of governments, technical guidance from UN agencies and research institutions, and the awareness and support among consumers" (GAIN 2006). While a voluntary approach may result in some positive changes, evidence from the iodization of salt suggests it is insufficient, as will be explained.

According to UNICEF, iodine deficiency is "the world's leading cause of preventable mental retardation and impaired psychomotor development in young children" (UNICEF 2006a). Iodization of salt has been recommended as a solution by the WHA. In its 2005 evaluation WHO reported progress, but noted:

> In most countries the use of iodized salt in processed foods is not mandatory or even regulated. . . . The challenge is to reinforce salt iodization programmes in the remaining 54 affected countries while ensuring the long-term sustainability of control programmes in the others. The main constraints are related to delivery of iodized salt, especially to the most vulnerable populations, commitment of small salt producers, programme monitoring, and adequacy and enforcement of relevant legislation. (WHO 2005, 2)

This raises the question if the voluntary, "partnership" approach advocated by GAIN would be sufficient to ensure the global community meets its human rights obligations on the right to food. Relying on corporations to change harmful practices voluntarily and take positive action may even be counterproductive in diverting attention and resources from regulatory routes.

While voluntary measures are failing to deliver required changes in this and other areas of concern, regulation of the private sector has not kept pace with the growth in its power. The UN Commission on Transnational Corporations set up by the UN Economic and Social Council in the 1980s proposed a Code of Conduct on Transnational Corporations, but the move toward liberalization effectively killed off this initiative. As Judith Richter recalls in *Holding Corporations Accountable*, this was laid to rest in 1992, when the president of the UN General Assembly reported that "no consensus was possible . . . at present" and that "delegations felt that the changed international environment and the importance attached to encouraging foreign investment required a fresh approach." The commission was wound up after drafting regulations on environmental issues for presentation at the 1992 UN Conference on Environment and Development—the Rio Earth Summit (Richter 2001, 11).

Corporations are not always against internationally binding regulations. The International Chamber of Commerce has advocated strongly binding regulations for contract law, intellectual property rights, and brand protection, for example. At the same time it has called for de-regulation in other areas, a call that was heeded by the UN secretary-general, who proposed at the World Economic Forum in 1999 "a global compact of shared values and principles that will give a give a human face to the global market (quoted in Richter 2001, 14).

The UN-ICC Global Compact was launched on 5 July 1999 and is not only entirely voluntary, it explicitly is not intended to be monitored or enforced: "The initiative is not designed, nor does it have the mandate or resources, to monitor or measure participants' performance" (UN Global Compact 2006). In other words, it is not intended to regulate the corporations.

Businesses lobby against regulations at the national level, and political energy has been diverted as a result into developing voluntary codes such as the Organization for Economic Cooperation and Development (OECD) Guidelines for Multinational Enterprises, which require corporations to abide by human rights and environmental norms (OECD 2000). The nonbinding status of the guidelines is spelled out as the first point of principle:

> The *Guidelines* are recommendations jointly addressed by governments to multinational enterprises. They provide principles and standards of good practice consistent with applicable laws. Observance of the *Guidelines* by enterprises is voluntary and not legally enforceable.

The guidelines state that enterprises should

> respect the human rights of those affected by their activities consistent with the host government's international obligations and commitments.

This would include the right to food.

There is no international reporting mechanism for the OECD guidelines, though parties can register complaints with the OECD contact point in the home country or other OECD or designated country with a connection to the corporation or incident. The guidelines charge the contact point with arbitrating between the complainant and corporation to try to resolve differences. Such an approach may be appropriate in a labor dispute if a corporation was refusing to recognize representatives of the workforce, but is not so relevant when an NGO monitoring body is attempting to stop a corporation violating international standards. In such cases it is not negotiation that is needed, but investigation, judgment, and effective sanctions.

While food is not specifically referred to in the guidelines, requirements on care for the environment and consumer protection are relevant. For example, failure to abide by the International Code of Marketing of Breast-milk Substitutes and subsequent, relevant resolutions of the WHA comes within the OECD's "Consumers Interests" provisions, which state in part that enterprises should "not make representations or omissions, nor engage in any other practices, that are deceptive, misleading, fraudulent, or unfair."

A company proved to have done so needs sanctions levied against it to discourage further malpractice, rather than a process of arbitration.

Various bodies have proposed that monitoring and enforcement systems should be instituted at the international level. The European Parliament adopted a white paper on EU standards for European enterprises in developing countries. At the international level the white paper, "EU Standards for European Enterprises Operating in Developing Countries: Towards a European Code of Conduct,"

- Recommends that the European Union seek to work en bloc to strengthen existing ILO and OECD instruments, in particular in the review now underway in the OECD, and within the United Nations, to ensure more powerful and effective monitoring and enforcement mechanisms, and that EU efforts notably go into reviving the UN Commission on TNCs for it to be entrusted with concrete tasks in the context of the monitoring and implementation of Codes, along with the OECD Committee for International Investment and Multinational Enterprises and the ILO's Department for Multinational Enterprises;
- Strongly recommends that in connection with negotiations on investment agreements which could be concluded in either the OECD or the WTO, the European Union not only contribute to establishing the legitimate rights of multinational enterprises, but also their duties—with due regard to the present minimum applicable international standards—in the field of environment, labour and human rights; recommends that a monitoring mechanism affording every guarantee of im-

partiality and independence be incorporated in such an agreement. (European Union 1999)

Although the parliament supported these measures on 15 January 1999 it did not have the authority to implement them, aside from holding its own public hearings. The first public hearing, held in November 2000, was into Nestlé's baby food marketing practices. Nestlé refused to attend the hearing, sending instead an auditor who could not respond on behalf of the company. The European Parliament rapporteur on corporate responsibility, Richard Howitt MEP, commented to the *Independent* newspaper that Nestlé had shown "utter contempt for a properly constituted public hearing. Not to attend reveals a combination of arrogance and distance which has set their cause back" (Castle 2000). Mr. Howitt called, among other things, for the European Commission to review its monitoring of export measures as the commission refused to accept complaints about the practices of European-based corporations from NGOs in developing countries.

The European Commission, which the parliament called on to act to regulate European-based transnationals at regional and global levels, instead claimed the OECD Guidelines for Multinational Enterprises were sufficient and set up a Multi-stakeholder Forum on Corporate Social Responsibility (CSR) in 2002 to debate encouraging business to change practices voluntarily. CSR is the central element of the European Union's approach to bringing TNCs to respect human rights norms.

TNCs are headquartered in rich, industrialized nations. These nations, acting on behalf of their corporations, are able to use their political power to prevent binding international standards from being introduced. The contribution of global business to national revenues can be significant. Indeed, income from Nestlé enterprises was credited with lifting the income of the entire European region at a time when other industries, such as oil, faced a dip in profits in 2006 (Reuters 2006). This raises the question of whether such governments would ever take action that could hamper the ability of their transnationals to make profits, particularly if doing so would enable transnationals headquartered in other countries to gain their business.

A way to resolve the issue of government action potentially harming the competitiveness of its corporations and so the national economy, is for action to be taken at the international level. The global community of nation-states could introduce international global regulatory systems. Indeed, it is argued here that the global community has an *obligation* to do so under existing human rights commitments.

If such systems are to be introduced, the terms of reference and monitoring and enforcement mechanisms need to be defined. This chapter will now explore how global standards for business enterprises could be determined, monitored and enforced and whether more fundamental changes to the nature of corporations are relevant, perhaps creating the classification of globally-incorporated company.

While the discussion is applicable to ensuring all human rights are not violated, issues relevant to the right to food include:

- Environmental standards, so that pollution or extraction of resources is not prejudicial to agriculture.
- Food standards, so that food is of adequate nutritional quality and safety and that a precautionary principle is followed for novel foods, such as genetically modified organisms.
- Labor standards, so that employees receive a living wage enabling them to purchase food.
- Marketing standards, so that labels contain correct and necessary information, unhealthy foods are not promoted to vulnerable groups such as children, and practices such as breastfeeding are protected.
- Fair trading standards, so that the interests of producers, such as small farmers, are not prejudiced by corporate domination of supplies of agricultural inputs such as seeds, and of purchasing and distribution chains. When prices paid to producers are driven down and access to markets restricted, their food security can be affected.

This is an opportune time to be considering regulatory mechanisms. In 2005 the UN secretary-general appointed a special representative on the issue of human rights and transnational corporations and other business enterprises. The mandate includes identifying and clarifying standards of corporate responsibility and accountability with regard to human rights (United Nations Secretary-General 2005). In a report presented to the UN Human Rights Council, Special Representative John Ruggie concluded:

> The permissive conditions for business-related human rights abuses today are created by a misalignment between economic forces and governance capacity. Only a realignment can fix the problem. In principle, public authorities set the rules within which business operates. But at the national level some governments simply may be unable to take effective action, whether or not the will to do so is present. And in the international arena states themselves compete for access to markets and investments, thus collective action problems may restrict or impede their serving as the international community's "public authority." The most vulnerable people and communities pay the heaviest price for these governance gaps. (Ruggie 2007, para. 81)

Professor Ruggie requested an extension of his mandate to continue to consult and develop recommendations.

HOW SHOULD GLOBAL STANDARDS FOR
BUSINESS ENTERPRISES BE DETERMINED?

Transnational corporations sometimes have a negative impact on the right to food. The baby food industry's impact in changing breastfeeding cultures to bottle-feeding cultures is well known (IBFAN 2004). Processed foods are often criticized for having too high levels of salt, sugar, and fat, particularly saturated fats. Unhealthy foods are targeted at children through advertising during children's television in some countries. Impact on the environment, such as the extraction of water or dispersal of pollutants, can compromise the ability of surrounding communities to meet their food needs.

Initiatives intended to prompt a change in policy and practice, such as the Global Strategy on Diet, Physical Activity and Health and the International Code of Marketing of Breast-milk Substitutes are not binding on corporations unless given force in national measures. International initiatives such as the UN Global Compact and OECD Guidelines for Multinational Enterprises in their present form do not provide an enforcement mechanism.

Before discussing enforcement mechanisms it is necessary to consider how the global standards for business enterprises should be developed, drawing on the experience of existing standards.

Human rights norms do provide some guidance. In particular, General Comment 12, prepared by the United Nations Committee on Economic, Social and Cultural Rights in 1999, provides part of the answer as to the regulation of TNCs. Although ultimate responsibility for realizing the right to food lies with States:

> All members of society—individuals, families, local communities, non-governmental organizations, civil society organizations, as well as the private business sector—have responsibilities in the realization of the right to adequate food. The State should provide an environment that facilitates implementation of these responsibilities. The private business sector—national and transnational—should pursue its activities *within the framework of a code of conduct conducive to respect of the right to adequate food, agreed upon jointly with the Government and civil society.* (UN ECOSOC 1999, para. 20, emphasis added)

In the Norms on the Responsibilities of Transnational Corporations and Other Business Enterprises with Regard to Human Rights, approved on 13 August 2003 by the Sub-Commission on the Promotion and Protection of Human Rights, it is acknowledged that

> transnational corporations and other business enterprises, their officers and persons working for them are also obligated to respect generally recognized responsibilities and norms contained in United Nations treaties and other international instruments. (UN CHR 2003)

The Norms have not yet been endorsed by the responsible parent body, formerly the Commission on Human Rights and now the Human Rights Council. In their review of the situation, which argues the Norms are the "right vehicle through which to develop a framework for corporate accountability for human rights abuses at the international level," Kinley and Chambers recall why endorsement was not immediately forthcoming:

> In response to the promulgation of the Norms, business leaders were quick to reiterate and highlight both the benefits that corporate enterprise bring to all societies, and their voluntary efforts to regulate the few instances where corporations are responsible for bad business practices and human rights abuses. It was on these bases that business leaders mounted critiques, not only of the Norms document itself, but also of any expansion of the concept of corporate liability for human rights responsibilities that went beyond the current model of self-regulation through codes of conduct, social responsibility policies and the like.
>
> The corporate lobby made some headway. When the Norms came before the UN Commission on Human Rights, at its 60th Session in 2004, they encountered a frosty reception from member states already primed with the concerns of the corporate sector. (Kinley and Chambers 2006)

The Norms envision that:

> Transnational corporations and other business enterprises shall respect economic, social and cultural rights as well as civil and political rights and contribute to their realization, in particular the rights to . . . adequate food and drinking water. (UN CHR 2003)

No explanation is given as to what contributing to the realization of the right to food should entail. The Human Rights Council, formed under General Assembly Resolution 60/251 of 15 March 2006, assumed the mandates, mechanisms, functions, and responsibilities of the Sub-Commission on 19 June 2006, and it remains to be seen if and how the Norms will be developed further.

Under the Norms, states would have a responsibility to develop a code of conduct that transnational corporations are obligated to respect. TNCs should also respect, it is argued, existing generally recognized responsibilities and norms, including the right to adequate food and also, as specified in the Norms, drinking water. Whether the Norms are the vehicle for pursuing this aim or not, this chapter recommends that the principle of monitored and enforced regulations at the global level is accepted as necessary action by states to protect the right to food. In a globalized world, something business interests profess is inevitable, it is surely also inevitable that global regulation of transnational corporations will be introduced to legitimize their existence as well as provide checks and balances on their power. The focus should be on how the regulations are to be developed.

The impact of corporations on food is often treated only as a trade issue, but to address the potential negative health impacts of trade, it should be treated as a health issue as well. This was the approach taken with the one existing set of international standards seeking to regulate an industry sector, the International Code of Marketing of Breast-milk Substitutes. The code was adopted as a "minimum requirement" for all countries under Resolution 34.22 of the World Health Assembly, the world's highest health policy setting body. The UN Committee on the Rights of the Child increasingly looks to whether governments have implemented the code and subsequent, relevant resolutions when reviewing compliance with the Convention on the Rights of the Child.

The International Code of Marketing of Breast-milk Substitutes was developed through a process of consultation with all stakeholders, including health professionals, civil society, and the baby food industry under the auspices of WHO and UNICEF. Manufacturers and distributors of products within the scope of the code are called upon to abide by it independently of government measures taken to implement it at the national level. However, there is no monitoring or enforcement mechanism at the international level to ensure that they do so.

The standards in the code and subsequent relevant resolutions are seen by civil society groups such as the International Baby Food Action Network (IBFAN) as a valuable tool for protecting infant health and a mother's rights to receive information free from commercial pressure (IBFAN 2004). Particularly important is the World Health Assembly's review of progress in implementation, which takes place every two years, generally leading to a further resolution addressing changes in marketing practices and scientific knowledge and questions of interpretation.

This is a good model for the development of other standards relating to food security. WHO and UNICEF were appropriate lead agencies for the issue of infant and young child feeding. According to WHO:

> WHO's objective, as set out in its Constitution, is the attainment by all peoples of the highest possible level of health. Health is defined in WHO's Constitution as a state of complete physical, mental and social well-being and not merely the absence of disease or infirmity. (WHO 2006b)

And UNICEF:

> UNICEF is the driving force that helps build a world where the rights of every child are realized. (UNICEF, 2006b)

While the code came into being some years before the Convention on the Rights of the Child, its promotion is now seen as a necessary part of UNICEF's mandate to protect child rights.

The aim of the International Code of Marketing of Breast-milk Substitutes is:

> To contribute to the provision of safe and adequate nutrition for infants, by the protection and promotion of breastfeeding, and by ensuring the proper use of breast-milk substitutes, when these are necessary, on the basis of adequate information and through appropriate marketing and distribution. (WHO 1981, Art. 1)

It is entirely appropriate that bodies concerned with health and child rights take the lead on developing such a marketing code.

Although regulations to protect the right to adequate food impact on trade, the financial interests of the private sector should not be placed on the same level as health and child rights. If the Code had resulted from a *negotiation* among stakeholders it would have been far weaker than it is, as shown by the fact that industry opposed key provisions throughout the drafting process and opposed its adoption by the World Health Assembly. While flawed, the code is as strong as it is because industry comments were taken as part of a *consultation*. While it was correct to consider the views of industry, it would have been a disservice to mothers and infants to negotiate away their rights to reach a deal the industry would have found financially acceptable.

The difference between *consultation* (meaning "seek information or advice from") and *negotiation* (meaning "try to reach an agreement or compromise by discussion") is important (Weiner and Simpson 2006). It may be that an uncompromising position has to be taken on certain issues to protect the right to food and all other human rights. It is appropriate that business interests express their views. But if there is a conflict between rights and, say, profits, it is entirely reasonable that health and human rights win the day.

The baby food industry found the code too robust. Ernest Saunder, vice president of Nestlé, writing as the president of International Council of Infant Food Industries, of which Nestlé was a founding and prominent member, to the WHO's director general, 26 January 1981 states:

> The World Industry has found this present draft code unacceptable . . . highly restrictive . . . irrelevant and unworkable. . . . The various provisions, if applied, could have a negative effect on child health. (ICIFI 1981)

The World Health Assembly disagreed, voting for the code by 118 votes to 1, with 3 abstentions. In this way, the global community signaled its support for the code. The principle that the UN's premier health body should take the lead on health issues is again entirely reasonable.

Since then, the WHA has called for the UN Codex Alimentarius Commission, which sets food standards,

> to continue to give full consideration, when elaborating standards, guidelines and recommendations, to those resolutions of the Health Assembly that are relevant in the framework of its operational mandate.

The Assembly has further directed a call to states

> to ensure that all national agencies involved in defining national positions on public health issues for use in all relevant international forums, including the Codex Alimentarius Commission, have a common and consistent understanding of health policies adopted by the Health Assembly, and to promote these policies. (WHA 2005)

Codex is a body under the umbrella of WHO and the Food and Agriculture Organization of the United Nations (FAO). This is a hugely influential body. According to the Codex Alimentarius Commission:

> The Codex Alimentarius, or the food code, has become the global reference point for consumers, food producers and processors, national food control agencies and the international food trade. The code has had an enormous impact on the thinking of food producers and processors as well as on the awareness of the end users—the consumers. Its influence extends to every continent, and its contribution to the protection of public health and fair practices in the food trade is immeasurable. (FAO 2005)

Codex standards have power in international law because the World Trade Organization (WTO) Agreement on the Application of Sanitary and Phytosanitary Measures (SPS Agreement) and the WTO Agreement on Technical Barriers to Trade (TBT Agreement) reference them. In a trade dispute the World Trade Organization could rule a nation's food safety measures as illegal if they are out of step with Codex standards and permit other countries to levy punitive tariffs to recoup losses.

While WHO is focused on health, FAO states:

> FAO's mandate is to raise levels of nutrition, improve agricultural productivity, better the lives of rural populations and contribute to the growth of the world economy. (FAO 2006)

Having the goal of growing the world economy may on occasion conflict with protecting health and protecting the right to food. Codex standards are developed through negotiation, requiring compromise with business interests, whose representatives dominate meetings. To illustrate,

IBFAN has documented how meetings discussing baby food standards have 50 percent or more participants from industry, including on government delegations, while public interest groups have a minor presence. In a 2003 review, IBFAN called on WHO to strengthen its management of the Codex Alimentarius Commission.

Thus, while existing United Nations bodies are appropriate fora for developing regulatory standards, there is a need to strengthen the public interest mandate of the bodies to ensure they introduce measures that are necessary, not only those that will be readily tolerated by the private sector.

If necessary measures are introduced in the face of industry opposition, then that opposition is likely to continue unless further action is taken. Twenty-five years after the baby food industry described the International Code of Marketing of Breast-milk Substitutes as "irrelevant and unworkable" it still refuses to bring policies and practices into line with it and the subsequent resolutions adopted to address questions of interpretation and changes in marketing practices and scientific knowledge. Only where national measures are introduced and authorities monitor and enforce compliance or there is strong campaigning by civil society are violations stopped. Where violations are stopped, this contributes to increases in breastfeeding rates and, inevitably, reduced sales of breastmilk substitutes and company profits. The fact that companies can comply when forced to do so demonstrates the code and resolutions are not in themselves unreasonable. It is the impact on profits that concerns company executives and leads to their lobbying for voluntary measures. It is necessary for the global community to put health before profits.

To summarize the above argument, if we are serious about protecting the right to food from abuse by transnational corporations it is essential that regulations are developed under the auspices of bodies whose primary concern is the right to food, rather than trade and company profits. Business interests should be consulted as appropriate, but the right to food should not be put up to negotiation to satisfy commercial interests. If necessary measures do not achieve the support and agreement of business interests, then it needs to be accepted that coercion, through monitoring and enforcement at national and international levels, is necessary.

MONITORING COMPLIANCE WITH GLOBAL STANDARDS

It is insufficient to develop standards for regulating transnational corporations with regard to the right to food if these are not monitored and enforced. The global community should take responsibility for introducing monitoring mechanisms at the global level to ensure that company self-monitoring and national measures are effective and to provide protection when they are not. Doing so does not usurp the power of the nation-state, but recognizes that the transnational nature of certain business interests requires checks and balances at global, as well as national, levels.

This principle was recognized in the Norms on the Responsibilities of Transnational Corporations and Other Business Enterprises with Regard to Human Rights, which propose:

> Transnational corporations and other business enterprises shall be subject to periodic monitoring and verification by United Nations, other international and national mechanisms already in existence or yet to be created, regarding application of the Norms. This monitoring shall be transparent and independent and take into account input from stakeholders (including nongovernmental organizations) and as a result of complaints of violations of these Norms. Further, transnational corporations and other business enterprises shall conduct periodic evaluations concerning the impact of their own activities on human rights under these Norms. (UN CHR 2003, para. 16)

The International Code of Marketing of Breast-milk Substitutes provides one of the few efforts at the international level to monitor and enforce standards for corporations relevant to the right to food. The code guides the oversight activities of the nongovernmental International Baby Food Action Network. There is as yet no coordinated governmental action at the global level apart from the biennial reviews by the World Health Assembly. However, there has been governmental action on a regional basis. To illustrate, the European Union Council of Ministers adopted the Council Resolution of 18 June 1992 on the marketing of breastmilk substitutes in third countries by Community-based manufacturers (92/C 172/01) which applies to companies manufacturing or headquartered in the European Union and states:

1. The Community will contribute to the application of appropriate marketing practices for breastmilk substitutes in third countries.
2. For the implementation of point 1, the Commission will instruct its delegations in third countries to serve as contact points for the competent authorities. Any complaints or criticisms with respect to the marketing practices of a manufacturer based in the Community could be notified to them.
3. The Commission will be ready to examine such cases and to assist in the search for a satisfactory solution for all parties concerned.
4. This resolution will be communicated by the Commission to the countries concerned through the official channels.
5. The Commission will forward to the European Parliament and to the Council every two years a report on the results of the application of this resolution. (Council of the European Communities 1992)

The International Code of Marketing of Breast-milk Substitutes is mentioned in the preamble to the council resolution. On the basis of this explicit recognition, members of IBFAN in a number of countries have registered cases of violations of the code to the commission. The commission has not taken up a single case, arguing that civil society groups are not "competent authorities." However, this wording about competent authorities was introduced in the resolution for the stated purpose of including civil society alongside government authorities. At a public hearing into Nestlé baby food marketing held under the auspices of the European Parliament Committee for Economic Development and Cooperation in November 2000, the commission was called on to review its interpretation of "competent authority."

When introducing mechanisms on this and other issues relating to the right to food, the global community should accept the principle that civil society should be empowered to report breaches of international measures. Government authorities may be reluctant to report breaches, fearing such action could be construed as obstruction to trade or otherwise undermine relationships with powerful countries or economic blocs.

At the international level the obvious body to monitor and enforce the code and resolutions is arguably the World Health Organization, the executive body responsible for enacting the policies set by the World Health Assembly. However, WHO does not have and does not appear to want this mandate. When asked, WHO specifically states it does not report on company compliance, only steps taken by governments to implement the code and resolutions. Neither does the Codex Alimentarius Commission have a policing role.

If the standard setting bodies are not to be enforcement bodies, is there potential to use existing international mechanisms, such as the International Criminal Court (ICC) for redress if national measures are ineffective?

The ICC has a mandate only for investigating and adjudicating war crimes, crimes against humanity and genocide by individuals, and international aggression by states. The definition of "crimes against humanity" in the Rome statute that set up the ICC does not lend itself to prosecuting abuses of the right to food perpetrated by transnational corporations. The special representative of the secretary-general (SRSG) on the issue of human rights and transnational corporations and other business enterprises suggested in his 2007 report to the UN Human Rights Council that the fact that corporations are seen in law as legal persons could have relevance in international law. As extraterritorial measures can be taken against individuals by some states for breaches of human rights, the same measure could be applied against corporations. This argument could have had relevance to the ICC if its mandate had been different:

> The ICC preparatory committee and the Rome conference itself debated a proposal that would have given the Court jurisdiction over legal persons (other than states), but differences in national approaches prevented its adoption. Nevertheless, just as the absence of an international accountability mechanism

did not preclude individual responsibility for international crimes in the past, it does not preclude the emergence of corporate responsibility today. (Ruggie 2007, para. 21)

If the mandate were extended, the prosecutor of the court does have the power to investigate crimes on his own initiative and could decide to accept reports from civil society organizations. However, civil society organizations are not specifically named as having the right to refer cases. Named bodies are states and the UN Security Council (International Criminal Court 2002).

A procedure for empowering communities to prompt investigations by the prosecutor of the ICC or another court given jurisdiction over transnational corporations could be that of a civil public action. This approach is used at a national level in countries such as Brazil, and a similar approach could be followed. Under the Brazilian constitution the Public Ministry is a semiautonomous part of the civil service, meaning it is resistant to political interference as it has guaranteed funding and its head is appointed by the government from a short list prepared by the Public Ministry itself. The Public Ministry has been involved in investigating cases of corruption and was instrumental in the impeachment of a past president of Brazil, Fernando Collor. A civil public action is an investigation prompted by a citizen's petition presented to a public prosecutor of the Public Ministry. For example, if a community finds its water supply is depleted or polluted due to the action of a corporation, it can present a petition and trigger an investigation. If the public prosecutor finds there is a case to answer they will take the case through the courts. This can be time consuming. When the citizens of São Lourenço initiated a civil public action over the damaging environmental impact of a Nestlé bottling plant, it took five years to reach a settlement with the prosecutor, which was achieved in March 2006. Another possible mechanism would be for designated nongovernmental organizations to have the right to file cases at a new or existing international court mandated to hear such cases. Again, the global community can learn from experiences at the national level. In India the Infant Milk Substitutes Act (1992, revised 2003) empowers four NGOs to file cases against baby food companies. The law has the sanction of imprisonment. The four cases brought to date have resulted in companies rapidly changing their practices. Indeed, Johnson and Johnson decided to leave the feeding bottle market in India and later the whole world. Nestlé changed its labels after a case brought in 1995 to include warnings in Hindi on labels, but it continues to contest the case and launched an unsuccessful attempt at having the law overturned.

There have been some moves to allow NGOs to register complaints to nonjudicial bodies at the international level. As described above, the European

Parliament has envisioned a Monitoring Platform, a committee that would receive complaints from NGOs and members of the public and investigate those that seem to have merit. The UN Global Compact, though stating it is not intended to have a monitoring function, does allow people and organizations to report breaches of its code of conduct so it can investigate whether it has been brought into disrepute.

Nongovernmental organizations can file complaints with other bodies, such as the Committee on the Rights of the Child and the Committee on Economic, Social and Cultural Rights. While their conclusions are addressed to governments, not nonstate parties such as corporations, the principle is relevant and important.

An enforcement mechanism that is open to complaints by all might receive a large number, many without merit; however, this is perhaps preferable to limiting referrals to states parties. As has been found with the European Union's export measures for baby foods, governments are reluctant to register complaints about the behavior of transnational corporations of a powerful trading partner.

There are proposals for more radical solutions. For example, George Monbiot proposes an international Fair Trade Organization that has powers to regulate international business and impose meaningful sanctions to ensure human rights and environmental standards are respected (Monbiot 2003). The "simultaneous policy" campaign, originating from a book of the same name, provides a democratic space where such proposals are being debated and calls for multilateral action to implement the policies developed and approved by people across the world (Bunzl, 2001).

ENFORCEMENT OF GLOBAL STANDARDS

If a corporation is found guilty of breaching global standards aiming to protect the right to food, there needs to be a mechanism to stop continued or future breaches and to provide redress.

Prosecutions and fines can be viewed by corporations with multibillion dollar turnovers as a business cost. Nestlé was fined in Costa Rica at the end of 1999 for breaking laws relating to the labeling of breastmilk substitutes. When the government implemented the code and resolutions in legislation in 1994, companies were given one year to bring their labels into line. Nestlé was repeatedly warned after this that its labels did not comply. At one stage, in August 1996, Nestlé did present labels that satisfied the Ministry of Health and Economy, but these were not placed on the market. Instead Nestlé continued using labels that had been rejected. In September 1999, legal action was taken. Nestlé did not attend the court hearing and was convicted in absentia and fined about $1,000, an amount Nestlé itself described accurately as "a small fine."

In the United Kingdom, Wyeth was fined £60,808 (including costs) for illegal advertising of infant formula in 2003—equivalent to three minutes worth of sales for the company. The trial lasted eight days and set important legal precedents showing the type of advertisement at the center of the case was illegal under UK Law. However, similar advertisements continue to be placed, and enforcement authorities have not taken these to court, perhaps viewing the time and effort as unjustified given that the fine has not acted as a deterrent.

Fines framed in terms of company turnover may be a more effective sanction. To illustrate, in the European Union corporations can be fined up to 10 percent of their turnover if convicted in antitrust investigations. In 2001 fines were levied against eight pharmaceutical companies for price fixing in the vitamin market, amounting to £855.22 million ($753 million). The lead company, Hoffman-La Roche, was fined 2.6 percent of total sales. It set aside $3.04 billion to fight legal battles and pay fines in the United States, EU, and Australia. In 1999 Roche was one of three companies that agreed to settle for $725 million in the United States. In Australia three companies, including Roche, settled for US$30.5 million in 2006. Roche sold its vitamin business in September 2002, while remaining liable for payment of fines arising from the price fixing (Watson 2001; Rubin 2003; AFX 2006). The global nature of the malpractice demonstrates the central control of transnational corporations. While rich nations have been able to pursue the well-resourced companies through the courts to gain compensation for the price fixing, poorer nations have not been part of the settlements. Collective action by the global community at the international level could rectify this situation in future cases.

Regulations that require companies to withdraw offending products from the market can be an effective sanction. This involves cost and harms a corporation's all-important image. There have been numerous cases of formula being recalled for failing to comply with contamination guidelines. In 2005, for example, Nestlé was ordered to recall Neslac from the Chinese market for too high levels of iodine, something it at first resisted, prompting a consumer boycott. In 2003 Nestlé had to withdraw a batch of Beba infant formula from the European market after the death of a child from meningitis was linked to Enterobacter sakazakii contamination of the formula. Powdered infant formula is not a sterile product. The European Food Standards Agency has the power to order such recalls. However, despite the recall in most of Europe, in Nestlé's home country of Switzerland, the formula remained on sale because it was outside the jurisdiction of EFSA. In 2005 it was found that Nestlé and Milupa formula in several European countries was contaminated with a chemical from the ink on the packaging. In Italy, law enforcement officers moved into shops to seize products from the shelves and from the vehicles of distributors. Enforcement mechanisms introduced by the global community could follow a similar approach.

An international court could have the power to imprison executives of companies guilty of serious breaches of global standards, learning from experience at the national level. The Indian Infant Milk Substitutes Act, referred to above, has a sanction of imprisonment. Though that has not yet been invoked it has become a common sight in recent years to see executives of companies such as Worldcom and Enron imprisoned in the United States for other forms of corporate crime.

Another graphic example of the power of such sanctions comes from the campaign to improve food quality. Saturated fats or trans fats used in processed foods are blamed for contributing to the pandemic of obesity and noncommunicable diseases. They are used because they are cheaper and have a longer shelf life than healthier unsaturated fats. Trans fats were widely used in foodstuffs in Denmark until 2003, as in other countries. In 2003 the Danish government enacted legislation requiring manufacturers to reduce content of trans fatty acids in the oils and fats to no more than 2 grams per 100 grams. Manufacturers were allowed to sell food manufactured before the law came into force and were given a six-month period during which trans fat content in food products could be up to 5 grams per 100 grams of the product. From December 2003 sanctions of up to two years in prison have applied for selling foods with higher-than-permitted levels of trans fats ("Denmark's Trans Fat Law" 2003).

Manufacturers appear to have complied with the regulations in Denmark while not changing practices elsewhere. In April 2006, Dr. Steen Stender of Gentofte University Hospital in Hellerup, Denmark, wrote to WebMD with details of a survey of fast food he had conducted while traveling (Hitti 2006). WebMD reported Stender as stating "the content of trans fatty acids varied from less than 1 gram in Denmark and Germany, to 10 grams in New York (McDonald's) and 24 grams in Hungary (Kentucky Fried Chicken)." And "The cooking oil used for French fries in McDonald's outlets in the United States and Peru contained 23 percent and 24 percent trans fatty acids, respectively, whereas the oils used for French fries in many European countries contained only about 10 percent trans fatty acids, with some countries as low as 5 percent (Spain) and 1 percent (Denmark)." Questioned by WebMD, McDonald's stated, "McDonald's continues to work diligently on ways to reduce TFA levels in our fries. . . . Our reduction in the U.S. is taking longer than anticipated, as we have previously announced. However, we continue to progress in our testing and we are determined to get it right for our customers." Kentucky Fried Chicken sent an e-mail to WebMD stating, "Our product offerings vary from country to country to reflect local taste preferences, and we do make nutritional information available to our customers."

While Denmark's law has prompted changes, elsewhere in Europe a voluntary corporate social responsibility approach is being pursued to implement the World Health Assembly's Global Strategy on Diet, Physical Activity and Health (WHA 2004). The European Union has set up a European Platform for Action on Diet, Physical Activity and Health to "bring together all relevant players active at European level that are willing to enter into binding and verifiable commitments aimed at halting and reversing current overweight and obesity trends." In its green paper on Promoting Healthy Diets and Physical Activity, the commission reports, "Platform members are planning far-reaching commitments for 2006" (European Commission 2005). These commitments are from organizations such as the European Snacks Association, which has undertaken to improve product labeling and "to further develop products reduced in fat, saturated fat or salt and to make these products more available" (European Commission 2006). So while Denmark's regulatory approach has forced compliance and protected the public from health-damaging foods, the voluntary approach puts the onus on consumers to select the healthy option, which is likely to be sold at a higher price with claims as to its health benefits. The global community should learn from this experience and pursue regulatory systems backed by strong sanctions in addition to encouraging voluntary action to achieve necessary changes in business practices.

While seizure of goods and sanctions such as imprisonment are obviously applicable to cases where corporations market products that infringe on the right to food, there are other ways in which such sanctions can help protect this right. For example, a transnational may be infringing the right to food of the people in a community by depleting or polluting its water supplies, monopolizing supply chains or appropriating agricultural land. Seizing products whose production has infringed the right to food at any point in the supply is likely to be effective at changing company practices, as is seizing products that harm the end consumer.

The global community could also ensure that states take action to hold their corporations to account. One suggestion put forward for debate in the "simultaneous policy" campaign referred to previously is that an enforcement system similar to that of the World Trade Organization should be used. At present, governments can file cases at the WTO if another government seeks to gain competitive advantage through protectionism, technical trade barriers, or subsidies that have not been sanctioned in international agreements. This mandate could be extended to include gaining an unfair competitive advantage through failing to hold corporations headquartered in the country to account against global standards. Alternatively, the Fair Trade Organization proposed by George Monbiot could have this mandate. Punitive tariffs could be levied on imports from a country found to allow its corporations to violate agreed-upon standards. This would serve to transfer the wealth unfairly gained. The power of this approach has been demonstrated in past rulings of the WTO in trade disputes. For example, in 2003 the United States reversed protectionist tariff increases on steel imports following a ruling against it by the WTO. The European Union initiated plans to impose $2.2 billion of carefully targeted punitive tariffs on U.S. exports to prompt observance of the WTO ruling (Crustinger 2003).

Effective monitoring and enforcement mechanisms at the global level would drive standards up, whereas voluntary approaches always run the risk of collapsing if one corporation fails to comply. The experience of implementation of the marketing requirements for breastmilk substitutes at the national level is relevant. In some countries with independently monitored and enforced legislation, not only are violations stopped, but companies denounce competitors who seek to gain market share by breaking the regulations. In contrast, the voluntary ban on advertising of infant formula in the United States collapsed when Nestlé entered the market in the 1980s and refused to comply. Today all companies advertise infant formula in the United States.

CHANGING THE NATURE OF CORPORATIONS

A publicly listed company (a company with shares issued on a stock market) is required to put the interests of its shareholders before the interests of others. A private firm can follow the whims of its owners, and cooperatives generally give greater weight to the interests of members. Most, though not all, transnational corporations are publicly listed companies (the world's largest grain trader, Cargill, is exceptional as it is in private hands).

Putting shareholder interests first means, in practice, satisfying the demand for dividends and maintaining the value of the shares, achieved by increasing profits. Nestlé's chairman and onetime chief executive officer, Peter Brabeck-Letmathe, has undertaken to deliver 5–6 percent year-on-year growth. Failure to do so can reduce the share price as investors sell to move their money elsewhere, thus increasing the risk of a business being subject to a hostile takeover. Reduced shareholder confidence and share price also undermines a company's credit rating, thus making it more expensive to borrow money. To maintain the share price, executives have to force costs down, take business away from rival companies and create new markets.

While this drives efficiency and innovation, there are negative consequences. Under this paradigm, abiding by human rights and environmental standards only gains significance if violations have sufficient financial cost associated with them. This can be achieved by making the company legally responsible. Even then, a company may decide it is worth paying the fines instead of changing behavior. Consumer action, such as boycotts, can force ethical issues onto the balance sheet. Making ethical issues a selling point through ethical marking, such as the Fairtrade mark, can also have an impact. Several transnationals have tried to gain a share of the market with their own fair trade products.

In addition to giving malpractice a financial cost, changing the nature of corporations could improve respect for the right to food and human rights generally. The global community can learn from moves to do this at regional and national levels and respond to the rise of transnational corporations by creating a register of globally incorporated companies. The requirement to register could be on the basis of turnover and territorial extent (the number of countries in which a company is active). Registration would be with a global authority that would require registered companies to provide specified information on their activities, including how these may impact on the right to food. As with information supplied to a national register, this would be subject to external audit, sanctions if false information is supplied, and court proceedings if illegal activities are suspected.

While business leaders will no doubt throw up their hands in horror at such suggestion, they have already advocated the voluntary United Nations reporting system, the Global Compact. In addition, at regional level politicians have called for corporations to be incorporated not just at national, but international level. The EU Parliament white paper "EU Standards for European Enterprises Operating in Developing Countries: Towards a European Code of Conduct" called on the European Commission to

> ensure that consideration is given, with an appropriate legal basis, to incorporating core labour, environmental and human rights international standards when reviewing European company law, including the new EC Directive on a European-incorporated company. (European Union 1999, para. 27)

These suggestions have not yet been taken up by the EU Commission.

In the United Kingdom, the Corporate Responsibility Coalition (CORE) successfully lobbied for a change in UK company law, making it a legal requirement to report on a company's social and environmental impacts including down company supply chains. It is also calling for UK law to provide recourse to those harmed by UK-based enterprises operating in other countries. These moves were opposed by business interests (Corporate Responsibility Coalition 2006).

If the act of incorporation of a business were to require it to respect the right to food and other human rights, this would empower various actors, such as company insurers, to hold the corporation accountable by means other than legal action. The very fact that a corporation had a legal obligation could mean that failure to comply would increase its liability if any claim for damages were to be made against it. Therefore insurers and investors would wish to know that liabilities are reduced by compliance.

Shareholders or legislation itself could require a named director to take responsibility to ensure compliance. The director could be personally answerable before the courts for failing to fulfill his or her obligations, as a finance director is liable if accounts are not kept in accordance with legislation.

The basis of incorporation could be radically changed. For example, Shann Turnbull has proposed that shareholders be offered tax incentives to transfer their ownership to other stakeholders so creating "network firms."

> An outstanding example of network firms organised into networks of groups, are the stakeholder-controlled enterprises located around the town of Mondragon in Northern Spain. A World Bank study found that these firms were more efficient than investor owned firms. Like mutual enterprises, the stakeholder firms do not require equity investors to bring them into existence or to make them efficient. Over 80% of investor owned firms typically fail in their first five years compared with less than 1% of the Mondragon firms.
>
> Network governance [non-hierarchical governance] is found in the most complex and dynamic industries like fashion textiles, movie making, electronics and biotechnology. In such industries it is common for firms to both co-operate and compete with each other because of their respective specialisation of talent, knowledge or production techniques.
>
> Network governance is also found in all sustainable non-trivial employee-owned firms. The John Lewis Partnership that operates chain stores in the UK illustrates both network governance and its competitive advantages. The Partnership, like Mondragon, is a major business with over 50,000 employees. It demonstrates how contestability for corporate control through the stock market is not required to produce efficiency and competitive advantages. Another example is VISA International Inc. that has a network of over 1000 boards of directors within the one legal entity. Each board has absolute autonomy over a particular function or geographical area.
>
> The absence of a public market for shares in these firms eliminates the ability for senior management to ramp up the share price by one means or another, cash-up their stocks options and then depart. By not having shares publicly traded, network firms grow organically rather than through acquisitions. Many acquisitions are driven by the ambition of a CEO for greater power, influence and remuneration that commonly results in the loss of shareholder value. (Turnbull 1999)

Corporations more closely linked and responsible to the communities in which they operate are less likely to abuse the rights of those communities.

Within the simultaneous policy (SP) discussion, where global policies are developed by people coming together across the world, there is a suggestion for remodeling companies to become stakeholder-governed organizations (Simpol-UK 2006). Though such discussions have no status until approved by registered SP adopters, which may or may not happen, this demonstrates that there are routes other than conventional international politics to achieve such an end.

As described above, the European Parliament unsuccessfully called for the responsibilities of transnational corporations to be modified in legislation for the EU-incorporated company. Extrapolating from this proposal there is the possibility for the international community, through the United Nations, to rethink and redefine the nature of corporations in creating an official legal basis for the globally incorporated company. Businesses with a turnover and territorial extent above set criteria could be required to register with a global authority, with registration requiring a binding commitment to respect the right to food and other human rights, environmental standards, and other criteria. As with national registers, documentation would be required on an annual basis to demonstrate compliance to the authority, with suitable checks and balances, such as external auditing and legal obligations on named directors to assure the accuracy of data. To give confidence, the authority could also accept complaints from other stakeholders, including nongovernmental organizations, and conduct investigations, bringing cases before an international court if breaches are found.

The world's largest food company, Nestlé, claims there is not a country on the planet where its products are not sold. Is it not time that global companies were held to account by the global community?

CONCLUSIONS AND RECOMMENDATIONS

Due to the ever-increasing power of transnational corporations, which rivals that of states, and their impact on the right to food, it is essential that corporations be regulated at the global level.

Where there is regulation, independently monitored and enforced, companies can comply when compelled to do so. Leaving responsibility for legislating, monitoring, and enforcement at the national level is an abrogation of responsibility by the global community of nations, as only the richest countries will have the resources and political capacity to take action, though even in rich countries this is often lacking.

There have been past attempts at regulating business interests at the international level, be it through a trading block such as the European Union or through a United Nations initiative such as the measures once proposed by the UN Centre on Transnational Corporations. These have not progressed, due to resistance from the business community and its strategy of promoting voluntary approaches as a more effective way to achieve change. The fact that so little change has been achieved shows the voluntary approach is at best too limited and at worst an unwarranted distraction from binding regulations.

Several possibilities for achieving effective regulation, monitoring, and enforcement have been discussed. The route could be through a new or reformed international court, an authority to register and monitor globally incorporated companies, requirements on home countries to enforce standards on their corporations, or a change in the rules under which publicly listed (shareholder) corporations operate or are even incorporated. What is clear, in all of these cases, is the need for governments to act collectively as the global community to respond to the growth in size and power of companies.

It may be many years before the political will is there to make corporations answerable before an international criminal court or to achieve other possible balances on the power of corporations. But that does not mean it is wrong to discuss the possibilities. Corporations rival the power of governments in terms of their economic might and too often infringe the right to food and other human rights. For their own legitimacy in a globalized world, corporations will sooner or later have to accept regulation at a global level.

In the shorter term we can look to action that is perhaps more politically expedient. In this spirit the following recommendations are made, drawn from the preceding discussion.

It is recommended that:

1. The World Health Organization, Food and Agriculture Organization of the United Nations, or other suitable United Nations body or UN special rapporteur with a focus on health should develop proposals for regulatory systems for companies that impact on the right to food. This should include the creation of a United Nations global authority for regulating transnational corporations to be tasked with implementing the proposals. The proposals should be determined through a process of *consultation* with health experts, Nongovernmental organizations and business interests, not a process of *negotiation*. Endorsement of the proposals should be sought from the World Health Assembly as the world's highest health-policy-setting body, and other bodies, such as the World Trade Organization and Codex Alimentarius Commission, should incorporate the proposals in future activities once approved, as appropriate.

2. The global authority for regulating transnational corporations should specify the information required from corporations to enable reporting on their impact. It should develop criteria (if these are not included in the proposals in point 1) to specify the corporations coming within its remit based on turnover and territorial extent, and compile a list of corporations meeting the criteria.

3. The global authority for regulating transnational corporations should accept complaints of breaches of human rights norms relating to the right to food from nongovernmental organizations as well as government authorities and conduct a transparent investigation, publishing the results of its findings.

4. National governments acting individually, and also collectively through the proposed global authority for regulating transnational corporations, should examine the basis of incorporation of businesses within their territory and consider introducing a legal requirement to respect the right to food and other human rights. Responsibilities for reporting and the duties of directors in this regard should be considered at the same time. Present standards used should be shared through the global authority for regulating transnational corporations with a view to identifying core provisions for a globally incorporated company to be registered with and monitored by the global authority. These provisions can also form the basis for a minimum standard applied at national level.

5. Nongovernmental organizations should continue to monitor the impact of corporations on the right to food and call for action at the global level for meaningful monitoring and enforcement of standards to ensure the right to food is respected; to continue to collate case studies; and to register complaints with appropriate existing national, regional, and global bodies and those filling the functions set out above, should they come into being.

6. The United Nations System Standing Committee on Nutrition should endorse the above recommendations and advocate the provisions of funds for preliminary work in developing proposals for the global authority for regulating transnational corporations.

REFERENCES

AFX News. 2006. "Roche, BASF, Aventis Settle Australian Vitamin Cartel Action Out of Court." 17 July. www.finanznachrichten.de/nachrichten-2006-07/artikel-6710893.asp.

Anderson, S., and J. Cavanagh. 2000. *Top 200: The Rise of Global Corporate Power.* Corporate Watch. www.globalpolicy.org/socecon/tncs/top200.htm.

Bunzl, John. 2001. *The Simultaneous Policy: An Insiders Guide to Saving Humanity and the Planet.* London: New European Publications.

Cargill. 2005. "Cargill Reports Fourth-Quarter and Fiscal 2005 Earnings." Press release. www.cargill.com/news/news_releases/news4/050823earn.htm.

Castle, Stephen. 2000. "Adidas Boycotts EU Ethics Hearing." *Independent* (London), 23 November. http://news.independent.co.uk/europe/article152252.ece.

Clausing, Kimberly A. 2001. *The Behavior of Intrafirm Trade Prices in U.S. International Price Data.* U.S. Department of Labor, Bureau of Labor Statistics, BLS Working Paper 333 (January 2001). Cited in *Interim Report of the Special Representative of the Secretary-General on the Issue of Human Rights and Transnational Corporations and Other Business Enterprises.* UNHCHR (2006) http://daccessdds.un.org/doc/UNDOC/GEN/G06/110/27/PDF/G0611027.pdf?OpenElement.

Corporate Responsibility Coalition. 2006. www.corporate-responsibility.org/.

Council of the European Communities. 1992. *Council Resolution of 18 June 1992 on the Marketing of Breast-milk Substitutes in Third Countries by Community-based Manufacturers* (92/C 172/01). http://ec.europa.eu/food/food/labellingnutrition/children/df14_en.pdf.

Crustinger. 2003. "Bush Decides to Lift Steep Steel Tariffs." Associated Press, 4 December. www.tradeobservatory.org/showFile.php?RefID=18876.

Dalmeny, K., E. Hanna, and E. Lobstein. 2003. *Broadcasting Bad Health: Why Food Marketing to Children Needs to Be Controlled.* International Association of Consumer Food Organizations.

"Denmark's Trans Fat Law." 2003. Executive Order No. 160 of 11 March 2003 on the Content of Trans Fatty Acids in Oils and Fats etc. English translation as cited by tfX: The Campaign against Trans Fat in Foods. www.tfx.org.uk/page116.html.

European Commission. 2005. *Promoting Healthy Diets and Physical Activity: A European Dimension for the Prevention of Overweight, Obesity and Chronic Diseases.* Green paper. http://ec.europa.eu/health/ph_determinants/life_style/nutrition/documents/nutrition_gp_en.pdf.

———. 2006. *EU Platform on Diet, Physical Activity and Health: Synopsis of Commitments 2006* (first update, 29 March). http://ec.europa.eu/health/ph_determinants/life_style/nutrition/platform/docs/synopsis_commitments.pdf.

European Union. 1999. *EU Standards for European Enterprises Operating in Developing Countries: Towards a European Code of Conduct.* http://europa.eu.int/eur-lex/pri/en/oj/dat/1999/c_104/c_10419990414en01800184.pdf.

FAO (Food and Agriculture Organization of the United Nations). 2005. *Understanding the Codex Alimentarius.* www.fao.org/documents/show_cdr.asp?url_file=/docrep/008/y7867e/y7867e00.htm.

———. 2006. "FAO's Mandate." www.fao.org/UNFAO/about/mandate_en.html.

GAIN (Global Alliance for Improved Nutrition). 2006. "About GAIN, Partners in Food Fortification." www.gainhealth.org/.

Guardian. 2002. "Fat Is a Financial Issue." *Guardian.* 27 December. www.guardian.co.uk/food/Story/0,2763,865377,00.html.

Hitti, Miranda. 2006. "How Much Trans Fat in Those Fries? It Depends Where in the World You Buy Them, Study Shows." *WebMD*, 12 April. www.webmd.com/content/Article/121/114064.htm?pagenumber=1.

IBFAN (International Baby Food Action Network). 2004. *Checks and Balances in the Global Economy: Using International Standards to Stop Corporate Malpractice—Does It Work?* Cambridge: IBFAN.

ICIFI (International Council of Infant Food Industries). 1981. Letter. www.babymilkaction.org/pdfs/saunders81.pdf.

International Criminal Court. 2002. *Rome Statute of the International Criminal Court.* www.icc-cpi.int/library/about/officialjournal/Rome_Statute_120704-EN.pdf.

Kinley, David, and Rachel Chambers. 2006. *The UN Human Rights Norms for Corporations: The Private Implications of Public International Law.* Oxford: Human Rights Law Review, Oxford University Press. http://papers.ssrn.com/sol3/papers.cfm?abstract_id=944153.

Lang, Tim, and Michael Heasman. 2004. *Food Wars: The Global Battle for Mouths, Minds and Markets.* London: Earthscan.

Lang, Tim, and E. Millston. 2002. *The Atlas of Food*. London: Earthscan Books.

Monbiot, George. 2003. *The Age of Consent*. London: HarperCollins.

Nestlé. 2006a. *The Nestlé Sustainability Review*. Vevey, Switzerland: Nestlé. www.Nestlé.com/NR/rdonlyres/F16BB594-F86F-4EDA-81AD-4C5F7 17FBA33/0/Sustainability_Review_English.pdf.

———. 2006b. Spring press conference, February 23, 2006. Powerpoint presentation. www.ir.nestle.com/NR/rdonlyres/6E296A6C-9B70-497E-93AD-EB218689 FA69/0/2006FirstQuarterSalesConferenceCall.pdf.

OECD (Organization for Economic Cooperation and Development). 2000. *The OECD Guidelines for Multinational Enterprises*. www.oecd.org/dataoecd/56/36/1922428.pdf.

Reuters. 2006. "European Shares Gain as Earnings Please." 25 April. http://today.reuters.com/business/newsarticle.aspx?type=tnBusinessNews&sto ryID=nL25756472&imageid=&cap=.

Revill, Jo. 2004. "Sugar's Secret Sweetener Offer to Health Chiefs." *Observer*, 3 October. www.guardian.co.uk/medicine/story/0,,1318634,00.html.

Richter, Judith. 2001. *Holding Corporations Accountable*. London: Zed Books.

———. 2002. *Codes in Context: TNC Regulation in an Era of Dialogues and Partnerships*. Corner House briefing, February. Sturminster Newton, UK: Corner House. www.the cornerhouse.org.uk/item.shtml?x=51978.

Rubin, Allan. 2003. "Vitamin Price Fixing Lawsuits." 28 December. www.therubins .com/legal/vitamsuit.htm.

Ruggie, John. 2007. *Business and Human Rights: Mapping International Standards of Responsibility and Accountability for Corporate Acts*. Report of the Special Representative of the Secretary-General (SRSG) on the issue of human rights and transnational corporations and other business enterprises. United Nations A/HRC/4/035. www.ohchr.org/english/bodies/hrcouncil/docs/4session/A.HRC.4 .35.Add.3.pdf.

Simpol-UK. 2006. "Policy Zone" website section. www.simpol.org.uk/.

Turnbull, Shann. 1999. "Corporate Governance: Its Scope, Concerns and Theories." *Corporate Governance: An International Review* 5, (4): 180–205. www.capitalownership .org/lib/turnbull4.html.

UN CHR (United Nations Commission on Human Rights). 2003. *Norms on the Responsibilities of Transnational Corporations and Other Business Enterprises with Regard to Human Rights*. www.unhchr.ch/huridocda/huridoca.nsf/(Symbol)/E.CN.4 .Sub.2.2003.12.Rev.2.En?Opendocument.

UN ECOSOC (United Nations Economic and Social Council). 1999. *Substantive Issues Arising in the Implementation of the International Covenant on Economic, Social and Cultural Rights*. General Comment 12 (Twentieth Session, 1999) "The Right to Adequate Food" (art. 11). Geneva: ECOSOC E/C.12/1999/5. www.unhchr.ch/tbs/doc.nsf/ MasterFrameView/3d02758c707031d58025677f003b73b9?Opendocument.

———. 2002. *Millennium Development Goals*. www.un.org/millenniumgoals/.

UN Global Compact. 2006. *Global Compact: Note on Integrity Measures*. www.unglobal compact.org/AboutTheGC/gc_integrity_mesures.pdf.

UNICEF (United Nations Children's Fund). 2006a. *Iodine Deficiency Disorders: The Challenge*. http://childinfo.org/areas/idd/.

———. 2006b. "About UNICEF: Who We Are." www.unicef.org/about/who/index .html.

UN Secretary-General. 2005. "Secretary-General Appoints John Ruggie of United States Special Representative on Issue of Human Rights, Transnational Corporations, Other Business Enterprises." Press release, 28 July. www.un.org/News/Press/docs/2005/sga934.doc.htm.

Vorley, Bill. 2003. *Food, Inc. Corporate Concentration from Farm to Consumer*. London: UK Food Group. www.ukfoodgroup.org.uk/.

Watson, Rory. 2001. "Vitamin Cartel Companies Given Record Fines." *British Medical Journal* 323 (1 December): 1271.

Weiner, E. S., and J. A. Simpson. 2006. *Compact Oxford English Dictionary*. Oxford: Oxford University Press.

WHA (World Health Assembly). 2004. *Global Strategy on Diet, Physical Activity and Health*. www.who.int/gb/ebwha/pdf_files/WHA57/A57_R17-en.pdf.

———. 2005. *Infant and Young-child Nutrition*. Resolution 58.32. WHO. www.who.int/gb/ebwha/pdf_files/WHA58/WHA58_32-en.pdf.

WHO (World Health Organization). 1981. *The International Code of Marketing of Breast-milk Substitutes*. www.who.int/nutrition/publications/code_english.pdf.

———. 2005. *Implementation of Resolutions* (Progress Reports). A58.23. www.who.int/gb/ebwha/pdf_files/WHA58/A58_23-en.pdf.

———. 2006a. *Implementation of Resolutions* (Progress Reports). A59.23 www.who.int/gb/ebwha/pdf_files/WHA59/A59_23-en.pdf.

———. 2006b. "About WHO." www.who.int/.

5

International Obligations for Infants' Right to Food

Arun Gupta

The right of infants to adequate food and nutrition needs to be viewed within the context of existing human rights principles. In the many dialogues and debates about nutritional security and human rights, the nutritional rights of infants are usually forgotten. It is often presumed that infant feeding is a natural process, in the private domain between the infant and its mother, an area that rarely needs interventions from outside. Yet infancy is the period when human life is most vulnerable. The majority of deaths of children under five years of age take place during infancy, before the child is one year old. Evidence is increasingly highlighting the role of adequate nutrition in preventing these deaths.

For the infant there are three necessary components of good nutrition: adequate and proper diet (food), good and loving care in a healthy environment, and access to health care services. These components can make a difference not just between life and death, but also in terms of physical, mental, emotional, and intellectual development, impacting even future earning capacity. Optimal infant nutrition includes optimal breastfeeding, which in turn includes timely initiation of breastfeeding within one hour of birth, exclusive breastfeeding for the first six months, and continued breastfeeding for six to twenty-four months along with adequate complementary feeding after six months. Optimal infant nutrition contributes enormously to the survival and best potential development of infants; in fact, it lays the foundation for a healthy life.

Optimal infant nutrition is clearly linked to a reduction in infant mortality. Achieving universal optimal breastfeeding during infancy could cut under-five child deaths by nearly one-sixth; and ensuring that breastfeeding starts within one hour of birth could cut newborn deaths by more than one-fifth.

Thus it is critical to first recognize and clearly state the infant's human right to nutritional security and secondly initiate widespread action to ensure this right.

Apart from the fact that infants need more attention, there are problems of inequity and poverty that are linked to high infant and neonatal mortality in developing and resource-poor countries. Undernutrition is also at it highest in these nations. Although postneonatal and child mortality rates have declined dramatically in many developing countries in recent decades, neonatal mortality rates have remained relatively unchanged. Neonatal mortality now accounts for approximately two-thirds of the 8 million deaths in children less than one year of age, and nearly four-tenths of all deaths in children less than five years of age. Worldwide, 98 percent of all neonatal deaths occur in developing countries, mostly at home (Moss et al. 2002). A global ecological risk assessment (Lauer et al. 2006) of deaths and years of life lost due to suboptimal breastfeeding among children in the developing world revealed that attributable fractions for deaths due to diarrhea disease and lower-respiratory-tract infections are 55 percent and 53 percent, respectively, for the first six months of infancy, 20 percent and 18 percent for the second six months, and are 20 percent for all-cause deaths in the second year of life. The authors concluded that globally, as many as 1.45 million lives (117 million years of life) are lost due to suboptimal breastfeeding in developing countries. The fact that these countries need support both in terms of resources and building their capacity to deal with these situations calls for an international obligation in the human rights framework.

Women need accurate information and skilled support to succeed in adopting optimal breastfeeding practices. They also need financial as well other forms of assistance, such as food supplementation, to enable them to meet infants' nutritional rights. The global community has made several commitments in the past five decades to improve infant nutrition and survival. These commitments now need to be translated from rhetoric into action. This chapter calls for entitlement of some services as a road map to achieve optimal infant nutrition under a universal "Minimum Essential Program" (MEP).

THE STATE OF INFANT NUTRITION AND SURVIVAL

The report card on child nutrition published by UNICEF in 2006 showed that 146 million children under five years of age in the developing world are underweight. This means one out of every four children under the age of five is underweight for his or her age, and at increased risk of an early death. Undernutrition in under-fives is extremely high and unacceptable, particularly in Sub-Saharan Africa (28 percent) and South Asia (46 percent) (UNICEF

2006). Shrimpton et al. (2001) emphasized that child malnutrition sets in very early in life and accelerates during the second half of infancy. This highlights the fact that the window of opportunity for preventing childhood malnutrition is the first twelve months of life, or at most until eighteen months.

Infant mortality forms the bulk of under-five mortality, as shown in figure 5.1. In 2006 *Lancet* published the findings of an exercise to track intervention coverage for child survival in sixty countries that have the highest child mortality. The findings show that seven countries are on track to meet the Millennium Development Goal 4, thirty-nine are making some progress but need to accelerate action, and in fourteen countries the situation is a cause for serious concern (Bryce et al. 2006).

The Innocenti Declaration 2005 states in unambiguous terms: "Inappropriate feeding practices—sub-optimal or no breastfeeding and inadequate complementary feeding—remain the greatest threat to child health and survival globally" (UNICEF/WHO 2005). Available evidence makes it clear that the substantial reductions in child mortality required for achieving the Millennium Development Goals (MDGs) will not happen if undernutrition of children, including infants, is not addressed more effectively (WHO 2005).

It is not just the vulnerability of infants, it is also the criticality of timing: this is the period of significant brain development. It is thus imperative that action to reduce undernutrition in children under five should primarily target infancy.

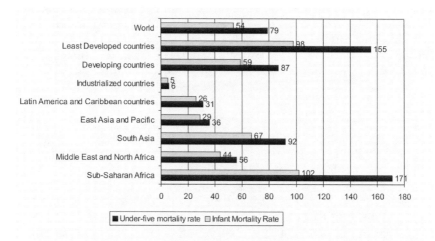

Source: Prepared by Arun Gupta based on data in United Nations Children's Fund, The State of the World's Children. New York: UNICEF, 2006.

Figure 5.1.　Under-five and Infant Mortality Rates, 2004

Based on data in United Nations Children's Fund, *The State of the World's Children*. New York: UNICEF, 2006.

The World Health Organization's (WHO) infant feeding recommendation states that breastfeeding is an unequalled way of providing the ideal food for the healthy growth and development of infants (WHO 2006). It is also an integral part of the reproductive process with important implications for the health of mothers. As a global public health recommendation, infants should be exclusively breastfed for the first six months of life to achieve optimal growth, development, and health. Thereafter, to meet their evolving nutritional requirements, infants should receive nutritionally adequate and safe complementary foods while breastfeeding continues up to two years of age or beyond.

Scientific evidence establishes compelling health and survival benefits of timely initiation of breastfeeding, as is evident from a study of 10,000 infants in rural Ghana. The initiation of breastfeeding within the first twenty-four hours of birth by all mothers has the potential to reduce neonatal mortality by 16 percent. If breastfeeding starts within the first hour, the reduction in neonatal deaths goes up to 22 percent (Edmond et al. 2006). This effect has been found to be independent of exclusivity of breastfeeding. Exclusive breastfeeding for the first six months and continued breastfeeding for the next six months has already been identified as the single most effective intervention to prevent childhood deaths. The *Lancet* series on child survival also provided a clear understanding that achieving universal coverage (90 percent) of exclusive breastfeeding could bring down child deaths by 13 percent to 15 percent. Adequate complementary feeding between six and twenty-four months could prevent an additional 6 percent of all such deaths (Jones et al. 2003). In Bangladesh, an increase in exclusive breastfeeding rates from 39 percent to 70 percent led to a 32 percent reduction in infant mortality (Arifeen et al. 2001). Such clear scientific evidence makes it imperative that the global community takes steps to enhance the practice of early initiation of breastfeeding within one hour and exclusive breastfeeding for the first six months to guarantee survival of infants.

Optimal nutrition for infants is critical not only for survival but also for early child and long-term human development. Most of the brain growth occurs during this period. Undernutrition impairs cognitive development, intelligence, strength, energy, and productivity of the individual, and thus of the nation as well (Karoly et al. 1998). Moreover, breastfeeding is not simply a matter of the physical transmission of nutrients; it also embodies caring and warmth through the closeness and contact. Lack of adequate breastfeeding in infancy has been linked to numerous ill health conditions in later life, such as cardiovascular problems and obesity (Dewey 2006). Thus, breastfeeding promotion is a sound means of tackling the double burden of malnutrition. Breastfeeding is thus a health service provided by the mothers.

THE STATE OF THE WORLD'S BREASTFEEDING

Countries are expected to implement the Global Strategy for Infant and Young Child Feeding (WHO 2003) to ensure infant feeding practices. Unfortunately, data on infant feeding practices are extremely hard to come by. Only thirty-eight of the sixty countries with the world's highest rates of child mortality had data available on the initiation of breastfeeding within an hour of birth. On the basis of the data we do have, the picture is dismal. The percentages of those practicing optimal infant feeding practices such as early initiation of breastfeeding (within one hour) are low. The percentages of those practicing early initiation vary from 9 percent to 72 percent, averaging at 36 percent (Bryce et al. 2006). The neonatal mortality rate for the thirty-eight countries for which data were available ranged from 15 to 70 for every 1,000 live births. In South Asia, the rate of initiation of breastfeeding within one hour was reported to be 15.8 percent in India and 24 percent in Bangladesh. These two countries contribute significantly to the unacceptably high global infant mortality rate. Sadly, Afghanistan, Bhutan, and Maldives do not yet have these data (IBFAN Asia Pacific 2006).

According to the UNICEF's 2006 report, only about one-third of the world's infants are exclusively breastfed for the first six months. The rates vary across regions and countries. For example, the rate is 43 percent in East Asia-Pacific, 41 percent in Eastern/Southern Africa, 20 percent in West/Central Africa, and 22 percent in CEE/CIS.

The global rate for timely complementary feeding is 51 percent. In developing countries, it varies from 67 percent in Sub-Saharan Africa and 60 percent in Middle East/North Africa to 44 percent in East Asia/Pacific and 45 percent in South Asia. This variation reflects the different levels of support women receive (UNICEF 2006).

To find out the state of national policy and program support to infant feeding, IBFAN Asia Pacific carried out an innovative project, the World Breastfeeding Trends Initiative (WBTi), to rank countries on the basis of their policies and programs on infant and young child feeding. The WBTi rates and ranks countries' performance on the implementation of the Global Strategy for Infant and Young Child Feeding using ten indicators for assessment of policies and programs, and an additional five indicators for resultant infant feeding practices. The study, so far completed in the South Asian Region, found that on almost all indicators, eight South Asian countries are struggling at the halfway mark. The exercise revealed gaps in almost every program meant to support optimal infant and young child feeding practices or fulfillment of infants' nutritional rights (IBFAN Asia Pacific 2006). The reports provide a key measure of progress on infant and young child feeding policy and programs and also signals areas that need accelerated efforts.

TURN INITIATIVES INTO OBLIGATIONS

Breastfeeding is nature's way of providing infants with optimal nutrition from the time of birth until they reach the age of six months when other foods need to be added. After six months, breastfeeding needs to be continued along with adequate complementary feeding for two years or beyond. As commercial interests took control over infant feeding practices, the decline of the natural practice of breastfeeding, together with the inherent dangers and difficulties of formula feeding led to an increase in "commerciogenic malnutrition" (Jelliffe 1972). Infants' nutrition status was further compromised by the medicalization of infant feeding, societal failure to assist mothers to breastfeed, lack of community support for breastfeeding, poor and often wrong advice of health care professionals and unsupportive hospitals, and women's work outside and inside their homes (Latham 1999).

Commercial pressures that distance the infant from achieving optimal nutrition have steadily increased with globalization. There are safeguards to protect optimal infant nutrition such as the International Code for Marketing of Breast-milk Substitutes and labor laws, but often there is pressure to ignore or undermine such safeguards. More and more women are entering the workforce, and their work is increasingly being shifted to the informal sector, where even the diluted labor laws do not apply. In the absence of education regarding breastfeeding at family and community levels, women often choose inappropriate infant-feeding practices, which prove even more dangerous in such difficult circumstances.

Ensuring optimal breastfeeding for all babies has been a major concern of international agencies and nations for many decades. In spite of its proven links to child survival and development, program managers dealing with child health or child development have failed to bring a program focus throughout the world to achieve optimal nutrition for infants, both in developing and developed countries. This is clear from the data available, considering the evidence that optimal infant nutrition is physically possible and does not require huge economic investments, technology, or infrastructure, but recognition that women require a supportive and caring environment at all levels including the family, the work place, and the health care system. The establishment of such an environment requires action by the state. The inability to achieve optimal infant nutrition needs to be examined and solutions sought.

A global movement to protect and promote breastfeeding began very early in the nineteenth century. The movement gained momentum in the 1970s and 1980s, when concerned civil society groups emerged, such as the International Baby Food Action Network (IBFAN) and then later the World

Alliance for Breastfeeding Action (WABA). Linked to several national movements and witnessing the large-scale damage to the health and survival of infants caused by inappropriate feeding practices, the breastfeeding support movement realized that mothers need accurate information, education, practical help, and support from all quarters of the community and the health care system to optimally breastfeed their infants.

This realization was reinforced by new findings in the 1980s that showed how hormones control milk flow from a mother's breast to the baby's mouth (Woolridge et al. 1985), and how this could be hindered by negative influences, and enhanced by positive confidence building of mothers. Since then, WHO, UNICEF, and other agencies involved in infant survival have given more clear guidance and further defined the specific and skilled support that a mother needs, particularly from the health care providers. The challenge is to provide this support to all women, and especially to poor nations where babies are facing high mortality rates. The global community has made several commitments, as shown in table 5.1. However these need to be translated into effective and coordinated action with the commitment of financial resources in order to provide real benefits to infants.

As early as 1952, the International Labour Organization (ILO) Maternity Protection Convention recognized the need for breastfeeding support and called for twelve weeks of paid maternity leave (ILO 1952). In 1979, WHO and UNICEF called a global meeting to address infant and young child feeding and the dangers of commercial marketing of formula on infant health. The conference led to the International Code of Marketing of Breastmilk Substitutes (WHO 1981) and subsequent World Health Assembly (WHA) resolutions. These instruments serve as milestones in the history of building support for the breastfeeding mothers.

Many subsequent actions at the global level lent support to the breastfeeding support movement. One of the most important is the Convention on the Rights of the Child (CRC), which has a clear monitoring mechanism at the UN. Also noteworthy is the World Health Assembly resolution of 2002 that adopted the Global Strategy for Infant and Young Child Feeding, a rights-based instrument. This resolution, which was later adopted by the UNICEF executive board, calls for coordinated actions to improve infant-feeding practices as a means to improve infant nutrition and survival and spells out specific obligations and responsibilities of a range of stakeholders at international and national levels.

Under the Global Strategy, obligations for international organizations include placing infant and young child feeding high on the global public health agenda and advocating for increased human, financial, and institutional resources for the universal implementation of this strategy. The strategy sets out

Table 5.1. International Commitments Supporting Infant and Young Child Feeding

Year	Organization	Document/Event	Summary
1952	ILO	Convention Number 95 Convention Number 103	Establishment of 12 weeks of leave of absence with at least 2/3 pay
1979	WHO/UNICEF	Joint Meeting on Infant and Young Child Feeding	Promotion of BF; appropriate weaning practices; strengthen education, training, information on feeding practices; promote health, social status of women; establish need for marketing codes for breastmilk substitutes
1981	World Health Assembly	International Code of Marketing of Breast-milk Substitutes	Control of marketing of breastmilk substitutes and supplements, bottles and teats
1982	FAO/WHO	Codex Alimentarius	Establishment of minimum quality and hygiene requirement for breastmilk substitutes
1986	World Health Assembly	Resolution 39.28	Limits placed on free and low-cost supplies; follow-up formulas unnecessary
1988	Expert working group in Bellagio, Italy	Bellagio Consensus	From a research review, establishes probability that full breastfeeding provides 98% protection from pregnancy during the first six months of life when the mother is amenorrheic
1989	WHO/UNICEF	Protecting, promoting and supporting breast-feeding; the special role for maternity services A Joint WHO/UNICEF statement	Establishment of "Ten steps for successful breastfeeding"

1990	32 Government and 10 International Organizations	Innocenti Declaration for the Promotion, Protection and Support of Breastfeeding	Promotion of exclusive breastfeeding until 4-6 months old and continued BF with appropriate supplements until at least 2 years of age; formation of national committees/programs to assure that the national health services meet the 10 steps by 1995; agreement to stop distribution of substitutes
1990	UN	Convention on the Rights of the Child (CRC)	Legal obligation of the member states to protect mothers and families; support of breastfeeding practices
1990	UNICEF and 79 Heads of State	World Summit for Children	Goal that all women exclusively breastfeed for six months and continue to BF with complementary foods thereafter into the second year
1991	UNICEF/WHO	Baby Friendly Hospital Initiative (BFHI)	Adoption of the ten steps; creation of a favorable environment for children in maternity wards; removal of formulas
1992	UN	Agenda 21, Rio 92	Protection of women so they may breast-feed for at least the first four months postpartum
1992	FAO/WHO/159 countries and European Community	International Conference on Nutrition Plan of Action	Declaration that breastfeeding is one of the nine strategic actions for reaching adequate nutritional development; calls for removal of obstacles to breastfeeding
1992	World Health Assembly	Convention on the Elimination of all Forms of Discrimination against Women (CEDAW)	Elimination of all forms of discrimination against working women
1992	UN	World Summit for Children follow-up	Establishment of intermediate goals for BFHI and the elimination of free samples by 1995

(continued)

Table 5.1. (*continued*)

Year	Organization	Document/Event	Summary
1994	World Health Assembly	Resolution 47.5	Unanimously adopted prohibition against free and low-cost supplies of breastmilk substitutes in all parts of the health system
1994	UN	Plan of Action, International Conference on Population and Development, Cairo, Egypt	Promotion of breastfeeding as a family planning method and strategy for infant survival
1995	UN	Plan of Action, Social World Summit, Copenhagen, Denmark	Access to education and information on breastfeeding benefits
1995	UN	Fourth Women's Conference Platform of Action	Support to working women's rights to accurate information, legal, economic, and emotional support for breastfeeding practices
1996	WHO	Resolution 49.15	Calls on member states to have health policies that are consistent with the international Code of Marketing of Breastmilk Substitutes, and avoid conflicts of interest
2000	ILO	Convention 183	Include women performing atypical work, fourteen weeks of maternity leave, breastfeeding works and security of job.
2001	WHA	WHA Resolution 54.2	Defines the period of exclusive breast-feeding for first six months, removes all ambiguities, calls for promotion
2002	WHA	WHA Resolution 55.25	Calls for urgent action by member states to develop, implement, and evaluate plans of action on infant and young child feeding

Year	Organization	Title	Description
2002	WHA	Global Strategy for Infant and Young Feeding. Adopted by WHA Resolution 55.25	Calls for comprehensive plans for action on infant and young child feeding by all member states and provides a framework for action, defines role and responsibility of governments, NGOs, professional bodies, and commercial sector
2002	UNGASS	World Fit for Children	Calls for reducing infant and young child malnutrition and mortality by promoting optimal infant and young child feeding
2003	UN	Framework for Priority Action on HIV and Infant Feeding	Provides a clear five-point framework for action to minimize infant mortality as a goal while implementing MTCT programs
2003	Asia Pacific Conference on Breastfeeding	The Delhi Declaration on Infant and Young Child Feeding	Calls for ten urgent actions to promote early and exclusive breastfeeding as well as complementary feeding with use of indigenous foods, code implementation, and others
2005	WHA	WHA Resolution 58.32	Calls for adopting global strategy; remove conflicts of interest in child health programs
2005	Global partners: WHO, UNICEF, WABA, IBFAN, LLLI, WELLSTART, ILCA, Academy of Breastfeeding Medicine, Regione Toscana	Innocenti Declaration 2005 on infant and young child feeding	Calls for allocating adequate resources for action plans to implement the Global Strategy for Infant and Young Child Feeding
2006	WHA	Resolution adopted on May 27, 2006	Calls upon member states to implement policies and programs to implement WHA resolutions and multilateral and bilateral donor arrangements and international financial institutions to direct financial resources for member states to carry out these efforts

targets for improving child survival through enhancing optimal infant and young child feeding, including in difficult circumstances like HIV and emergency situations.

The 1990 Innocenti Declaration on infant and young child feeding was renewed in 2005, and it endorses the framework of action of the Global Strategy and has given a Call for Action. The WHA resolution 59.21 of May 2006 recognized the contribution of optimal infant feeding practices to the achievement of the Millennium Development Goals and calls upon member states to renew their commitment to implement the Call for Action in the 2005 Innocenti Declaration. The resolution also calls on donors to commit resources for such implementation.

Home-based peer counseling; early and repeated contact with peer counselors; the Baby Friendly Hospital Initiative (BFHI) to ensure the ten steps to successful breastfeeding in health facilities; establishing lactation/breastfeeding support centers; providing individual counseling, group consultations, and assistance with specific breastfeeding problems, all these interventions have been found to be associated with a significant increase in exclusivity and duration of breastfeeding (Morrow et al. 1999; Kramer et al. 2001; Barros et al. 1995; Albernaz and Victora 2003; Bhandari et al. 2003; and CDC 1996). Country-level models of breastfeeding promotion programs are also available. For example, a three-country study from Ghana, Bolivia, and Madagascar showed that a sizable improvement in early and exclusive breastfeeding could be achieved at scale and within a relatively rapid time frame using the program approach. This study called for securing the commitment of governments and donors to invest in infant and young-child nutrition programs, particularly in the poorest regions of the world (Quinn et al. 2005).

Very low rates of optimal infant and young child feeding practices and high rates of infant mortality and undernutrition in almost half of the human population is a serious concern recognized in the UN's "A World Fit for Children" resolution and Millennium Declaration, UNICEF's *State of the World's Children 2006*, WHO's Annual Report 2005, and the World Bank's 2006 book, *Repositioning Nutrition as Central to Development*. It is time that global initiatives based on scientific evidence are escalated to fully benefit children, especially in developing countries to bring down infant mortality. For this, we must move toward initiating social change at the ground level that provides an environment to improve early and exclusive breastfeeding.

BREASTFEEDING AND HUMAN RIGHTS

Infants' and young children's need for food is met in different ways during two distinct time periods, birth to six months and six to twenty-four months. For the first six months, exclusive breastfeeding fulfills this need. As an essential component of adequate breastfeeding is feeding on demand, fulfillment of the infant's need for food requires that mothers stay close to their infants during the period of exclusive breastfeeding. However, many breastfeeding women, especially poor women, need to engage in economic and other activity, often outside the home, where they cannot take their infants with them. Many such women are extremely undernourished themselves. While they can still produce adequate milk to feed their infants, exclusive breastfeeding for such long periods can further jeopardize these mothers' health. Thus, fulfilling infants' right to adequate nutrition obliges the state to acknowledge women's rights to adequate nutrition, as well as their rights to other forms of support to enable them to exclusively breastfeed their infants without endangering either their own health or their economic status. Continued breastfeeding along with adequate complementary feeding fulfills the need for food from six to twenty-four months.

The rights of women and children to adequate food and nutrition can be located within the broader context of nutrition rights in modern international human rights law and principles. The human rights relevant to infant feeding are mainly found in the International Covenant on Economic, Social and Cultural Rights (ICESCR), the Convention on the Elimination of All Forms of Discrimination against Women (CEDAW), and the Convention on the Rights of the Child (CRC). The specific relevant articles found in these conventions that address the rights of infants and mothers, as well as the obligations of the state, are shown in box 5.1.

The international instruments obligate states to take appropriate measures to ensure the realization of the human right to adequate food for infants and everyone else within their jurisdiction. This information clearly spells out that a woman has the right to be fully informed, the right to adequate nutrition and health care, and the right if she is working outside the home to support so that she is able to provide optimal breastfeeding to her baby. In an analysis of breastfeeding in the human rights perspective, it was concluded that building mothers' capacity to perform is essential, as is action to enhance the capacity of the state to create an enabling environment for breastfeeding women (Engesveen 2005). Based on human rights principles, these rights should be available universally, and for those nations that, for whatever reasons, are not able to fulfill these rights, the international community must step in.

Creating an environment in which women are able to meet their infants' right to nutrition means that women may need to be supported financially through maternity entitlements. It also means that women working in the organized sector, whether in public or private sectors, should be given maternity leave of at least six months. The enabling environment should also include nutritional support for women. A breastfeeding woman needs

Box 5.1. Human Rights Related to Breastfeeding

Infants have the right to:

- Enjoyment of the highest attainable standard of health. Art. 24(1) CRC, Art. 12(1) ICESCR.
- Adequate nutritious food. Art. 24 (2)(c) CRC, Art. 11(1) ICESCR.
- Primary health care. Art. 24(2)(b) CRC.
- A standard of living adequate for the child's physical, mental, spiritual, moral and social development. Art. 27(1) CRC.

Mothers have the right to:

- Health care services and appropriate postnatal care. CEDAW 12.2, CRC 24.
- Education and support in the use of basic knowledge of child health and nutrition, the advantages of breastfeeding. CRC 24.2(e).
- Appropriate assistance in their child-rearing responsibilities. CRC 18.
- Adequate nutrition during pregnancy and lactation. CEDAW 12.2.
- Paid maternity leave or other equivalent, including job protection. ICESCR 10, CEDAW 11.2(b).
- Safeguarding of the function of reproduction in working conditions. CEDAW 11.1(f).
- Decide freely and responsibly the number and spacing of their children and to have access to the information, education, and means to enable them to exercise these rights. CEDAW 16.1(e).

States Parties are obliged to:

- Ensure that the institutions, services, and facilities responsible for the care or protection of children shall conform with the standards established by competent authorities, particularly in the areas of safety, health in the number and suitability of their staff, as well as competent supervision. Art. 3(3) CRC.
- Ensure to the maximum extent possible the survival and development of the child. Art. 6(2) CRC.
- Take appropriate measures to diminish infant and child mortality. Art. 24 (2)(a) CRC.
- Ensure the provision of necessary medical assistance and health care to all children with emphasis on the development of primary health care. Art. 24(2)(b) CRC.
- Combat disease and malnutrition, including within the framework of primary health care. Art. 24(2) (c) CRC.
- Take all effective and appropriate measures with a view to abolishing traditional practices prejudicial to the health of children. Art. 24(3) CRC.
- Take [in accordance with national conditions and within their means] appropriate measures to assist parents and others responsible for the child to implement this right and shall in case of need provide material assistance and support programs, particularly with regard to nutrition. Art.27 (3) CRC.

Source: Engesveen (2005).

almost 500 kcal of extra food a day, as she expends this amount through breastmilk. In many developing countries in Asia, women are extremely undernourished. While even the most undernourished woman can successfully lactate and breastfeed her child adequately, she does this by putting an immense strain on her own nutritional resources, which are inadequate to begin with. Thus, undernourished mothers need to be provided additional food while they are breastfeeding.

Creating an enabling environment where women can meet their infants' right to nutrition encompasses another equally important maternity entitlement—support services. In order to breastfeed successfully, women must have accurate information, practical help, and assistance. Two factors are vital to ensuring proper breastmilk supply: baby's suckling, which controls milk production, and women's confidence and state of mind, which controls breastmilk flow. Thus, women need to be physically close to their infants, and to be confident about their ability to feed their infants adequately. This often requires a behavior change that can be achieved through skillful counseling, which should ideally happen during pregnancy and at the family level. Many women give up breastfeeding because of the feeling or perception that they cannot produce enough milk. This can be corrected through one-to-one counseling and building their confidence. Where traditional beliefs interfere with successful breastfeeding, family-level counseling is helpful.

It is essential that states include women's maternity entitlements in a Minimum Essential Program (MEP) of services within the human rights framework. Such an MEP needs to be established by law and women's access to it ensured. Recourse mechanisms for those whose entitlements are not fulfilled should also be built in.

The Convention on the Rights of the Child (CRC) obliges states parties to take appropriate measures to diminish infant and child mortality. It also directs states parties to take appropriate measures "to ensure that all segments of society, in particular parents and children, are informed, have access to education and are supported in the use of basic knowledge of child health and nutrition [and] the advantages of breastfeeding" (Art. 24). And in Article 27, paragraph 3, the CRC also says that states parties "shall in case of need provide material assistance and support programs, particularly with regard to nutrition, clothing, and housing" (UN OHCHR 1989). The MEP can serve as a means to ensure optimal breastfeeding practices and fulfill the rights of children.

These measures also need to consider women's requirements for successful breastfeeding: women's right to appropriate postnatal care (Art. 24 CRC, Art. 12[2] CEDAW) and the right to paid maternity leave (Art. 10 ICESCR, Art. 11[2][b] CEDAW). Experts on human rights law have argued for an entitlement to the mother-baby dyad, considering that infants' right to good nutrition can only be realized if their mothers' rights are fully realized (Kent 2001, 2006).

Apart from these binding international human rights agreements, several nonbinding declarations and agreements, described earlier, call upon all nations to initiate serious action on nutrition security for infants. Experts in economics and health professionals agree that there is a need to focus on infants and young children if solutions to malnutrition in children are to be found (Ghosh 2004, 2006; Gupta and Rohde 1993, 2004; Gupta 2006). Economists also have argued for an allocation of specific financial resources for support of breastfeeding, as much as for immunization, if nations are to achieve optimal health and development of their infants (Smith and Ingham 2001). *Repositioning Nutrition as Central to Development: A Strategy for Large-Scale Action* (World Bank 2006) clearly recognizes that interventions to tackle child malnutrition must happen by the time the child is twenty-four months old, and promoting exclusive breastfeeding for the first six months is the fundamental first step toward achieving proper human development and poverty reduction. The report concludes that we know what needs to be done; action is required to scale up the coverage of interventions to reach all families. The *UNICEF 2006 Report Card on Nutrition* states that undernutrition contributes to 5.6 million under-five deaths per year and calls for swift action toward three proven strategies, one of which is the promotion of breastfeeding. WHO's *World Health Report 2005: Making Every Mother and Child Count*, calls for a focus on the period around birth, including early and exclusive breastfeeding. The World Health Assembly resolution 59.16 of May 2006 calls upon nations to commit to improving infant nutrition, and bilateral donors to commit resources for countries to improve infant and young child feeding practices. At the Child Survival Countdown Conference in London in 2005, it was established that achievement of MDG-4 would only be possible through large-scale action on what we know needs to be done. In a bid to track intervention coverage toward a countdown to 2015, there is an urgent need to make early breastfeeding within one hour and exclusive breastfeeding for the first six months key indicators for reaching the MDG-4 (Bryce et al. 2006). World leaders have agreed that the key is to focus on community-based approaches that include the promotion of exclusive breastfeeding and appropriate complementary feeding, if we want to accelerate achievement of MDG-4 (Veneman 2006).

It is ironic that, in spite of the volume of evidence that prevention is more effective (including cost effective) than cure, increasingly nations, UN agencies, and others have been putting their minds and resources on disease-control strategies like Integrated Management of Childhood Illnesses (IMCI) to control diarrhea, pneumonia, and malaria. While this is good, preventing these child diseases and undernutrition through community- or family-based interventions such as timely initiation of breastfeeding and exclusive breastfeeding do not receive the attention they need; nor are adequate financial resources made available to ensure their universalization. The fact that such preventive interventions can reduce the load on IMCI and thus reduce the finance gap that we look for to achieve MDGs deserves more focused attention.

MINIMUM ESSENTIAL PROGRAM (MEP) OF SERVICES AND SUPPORT

Infants' right to adequate food needs to be clarified and realized, as only one-third of the world's infants begin breastfeeding within one hour and are exclusively breastfed for the first six months. Just under half receive timely and adequate complementary feeding. Thus there is a need for a clear-cut program to provide a basic service and support package for pregnant and lactating women. This Minimum Essential Program (MEP) is proposed to be a basic minimum or essential service that includes "breastfeeding educational services." The MEP of services should ensure that all women have access to accurate information on optimal feeding practices and skilled counseling and practical support at birth and later. Other components that need to be included in the MEP are maternity benefits, which include leave for the first six months for women who are formally employed, and some financial support for lactating mothers who are poor. It would be ideal if all women could be financially compensated for devoting six months to exclusive breastfeeding. However, this may not be possible, or may not be as needed in particular situations; nations need to choose and prioritize. While some elements of the package could be provided for all women, other components, such as cash benefits and nutrition support, could be provided only to women of low socioeconomic status.

All countries should work toward making MEP a universal program under their food and nutrition security plans. Sufficient budgetary allocations need to be made by the countries, and for those that lack resources the international community should provide these. The MEP should provide the following three components as an entitlement.

1. Breastfeeding educational services
2. Practical support at birth and ongoing support
3. Leave and or cash maternity benefits

The cost calculations provided below are based on past experience, and can be adjusted according to local circumstances. These estimates serve as a guide.

1. Breastfeeding educational services /counseling services: All women should have access to accurate information and skilled counseling on optimal infant and young child feeding practices. Breastfeeding education services require training and capacity development of frontline health care providers. According to some estimates, training of care providers at the frontline and communication materials would cost about $3 per pregnant woman. After training, counseling at multiple contacts and home visits should be a part of the duty of frontline workers. The total cost for providing this service to about 75 million women in developing countries would work out to about $225 million per year.

2. Practical support at birth and ongoing support: Practical support at birth means that health providers should actively encourage and assist the woman to breastfeed within the first hour. Providing this service should be the legal duty of the care provider. It could be supported with an incentive to the care provider of perhaps two dollars for assistance at birth.

3. Leave and cash maternity benefits: Nations should devise methods to categorize women needing different levels of support. There should be paid maternity leave for six months for those who are in formal, organized employment, and support should also include nursing breaks and breastfeeding spaces at workplaces. However for women engaged in the unorganized sector, the state should create cash benefits to women, as a substitute for maternity leave. Such cash benefits can be critical in enabling poor women to provide exclusive breastfeeding to their infants for six months. A cash benefit of $20 per month per pregnant woman for six months ($120 per pregnant woman) might be a fair minimum. (This suggestion is based on experience in India's Tamil Nadu Childbirth Assistance Scheme.) The level of assistance could vary according to the cost of living in each country being supported.

Thus the total cost per woman supported if all three components of the MEP are to be delivered would work out to about $125.

When choosing the components of the MEP and deciding on which women are to be covered, many factors should be considered, including, for example,

- the critical role of breastfeeding in child survival, particularly that of exclusive breastfeeding on reducing diarrhea, pneumonia, and newborn infections;
- the major age-specific causes of infant mortality;
- the lower costs of prevention compared to curative services; and
- the rates of timely initiation of breastfeeding within one hour and exclusive breastfeeding for the first six months, or timely and adequate complementary feeding.

Achieving the MDGs, particularly MDG-4, demands that countries must review coverage of all key child-survival interventions and the status of policies and strategies for intervention delivery to ensure that all needed supports are in place to scale up coverage (Bryce et al. 2006).

All developing nations should consider this their priority and build action plans based on the framework of action in the Global Strategy for Infant and Young Child Feeding. These nations should also establish mechanisms for implementation and accountability and commit resources in their health and nutrition sectors' plans. If nations are unable to provide this package because of economic reasons or inadequate capacity to respond, the global community should come forward with the needed inputs of funds, capacity-building programs, and so forth. Bilateral and other donors should mobilize financial resources to make it happen.

RECOMMENDATIONS AND CONCLUSIONS

It is proposed that a "Global Fund for Infant Nutrition and Survival" should be set up, to support plans to scale up key breastfeeding interventions to prevent infant deaths. Beginning breastfeeding within the first hour deserves special attention, given the new evidence that it can hugely cut down neonatal mortality.

Such a fund could be established by single or multiple donors and should be dedicated specifically to national action plans for capacity building to scale up and implement various components of MEP, and for research on the key barriers to this action. The fund should focus national attention on infants and should support research on intervention-specific and coverage-level-specific impacts in different epidemiological and health systems contexts. It should promote evidence-based interventions to scale up rates of early and exclusive breastfeeding. The fund should be viewed as a preventive step aimed at reducing the need for immense funding for treatment of diarrhea, pneumonia, and neonatal infections by preventing these diseases in the first place. In addition and equally important, the fund could be used to implement the most neglected community-based care component of the IMCI strategy (Costello and Osrin 2005). The new secretary-general of the UN and WHO's director general should come forward to mobilize worldwide resources for this proposal. The World Health Assembly (WHA) should adopt a resolution to this effect, much as they supported setting up funding mechanisms for immunization of children.

The UN Committee on the Rights of the Child, which regularly monitors national actions on children's rights, should include coverage of key preventive interventions and verify when it monitors a country's performance. There is a need to clarify the importance of breastfeeding for infants and children up to twenty-four months in the General Comment on right to adequate food

UNICEF, which has already been assisting the Committee on the Rights of the Child, should be responsible for developing coordination plans specifically for this component of right to adequate food for infants. The Global Framework for Action on the Ending Child Hunger and Undernutrition Initiative (ECHUI) is based on a partnership of UNICEF and the World Food Programme (WFP). Its Outcomes 3 and 4 are relevant to building a Minimum Essential Program of the sort proposed here. Outcome 3 is "Capacities mobilized for direct community action on child hunger and undernutrition" and Outcome 4 is "Increased efficiency and accountability of global efforts to evaluation of the Initiative, programme interventions and impact for children." This promising initiative could adopt the idea of an MEP in its work plans (WFP and UNICEF 2006). The International Baby Food Action Network (IBFAN) and the World Alliance for Breastfeeding Action (WABA) should be involved as international partners for monitoring, evaluation, and capacity building for implementation of programs. In the beginning a few countries could be chosen to pilot the MEP. The lessons learned could then be applied while implementing MEP in other countries in a phased manner.

The world's more than 7 million infant deaths each year is morally unacceptable in the face of evidence that this number can be drastically and rapidly reduced. Most of the deaths are preventable. The time has come to turn global concern for infant health and deaths into a clear legal obligation, an obligation of not just individual nations but of the entire global community. The MEP of services could be the road map to turn the promises made into a reality, to ensure the realization of infants' rights to adequate food.

An international agreement is required to move the global community toward its commitments to recognize infants' right to adequate food and nutrition. Much more than rhetoric is needed to save infants and prevent unacceptable morbidity and mortality. Bringing down neonatal and infant mortality rapidly is imperative and can be achieved by infant nutrition interventions. The successful work of the GAVI Alliance (formerly known as the Global Alliance for Vaccines and Immunization) and the International Financing Facility for Immunization successfully put immunization on the priority map globally and nationally. Something similar needs to be done to move infant nutrition to a high priority on that map. A Global Fund for Infant Nutrition and Survival could fulfill this need. It has been shown that in the sixty countries with the highest infant mortality, the coverage of nutrition interventions is much below expected. There is a huge opportunity to promote timely initiation of breastfeeding and exclusive breastfeeding, and thus setting infants on the way to growing to their best potential and developing into healthy and productive adults. The potential economic benefits are tremendous. As the World Bank has indicated in its report, *Repositioning Nutrition as Central to Development*, there is loss of 2–3 percent GDP due to malnutrition.

The Global Fund could promote wider acceptance of the need for preventive and promotive interventions including promotion of early initiation of breastfeeding and exclusive breastfeeding for the first six months, which have the potential to make a major contribution toward achieving the Millennium Development Goal for reducing child mortality.

To achieve nutrition security for infants is no child's play; it requires resources that are at least equal to what we spend on immunization, as well as coordinated efforts and attention from the highest levels. Child survival is usually taken to mean children under five as a group. Very little attention is given to the fact that the majority of under-five children who die are under twelve months of age, or to the fact that most of their deaths are related to their nutrition. In the past, the available funds have been used mainly for promoting curative interventions. Where preventive interventions have been considered at all, often they have been linked to a marketable product such as immunizations. There is a need for a clear commitment to and funding for infant nutrition and survival, which means support for key breastfeeding interventions. Without this support it will not be possible to reach the Millennium Development Project's targets for reducing child mortality. With this support, ensuring that infants would be properly breastfed, we would help to ensure that all children could achieve their fullest mental, intellectual, emotional, and physical potential. Funds alone will not serve the purpose. There is a clear need to have MEP as a part of the right to food for infants. Decisive action should be taken at both the national and global level to establish the MEP program, together with adequate accountability mechanisms to assure that women's and infants' right to the MEP are realized.

ACKNOWLEDGMENTS

I wish to thank George Kent, Jon Rohde, Michael Latham, Annelies Allain, Radha Holla, Deeksha Sharma, and Rita Gupta for their valuable comments and inputs. I deeply appreciate the help and support of Amit Dahiya and Vasumati Arora.

REFERENCES

Albernaz, E., and C. G. Victora. 2003. "Impact of Face-to-face Counseling on Duration of Exclusive Breastfeeding: A Review." *Rev Panam Salud Publica* 14 (1): 17–24.

Arifeen, S. E., R. E. Black, L. E. Caulfield, G. Antelman, and A. H. Baqui. 2001. "Determinants of Infant Growth in the Slums of Dhaka: Size and Maturity at Birth, Breastfeeding and Morbidity." *Eur J Clin Nutr* 55: 167–78.

Barros, F. C., T. C. Semer, S. Tonioli Filho, E. Tomasi, and C. G. Victora. 1995. "The Impact of Lactation Centers on Breastfeeding Patterns, Morbidity and Growth: A Birth Cohort Study." *Acta Pediatrics* 84: 1221–26.

Bhandari, N., R. Bahl, S. Mazumdar, J. Martines, R. E. Black, and M. K. Bhan. 2003. Effect of Community-based Promotion of Exclusive Breastfeeding on Diarrhoeal Illness and Growth: A Cluster Randomised Controlled Trial." *Lancet* 361: 1418–23.

Bryce Jennifer, Nancy Terreri, Cesar G. Victora, Elizabeth Mason, Bernadette Daelmans, Zulfiqar Bhutta, Flavia Bustreo, Francisco Songane, Peter Salama, and Tessa Wardlaw. 2006. "Countdown to 2015: Tracking Intervention Coverage for Child Survival." *Lancet* 368: 1067–76. www.accessmylibrary.com/coms2/summary_0286-19599471_ITM.

CDC (Centers for Disease Control and Prevention). 1996. *Encuesta Nacional de Epidemiologiay Salud Familiar, Honduras.* Atlanta, GA: Centers for Disease Control and Prevention.

Costello, A., and D. Osrin. 2005. "The Case for a New Global Fund for Maternal, Neonatal and Child Survival." *Lancet* 366: 603–5.

Dewey, K. G. 2006. "Tackling the Double Burden of Malnutrition." UN Steering Committee on Nutrition, *SCN News* 32: 16–20.

Edmond, K. M., C. Zandoh, M. A. Quigley, S. Amenga-Etego, S. Owusu-Agyei, and B. R. Kirkwood. 2006. "Delayed Breastfeeding Initiation Increases Risk of Neonatal Mortality." *Pediatrics* 117: 380–86. http://pediatrics.aappublications.org/cgi/reprint/117/3/e380.

Engesveen, K. 2005. "Strategies for Realizing Human Rights to Food, Health and Care for Infants and Young Children in Support of the Millennium Development Goals: Role and Capacity Analysis of Responsible Actors in Relation to Breastfeeding in the Maldives." *SCN News* 30: 56–66.

Ghosh, S. 2004. "Child Malnutrition." Commentary. *Economic and Political Weekly*, 2 October.

———. 2006. "Food Dole or Health, Nutrition and Development Programme." *Economic and Political Weekly*, 26 August.

Gupta, A. 2006. "Infant and Young Child Feeding: An 'Optimal Approach.'" *Economic and Political Weekly*, 26 August.

Gupta, A., and J. E. Rohde. 2004. "Infant and Young Child Undernutrition: Where Lies the Solution?" *Economic and Political Weekly*, 4 December.

———. 1993. "Economic Value of Breastfeeding in India." *Economic and Political Weekly*, 26 June.

Horton, R. 2006. The Coming Decade for Global Action on Child Health. *Lancet* 367: 3–5.

IBFAN (International Baby Food Action Network). Asia Pacific. 2006. *World Breastfeeding Trends Initiative* (WBTi). www.worldbreastfeedingtrends.org.

ILO (International Labour Organization). 1952. IC 103 Maternity Protection Convention (Revised). Geneva: ILOLEX (The International Labour Organization's Database on International Labour Standards) http://ilolex.ilo.ch/.

Jelliffe, D. B. 1972. Commerciogenic Malnutrition? *Nutr Rev* 30 (9): 199–205.

Jones, G., R. W. Steketee, R. E. Black, Z. A. Bhutta, and S. S. Morris. 2003. "How Many Child Deaths Can We Prevent This Year?" *Lancet* 362: 65–71.

Karoly, L. A., C. P. Rydell, J. Hoube, S. S. Everingham, R. Kilburn, and P. W. Greenwood. 1998. *Investing in Our Children: What We Know and Don't Know about the Costs and Benefits of Early Childhood Interventions*. Santa Monica CA: RAND.

Kent, G.1998. "Women's Right to Breastfeed vs. Infants' Rights to Be Breastfed." *SCN News* 17: 18–19.

——. 2001. "Breastfeeding: A Human Rights Issue?" *Development* 44 (2): 93–98.

——. 2004. "Response to 'Breastfeeding and Human Rights,'" *Journal of Human Lactation* 20 (2): 146–47.

——. 2006. "Child Feeding and Human Rights," *International Breastfeeding Journal* 1. www.internationalbreastfeedingjournal.com/content/1/1/27.

Kramer, M. S., B. Chalmers, E. D. Hodnett, Z. Sevkovskaya, I. Dzikovich, S. Shapiro, J. P. Collet, I. Vanilovich, I. Mezen, T. Ducruet, G. Shishko, V. Zubovich, D. Mknuik, E. Gluchanina, V. Dombrovskiy, A. Ustinovitch, T. Kot, N. Bogdanovich, L. Ovchinikova, and E. Helsing; PROBIT Study Group (Promotion of Breastfeeding Intervention Trial). 2001. "Promotion of Breastfeeding Intervention Trial (PROBIT): A Randomized Trial in the Republic of Belarus." *JAMA* 285 (4): 413–20.

Latham, M. C. 1999. "A Mother's Right to Breastfeed: Removing the Obstacles." *Food and Nutrition Bulletin* 20 (3).

Lauer, J. A., A. P. Betran, A. J. Barros, and M. de Onis. 2006. "Deaths and Years of Life Lost Due to Suboptimal Breastfeeding among Children in the Developing World: A Global Ecological Risk Assessment." *Public Health Nutrition* 9 (6): 673–85.

Morrow, A. L., M. L. Guerrero, J. Shults, J. J. Calva, et al. 1999. "Efficacy of Home-based Peer Counselling to Promote Exclusive Breastfeeding: A Randomised Controlled Trial." *Lancet* 353: 1226–31.

Moss, W., G. L. Darmstadt, D. R. Marsh, R. E. Black, and M. J. Santosham. 2002. "Research Priorities for the Reduction of Perinatal and Neonatal Morbidity and Mortality in Developing Country Communities." *Perinatol* 22 (6): 484–95.

Quinn, V. J., A. B. Guyon, J. W. Schubert, M. Stone-Jiménez, M. D. Hainsworth, and L. H. Martin. 2005. "Improving Breastfeeding Practices on a Broad Scale at the Community Level: Success Stories from Africa and Latin America." *J Hum Lact* 21 (3): 345–54.

Shrimpton, R., C. G. Victora, M. de Onis, R. C. Lima, M. Blössner, and G. Clugston. 2001. "Worldwide Timing of Growth Faltering: Implications for Nutritional Interventions." *Pediatrics* 107 (5): 75.

Smith, J. P., and L. H. Ingham. 2001. "Breastfeeding and the Measurement of Economic Progress." *Journal of Australian Political Economy* 47: 51–72.

UNICEF (United Nations Children's Fund). 2004. *A Child Survival Report Card. Number 1*. New York: UNICEF.

——. 2006. *Progress for Children: A Report Card on Nutrition. Number 4*. New York: UNICEF.

——. 2006. *State of World's Children 2006*. New York: UNICEF.

UNICEF and WHO (United Nations Children's Fund and World Health Organization). 2005. *Innocenti Declaration on Infant and Young Child Feeding*. 22 November. Florence, Italy. http://innocenti15.net/declaration.pdf.pdf.

UN OHCHR (United Nations Office of the High Commissioner on Human Rights). 1989. *Convention on the Rights of the Child.* Art. 24 (2)(e). www.unhchr.ch/html/menu3/b/k2crc.htm.

UN SCN (United Nations System Standing Committee on Nutrition). 2004. *Working Group on Breastfeeding and Complementary Feeding: Contribution to Millennium Development Goals (MDGs).* 31st Session. New York. March.

Veneman, A. 2006. "Achieving Millennium Development Goal 4." *Lancet* 368: 1044–47.

WFP and UNICEF. (World Food Programme and United Nations Children's Fund). 2006. *Ending Child Hunger and Undernutrition Initiative.* Rome Italy, and New York: World Food Programme, and United Nations Children's Fund.

WHO (World Health Organization). 2003. *Global Strategy for Infant and Young Child Feeding.* Geneva: World Health Organization. www.who.int/child-adolescent-health/New_Publications/NUTRITION/gs_iycf.pdf.

———. 1981. *International Code of Marketing of Breast-milk Substitutes,* Geneva: World Health Organization.

———. 2003. *HIV and Infant Feeding—Framework for Priority Action.* Geneva: World Health Organization.

———. 2005. *Making Every Mother and Child Count.* World Health Report. Geneva: World Health Organization.

———. 2006. "World Health Organization's Infant Feeding Recommendation." www.who.int/nutrition/topics/infantfeeding_recommendation/en/index.html.

Woolridge, M. W., V. Greasley, and S. Silpisolnosol. 1985. "The Initiation of Lactation: Effect of Early Delayed Contact for Suckling on Milk Intake in the First Week Postpartum." *Early Hum Dev* 12: 269–78.

World Bank. 2006. *Repositioning Nutrition as Central to Development: A Strategy for Large-Scale Action.* Washington, DC: World Bank. http://web.worldbank.org/WBSITE/EXTERNAL/TOPICS/EXTHEALTHNUTRITIONANDPOPULATION/EXTNUTRITION/0,,contentMDK:20613959~menuPK:282591~pagePK:210058~piPK:210062~theSitePK:282575,00.html.

6

Global Action against Worm Infections, Measles, and Malaria

Michael C. Latham

The United Nations Millennium Summit held in New York in 2000 was attended by 147 heads of state or government. The assembly called for the alleviation of extreme poverty, disease, and environmental degradation using the existing wealth, the modern technology, and the global awareness that we have, as we enter the twenty-first century (Sachs 2005). United Nations secretary-general Kofi Annan expressed a strong conviction that the UN represents not only the governments of 191 member states, but more importantly the world's people, who have rights and responsibilities that have a global reach.

The assembly concluded by adopting the Millennium Declaration, which included an agreement to "halve the proportion of people who suffer from hunger" by the year 2015 (Sanchez et al. 2005). The Food and Agriculture Organization of the United Nations (FAO) in 2006 published its guidelines to support the progressive realization of the right to adequate food in the context of national food security (FAO 2005, 2006). Chapters in this book mainly argue that there are global obligations regarding the human right to adequate food. When the world is plagued by social injustice and increasing inequity, there surely are obligations not only with regard to food but also with regard to health care, educational opportunities, safe water, decent sanitation, and housing (Latham and Beaudry 2001).

The focus of the Millennium Development Goals (MDGs) on halving hunger is laudable. However, the actions proposed nationally and internationally seem largely focused on agricultural and other means to make more food available, and to ensure food security. This may reduce the percentage of people who go to bed hungry, when hunger is used as meaning an uneasy sensation caused by want of food. But the MDG reports also use the term "hunger" as a proxy for malnutrition. Their maps of "hunger hot spots" are based entirely on prevalence rates of underweight children. This form of malnutrition is not always due to a problem of food availability and lack of food security. Often it is due to childhood health problems, to lack of good child care, and to poor appetite (Latham 1997). Civil society, national governments, and all who are working to "halve hunger" need to appreciate that while lack of food contributes importantly to malnutrition, other causes, including infections and other diseases, are vitally important and need to be addressed. Ensuring a right to food by itself will not solve the nutrition problem. This chapter illustrates how addressing certain infections could reduce malnutrition and contribute importantly to halving hunger.

If, using a human rights approach, we are markedly to reduce malnutrition, then, as well as concentrating on food security, we must also reduce the burden of common infections that contribute importantly to hunger and malnutrition. Intestinal worms, measles, and malaria are three such infections for which control measures exist. However the countries where these infections are most prevalent have little capacity to deal with them. As a result, on the basis of moral considerations, and also on the basis of human rights law relating to food and health, the global community should be viewed as having an obligation to address these problems.

Intestinal helminths (worms) infect some 2 billion people, mainly in southern countries, and they contribute to malnutrition and anemia (Stephenson, Latham, and Otteson 2000). Measles is seldom fatal in northern countries, but it is an important cause of mortality in malnourished populations. Malaria causes over 1 million deaths a year in Africa alone. Established public health measures are available to reduce significantly the impact of these three infections on health and nutrition. There should be a clearly recognized obligation of the world community to deworm infected populations, to immunize children against measles, and to make available preventive measures (such as insecticide-impregnated bed nets) and effective medication for malaria.

There are established human rights to food and to health, with the correlative obligations being carried primarily, but not exclusively, by national governments. Under the broad principles in human rights law, and the limited capacity of many countries to take control measures, the global community ought to recognize certain specific entitlements that people have to services to help control these infections. The obligations fall on the global community as a whole, and how these obligations will be met needs to be addressed. A marked reduction in the prevalence of helminthic infections, much lower morbidity from malaria, and the elimination of measles would together have an enormous impact on hunger and malnutrition rates worldwide.

This book concentrates on the human right to adequate food. Article 12 of the International Covenant on Economic, Social and Cultural Rights (ICESCR) confirms the human right to enjoy "the highest attainable standard of physical and mental health." The second part of the article concludes that steps should be taken by the states parties to the covenant to achieve the full realization of the right to health. The direct responsibility for the implementation of human rights rests with individuals and families themselves, and then with the state. This requires, however, that the national government is able to fulfill this function. Many states have limited capacity fully to meet these obligations (Eide 1999), including the right to health. The UN rapporteur on the right to the highest attainable standard of health has written that "under international human rights law, developed states have some responsibilities toward the right to health in poor countries," and he further states, "as the right to the highest attainable standard of health migrates from the margins to the human rights mainstream, it presents human rights and health professionals with a range of new opportunities and challenges" (Hunt 2006).

In 2005 the People's Health Movement, an international alliance of health workers, launched a new campaign on the right to health. This right is reaffirmed in their declaration from the second People's Health Assembly, held in Cuenca, Ecuador, in 2005 (People's Health Movement 2006). Several UN agencies, including the World Health Organization (WHO) and United Nations Children's Fund (UNICEF), have mandates to promote the enjoyment of the human right to health, just as FAO has a mandate to promote the right to food. The bold words emanating from the Millennium Declaration clearly suggest a global agreement that the international community has obligations to assist poorer countries and people to be relieved of poverty, hunger, and disease.

WHY THESE THREE DISEASES?

Worms, measles, and malaria are addressed here because these three diseases contribute very importantly to hunger and malnutrition, and we have inexpensive means available to reduce their impact.

It is clear from publications of the WHO that the two most important immediate causes of death of children in poor countries are diarrhea and respiratory infections. Half of these deaths would not have occurred if the children had not been malnourished (Pelletier 1994). These diseases themselves are acute and therefore of short duration, but they kill because children have chronic undernutrition. Diarrhea and respiratory infections have multiple etiologies. These include many different viruses, bacteria, parasites, and even toxins and allergens. Therefore we do not have a vaccine or other weapon that could greatly reduce the prevalence of these infections. There is a new vaccine for Rotavirus, a common cause of diarrhea, but the cost of fifty dollars per dose is prohibitive.

Diarrhea is a major cause of mortality, particularly in children. It results in a great deal of nonfatal morbidity. It is estimated that diarrhea causes a billion episodes of illness annually, and in some countries it is the cause of more than 30 percent of hospital admissions. Because of the multiple etiologies of diarrhea, a wide variety of approaches are required to reduce incidence. Deworming and immunization against measles are two such measures. While oral rehydration therapy (ORT) has little impact on diarrhea incidence (Laxminarayan et al. 2006), it has been shown to be highly effective in reducing diarrheal deaths.

Actions to increase access to safe water and the provision of decent latrines and sanitation are cost effective measures to reduce the incidence of diarrheal disease. There is clear evidence that mortality from diarrhea is much lower in breastfed than in formula-fed infants. So protection, support, and promotion of breastfeeding is another measure that can reduce mortality from diarrhea.

Some of the respiratory infections, including pneumonia, that are causes of morbidity and a great deal of mortality, especially in children, could be prevented using existing vaccines. Measles vaccine is one of these. Multivalent pneumococcal conjugate vaccines could reduce the incidence of pneumococcal disease, but at fifty dollars per dose this is considered unaffordable to most people in nonindustrialized countries (Laxminarayan et al. 2006). Most countries do have in place programs for pertussis (whooping cough) and diphtheria immunization, and some countries use BCG to reduce tuberculosis. But actions to reduce morbidity and mortality from many common respiratory diseases require a wide variety of approaches, including environmental actions, and especially early good diagnosis and treatment in health facilities. Anthelminthics used to deworm children also reduce respiratory disease because, on their way to the intestines, helminths move through the lungs.

We do not have affordable straightforward actions that could greatly reduce morbidity and mortality from diarrhea and respiratory infections in the short term other than those mentioned here. We do have weapons that at reasonable cost could greatly reduce the impact of worms, measles, and malaria as important contributors to widespread malnutrition. In the case of measles there is a vaccine that could, at a relatively low cost, totally eliminate measles from a country or even the world. For intestinal worms, there are cheap safe medicines called anthelminthics which if widely used would reduce infections to levels where these infections were not contributing much to the prevalence of malnutrition or anemia. Transmission rates would also be reduced.

Malaria is more difficult to control, but there is clear evidence that wide use of insecticide-impregnated bed nets and early good treatment would reduce malaria cases and significantly cut malaria deaths, particularly in children. This would also reduce the contribution of malaria to malnutrition and anemia. Research has shown that treatment of helminthic worm infections lowers malaria morbidity (Druilhe, Tall, and Sokhna 2005).

THE THREE DISEASES

A. Worm Infections

Helminths are a class of organisms also called worms, some of which are parasitic, causing disease in humans. We live in a wormy world. At this moment probably 2 billion people carry a burden of worms, unwanted guests in their intestinal tracts (Stephenson, Latham, and Otteson 2000). In the past, these parasites have infected people worldwide, but now high prevalence rates exist mainly in the nonindustrialized countries. In the 1920s, recognizing the debilitating impact of hookworm infections in the southern United States, the Rockefeller Foundation assisted several states in a major and largely successful hookworm control project.

The three helminths of major concern here are roundworms, infecting about 1.4 billion; hookworms, infecting 1.3 billion; and Trichuris, infecting 1.05 billion people (Stephenson, Latham, and Otteson 2000). With successful control in northern countries these infections have become mainly poor people's diseases. The majority of persons infected do not die directly from these infections, but the quality of their lives is compromised. These infections contribute importantly to high rates of malnutrition and poor growth of children (Stephenson and Holland 1987) and hookworm infections are an important cause of anemia. They lead to anorexia or poor appetite (Latham et al. 1990); they may limit work productivity and school performance; they may adversely impact pregnancy; and they contribute to mortality. Although diseases like these have low case fatality rates, they kill a lot of people because so many people have the disease.

The World Bank, using disability-adjusted life years (DALYs) lost per annum, estimated 22.1 million life years lost for hookworm; 10.5 million for roundworms, and 6.4 million for Trichuris. The DALYs lost for these three worm infections combined is a whopping 39.0 million life years, while that for malaria is 35.7 life years lost, for vitamin A deficiency 11.8 million, and for diabetes 8.0 million life years lost (Stephenson, Latham, and Otteson 2000).

In the long term, control of intestinal worms should involve measures that will simultaneously reduce the prevalence of other infections that are spread by fecal contamination, including some forms of diarrhea. Reduction in poverty and improved levels of living combined with safe water supplies, good sanitation, and improved environmental and personal hygiene can all play a role. In nonindustrialized countries these measures are slow in coming for most families.

If the quality of life of the current generation of children is to be improved, and if we hope to reduce hunger markedly by 2015, then other measures are needed to reduce the impact of worm infections. There are safe, highly effective and relatively cheap drugs that make regular treatment of worm infections feasible. Farmers in northern countries deworm their piglets regularly, knowing that this improves their growth, yet we leave millions of children suffering retarded growth because they harbor worms.

The World Health Organization and many countries have approved provision of the anthelminthic drugs (notably albendazole and mebendazole) to population groups without individual diagnosis (Stephenson, Latham, and Otteson 2000) when prevalence rates are high. Many countries could piggyback drug dosage onto existing delivery systems, such as during vitamin A supplementation or when immunizations are given.

The argument here is that people worldwide have the moral right, and ought to have the clear legal right, to be rid of these burdens of worms inhabiting their guts, debilitating them in so many ways and sometimes leading to death. Civil society and nation-states have obligations to take steps to see that children, pregnant women, and others are treated regularly. Many nations in which these infections are prevalent have limited capacity to do this alone. Moral considerations and human rights law relating to food and health surely places an obligation on the global community to assist countries to deworm their populations.

The cost can be quite low. As an example, Cambodia launched a deworming program in 2002 to treat 2.8 million children at a cost of six U.S. cents per child that year. This successful program was followed by retreatment in 2003 at a cost of three cents per child (Sinuon et al. 2005). Thus, with a small expenditure a major impact could be made in a very few years. This would help reach the MDG objectives for halving hunger by 2015.

B. Measles

Measles, caused by a virus, has been a major epidemic disease for centuries. Recognized by its typical rash and fever, it often causes serious complications, especially diarrhea, pneumonia, middle ear disease, encephalitis, and death. It is among the top four childhood killers worldwide (Levine 2004). Measles contributes importantly to malnutrition, and in children who are vitamin A deficient it exacerbates xerophthalmia, often leading to blindness and death. Rarely fatal in northern, better-nourished populations (the United Kingdom recently reported its first measles death in a decade), it is a major killing disease in developing countries. In malnourished preschool-age children, fatality rates in Africa and South Asia are often 10–20 percent.

The widespread introduction of a highly effective live measles vaccine in 1963 led rapidly to a major decline in measles prevalence in the industrialized countries. But because of its cost, and the cold chain difficulties (this live vaccine needs refrigeration), the wide use of the vaccine in developing countries did not take place until the 1980s when WHO launched its Expanded Program on Immunization (WHO 2002). With the successful conquering of smallpox in 1978, excitement mushroomed in the public health community, and advocates pressed for total global measles eradication. They stated that this was desirable on humanitarian and fiscal grounds, and it is feasible on technological and epidemiological grounds (Hopkins et al. 1982). In the decade from 1985–1995 international assistance made it possible for some developing countries to immunize a high percentage of children one to six years of age. But for a host of reasons (including a diversion of focus and funds to other diseases, notably HIV/AIDS), measles immunization rates have seriously lagged. In many poor countries a large percentage of children have not been immunized against measles, and the disease is again contributing importantly to high rates of malnutrition, vitamin A deficiency–related blindness, and mortality. It is estimated that there are about 50 million cases of measles worldwide each year with about 1 million deaths (Levine 2004).

As long as measles has not been eradicated worldwide, it remains necessary for people in industrialized countries (where measles transmission has been largely eliminated) to continue measles vaccination and surveillance. This is very costly, and these costs would end if measles were eradicated worldwide. It cost the United States $124 million a year to keep itself free of smallpox for the twenty-five years prior to when smallpox was eradicated in 1978. Thus the $32 million that the United States invested in the global Smallpox Eradication Program was recouped in about three months once smallpox vaccination and control could be discontinued (Hopkins et al. 1982). With worldwide measles eradication, U.S. savings could be close to $800 million a year.

The argument here for the international community to be more involved in measles immunization is not fiscal, but rather the argument is made in terms of health rights. Children in every country should have a recognized right to be protected against measles. The main obligation would fall on nation-states to prevent measles, but the global community also should have recognized obligations in this regard. In the long run, it is in their own self-interest. For nations struggling, often unsuccessfully, to reach the MDG goal of halving hunger by 2015, eradicating measles transmission would contribute importantly to that goal.

Eliminating measles is feasible even in poor African countries. Six southern African countries that recorded 60,000 measles cases in 1996 reduced
this to 117 cases in 2000. This was due to intensive immunization and surveillance (Biellek et al. 2002).

C. Malaria

There are four human malaria parasites, or plasmodia, but it is Plasmod-
ium falciparum that causes the most serious, debilitating, and lethal
malaria. The disease has had a huge impact on social and economic development, and even on the geographic location of populations.

Malaria contributes importantly to malnutrition. The parasites destroy red
blood cells, and in malaria-endemic areas, the disease is a major contributor
to anemia incidence and severity. Restoration of hemoglobin levels in anemia requires a diet with adequate amounts of iron, folate, vitamin B12, protein, and other nutrients. Malaria worsens nutritional status because the
fever accompanying the disease leads to anorexia, or lack of appetite. Frequent attacks of malaria, particularly in children, may lead to many days
when very little food is consumed, thus leading to, or aggravating protein-
energy malnutrition. In an indirect way, malaria contributes to global
hunger by sickening many people, who then lose days of work in agriculture,
or of earning money to purchase food, and by requiring parents to spend
time in the care of sick children, thus reducing their time in productive employment. Malaria infections during pregnancy may result in infiltration of
the placenta and reduction in infant birth weights. Chronic malaria results
in splenomegaly, and in some cases very enlarged spleens occupying considerable space in the abdominal cavity, which in turn aggravates malnutrition.

Malaria transmission used to occur in northern countries including the
United States and the United Kingdom, but has, over the years, been largely
confined to some 100 countries in the tropics and subtropics (Benenson
1995). Some 1.6 billion people inhabit areas at risk of malaria. The global
malaria incidence is estimated to be 1200 million cases, resulting in 1.5
million deaths annually. The majority of this mortality occurs in Africa,
where malaria is by far the leading immediate cause of death for preschool-
age children.

In addition to Europe and North America, malaria transmission has
been successfully eliminated from much of the Caribbean, Australia and
New Zealand, and some countries in Latin America and Asia (Benenson
1995). Some countries in the subtropics, including South Africa, have
moved close to eliminating malaria transmission. Most have used several
different control measures, including mosquito control of breeding sites,
residual insecticide spraying in houses, and early successful treatment of
malarial infections.

Recently, in part because of the WHO Roll Back Malaria Campaign, the international community and some affected countries are talking a great deal about malaria control, but this is not matched by action (Rosenberg 2006). For many tropical African countries, total control is not in sight, and malaria continues to contribute very importantly to child deaths, malnutrition and reduced growth in children, anemia and poor pregnancy outcomes, and lower levels of economic development. It seems imperative that the global community act now to assist countries to reduce the prevalence of malaria.

The Roll Back Malaria Campaign; the Global Fund on AIDS, Tuberculosis, and Malaria; and large funding from the Gates Foundation, the U.S. Agency for International Development (USAID), and others offer a potential to realize recommendations here for much wider use of insecticide impregnated bed nets and good malaria treatment. Yet malaria incidence has risen in Africa in recent years.

Major efforts should be undertaken to ensure that all people at risk sleep under insecticide-treated bed nets and receive early good treatment for malaria. Good treatment does not include, as is now common, just giving chloroquine because it is cheap and has been the drug of choice since the 1970s. In many places, because the parasite is resistant to chloroquine, what is now needed is artemisin-based combination therapy (*Lancet* 2005b). It is a highly effective treatment, but many are saying that it is too expensive, at about forty cents per child treated. It is true this may be too costly for some parents, but for countries and the global community forty cents should not be too much to save an African child's life (Rosenberg 2006).

It has been clearly established that sleeping under an insecticide-impregnated bed net is very effective in reducing malaria transmission (Curtis 2005). These nets are relatively cheap, costing about three dollars per net. But many families cannot afford them. Some governments point out that it would use a large proportion of the national health budget to provide free nets to all at-risk people. Donors and the international agencies have not stepped forward adequately to fill the breech.

With malaria causing a great deal of disease, much disability, many lost work or school days, and millions of deaths, surely people should have the right to protection from, and treatment for, malaria. Families and communities even in the poorest areas of Africa have obligations to reduce malaria morbidity, and countries have important obligations to assist their citizens to obtain bed nets and receive good treatment for malaria. But many nations, particularly in sub-Saharan Africa, have limited capacity and inadequate funding to take the anti-malarial measures suggested here. The global community surely has an obligation to assist families to provide these simple, relatively effective and inexpensive measures to reduce malaria, and thus to reduce the impact of malaria in terms of illness, malnutrition, debility, and death.

Togo in West Africa in 2004 gave away bed nets free to every child who was brought for measles immunization. Rapidly, Togo had in place a potentially effective malaria control program that few other African countries have achieved (Rosenberg 2006). An editorial (*Lancet* 2005a) reported that a goal recommended by the Millennium Project was to distribute bed nets to all children in malaria endemic areas by 2007. Goals are laudable, but to achieve results, action must follow.

INTERNATIONAL PRECEDENTS

There are clear precedents in which the global community has stepped forward to assist poorer countries to control or eradicate a disease. In the successful campaign that led to the eradication of smallpox, the early stages relied mainly on national campaigns. The prime responsibility in cost and human resources rested with national governments. Largely as a result of Soviet Union insistence and their initial financial support, the World Health Assembly in 1959 voted overwhelmingly for a smallpox eradication campaign (Levine 2004). WHO provided technical assistance to countries, industrialized countries provided some funds, and a worldwide campaign to vaccinate millions of persons was launched. Although not couched in terms of rights of humans to be protected against smallpox, the campaign was an important recognition by the global community of its responsibility to eliminate a devastating disease.

The faltering global initiative on immunization against poliomyelitis, although led by WHO, and with major funding from Rotary International, has largely been based on local efforts. The successful international Onchocerciasis (river blindness) Control Program, launched in 1974, was the first large-scale health program led by the World Bank (Levine 2004).

The campaign against guinea worm disease represents an important example of national and international collaboration. Guinea worm is contracted when a person drinks water from a pond or well contaminated with small fleas infected with guinea worm larvae. It is an ancient disease that used to be prevalent worldwide, but it disappeared from many countries with the introduction of safe water. It became a poor person's disease, debilitating underprivileged, mainly rural communities especially in Africa and Asia. Unlike many other infections that can be controlled using a vaccine, or by effective curative medication, this is not possible with guinea worm. The intervention is dependent on behavior change and very active participation of civil society, not simply as recipients of an immunization. National governments, with international support, need to reach underprivileged, sometimes isolated people, and influence them on how better to handle water to prevent disease (Hopkins 1999).

For more than five decades international responsibilities to control epidemic or other communicable diseases have been recognized. Now we see this being extended to SARS (Severe Acute Respiratory Syndrome), bird flu, and to some extent HIV/AIDS. The global community has clearly accepted a duty to assist countries to deal with acute severe infections, even though some do not have a high incidence, do not cause many deaths, and have little impact on hunger and malnutrition. Similarly the global community feels responsibility and often acts quickly and generously in responding to acute disasters such as earthquakes, famines, and tsunamis.

International solidarity has rarely been as impressive as the response to the 2004 tsunami in Asia. Major catastrophes such as that, and the 2005 Pakistani earthquake often quickly stir international action on a grand scale. Similarly, in areas of conflict when large numbers of families are displaced and become refugees, for example in Rwanda, Burundi, Darfur in the Sudan, and others, international funds are mobilized and international professionals and volunteers rush to provide help. But by far the majority of deaths caused by malnutrition each year, and every year, occur not following natural catastrophes or in acute emergencies or as a result of conflict. Rather they happen in relatively stable countries. More than 5 million children die each year from causes linked directly or indirectly to malnutrition in nonindustrialized countries, a very large proportion of these in Asia rather than Africa (Gross and Webb 2006). These deaths, and this malnutrition remain relatively "hidden." Since they do not generate the attention and publicity of large events, they are not in the public eye and therefore do not produce as much moral indignation as do the acute catastrophes. This seems illogical and wrong and needs to be remedied. Surely the global community needs to move on from lofty words setting global targets and embark on a set of achievable actions designed to reduce malnutrition in nonemergency situations. As the World Bank has stated, "reducing malnutrition is central to reducing poverty. As long as malnutrition persists, development goals for the coming decade will not be reached" (World Bank 2003). The global community has an obligation to act.

Here the argument is that when individual states are unable to meet their obligations to provide interventions to reduce the impact of worm infections, measles, and malaria, then obligations fall on the global community. Let us not have to say in 2015 that our generation, our governments in the north, and our international agencies would not provide the relatively modest funds and expertise that are needed to reduce these infections, save lives, and reduce malnutrition.

RECOMMENDATIONS

It is not possible here to provide a detailed plan of action to implement the measures suggested to address worm infections, measles and malaria. A human rights approach, with exploration of the obligations of the global community to assist poorer countries to meet their obligations, seems appropriate.

- It is recommended that a group of concerned countries from the north and south very soon bring a resolution to a meeting of the World Health Assembly (WHA), which meets each year in Geneva. This resolution would call on all countries to follow specified guidelines to deworm infected populations, to eradicate measles, and to ensure good treatment and impregnated bed nets for all at risk of malaria. The WHA is the policy-making body of the WHO. Previous resolutions approved by WHA have led to major global improvements in health. These include the total control of smallpox (Levine 2004) and the 1981 WHO International Code of Marketing of Breastmilk Substitutes described in Mike Brady's chapter of this book.
- It is recommended that parallel with this WHA resolution, WHO should establish a unit to assist countries with these control measures and with capabilities to provide technical expertise and funding, and to ensure monitoring and surveillance.
- It is recommended that prior to the WHA resolution, leaders in WHO should hold high-level talks with UNICEF and the World Bank to elicit their support and commitments. It is further recommended that UNICEF, with its international mandate to uphold the rights of children and its history of assistance in controlling infectious diseases and malnutrition, should be heavily involved. Another recommendation is that the World Bank, which is placing a new focus on nutrition and is a major funder of projects to reduce hunger, also should pledge support, including major funding to assist countries in these efforts related to deworming, measles immunization, and malaria control. It is recommended that WHO also obtain pledges of assistance in this effort from major international nongovernmental organizations currently involved in health and nutrition activities in developing countries, and also from the private sector.

CONCLUSIONS

It is argued here that national governments supported by the global community and international organizations should take these strong new measures against worms, measles, and malaria. This should be done in recognition of the human rights to adequate food and health. Although individual countries have the primary obligations to ensure the realization of these human rights, the global community also has obligations in regard to these rights.

Worms, malaria, and measles contribute very importantly to hunger, malnutrition, morbidity, and mortality, particularly in Africa, Asia, and Latin America. Some governments have successfully acted on them, as in Cambodia's efforts to control intestinal worms, six southern African countries' successful progress to eradicate measles, and Togo's provision of free bed nets to all who come for measles vaccination. Actions such as these would markedly reduce the prevalence of these three infections. This in turn would result in marked reductions in malnutrition, as we move to end hunger in the world.

While the obligations relating to the human right to adequate food fall primarily on the states, there is a role for the global community (Eide 2005). This book identifies global obligations that are implied in the human rights to adequate food. The right-to-food guidelines (FAO 2005, 2006) clearly recognize that international assistance is needed to help many national governments.

In general, economic globalization has strengthened the powers of the large transnational corporations and weakened the powers of many governments (Latham and Beaudry 2001). This has lessened the ability of many governments in nonindustrialized countries in the south fully to meet their obligations in terms of their own citizens' rights to adequate food and health.

As George Kent says in chapter 1, "Human rights law already recognizes that some obligations are extraterritorial or, more precisely, extrajurisdictional." In this chapter, examples are provided of such international obligations, followed by suggested actions, to lessen the impact of three prevalent infections that contribute importantly to world hunger and malnutrition.

The movements against slavery, colonialism, and racism at first looked hopeless, as do current calls to the richest and most powerful in the world to extend justice for the poorest and most helpless (Sachs 2005). They called upon fundamental values of human rights and human potentialities. To move ahead and get closer to fulfilling rights to health and adequate food for all, we will need the poor themselves to call loudly for social justice, and this will have to be followed by a shift in attitudes and actions by the more privileged peoples and nations.

REFERENCES

Benenson, Abram S. 1995. *Control of Communicable Diseases Manual—Malaria.* 283–92, Washington, DC: American Public Health Association.

Biellek, R., S. Madema, A. Taloc, A. Kutsulakata, E. Allies, R. Eggens, N. Ngcobo, A. Sheanley, E. Mabuzane, E. Kufa, and J. Okuo-Bele. 2002. "First Five Years of Measles Elimination in Southern Africa 1996–2000." *Lancet* 359: 1564–68.

Curtis, C. 2005. "Insecticide-treated Nets against Malaria." *Trends in Parasitology* 21: 504–7.

Druilhe, P., A. Tall, and C. Sokhna. 2005. "Worms Can Worsen Malaria: Towards a New Means to Roll Back Malaria." *Trends in Parasitology* 21: 357–62.

Eide, Asbjørn. 1999. "Globalization, Universalization and Human Rights to Adequate Food." In *Not by Bread Alone: Food Security and Governance in Africa*, ed. A. Ogunrinade, 1–16. Johannesburg, South Africa: Witwatersrand Press.

———. 2005. "The Importance of Economic and Social Rights in the Age of Globalization." In *Food and Human Rights in Development,* ed. Wenche B. Eide and Uwe Kracht. Antwerp, Belgium: Intersentia.

FAO (Food and Agriculture Organization of the United Nations). 2005. *Voluntary Guidelines to Support the Progressive Realization of the Right to Adequate Food in the Context of National Food Security.* Rome: FAO. www.fao.org/docrep/meeting/009/y9825e/y9825e00.htm.

———. 2006. *The Right to Food Guidelines: Information Papers and Case Studies.* Rome: FAO. www.fao.org/docs/eims/upload/214344/RtFG_Eng_draft_03.pdf.

Gross, Reiner, and Patrick Webb. 2006. "Wasting Time for Wasted Children: Severe Child Undernutrition Must Be Resolved in Non-emergency Settings." *Lancet* 367: 1209–12.

Hogerzeil, H. V., M. Samson, J. V. Casanovas, and L. Rahmani-Ocara. 2006. "Is Access to Essential Medicines as Part of the Fulfillment of the Right to Health Enforceable through the Courts?" *Lancet* 368: 305–11.

Hopkins, Donald R., A. R. Hinman, J. P. Koplan, and J. M. Lane. 1982. "The Case for Global Measles Eradication." *Lancet* (19 June):1396–98.

Hopkins, Donald R. 1999. *Perspectives from the Dracunculiasis Eradication Programme: Morbidity and Mortality Weekly Reports.* Atlanta, GA: CDC, 48:43–49.

Hunt, P. 2006. "The Human Rights to the Highest Attainable Standard of Health: New Opportunities and Challenges." *Transactions of the Royal Society of Tropical Medicine and Hygiene* 100:603–7.

Lancet. 2005a. Editorial: "The Roll Back Malaria Campaign." *Lancet* 361: 1904.

———. 2005b. Editorial: "Artesimin Combination Therapy (ART) for Malaria." *Lancet* 366: 1908–9.

Latham, Michael C., Lani S. Stephenson, Kathleen M. Kurz, and Stephen N. Kinoti. 1990. "Metrifonate or Praziquantel Treatment Improves Physical Fitness and Appetite in Kenya School Children with Hookworm Infections." *American Journal of Tropical Medicine and Hygiene* 43: 170–79.

Latham, Michael C. 1997. *Human Nutrition in the Developing World.* Rome, Italy: FAO.

Latham, Michael C., and Micheline Beaudry. 2001. "Globalization and Inequity as Determinants of Malnutrition: A Clear Need for Activism." *Ecology of Food and Nutrition* 40 (6): 597–617.

Laxminarayan, R., A. J. Mills, J. G. Breman, A. R. Measham, G. Alleyne, M. Claeson, P. Jha, P. Muzgrous, J. Chow, S. Shahid-Salles, and D. T. Jamison. 2006. "Advancement of Global Health: Key Messages from the Disease Control Priorities Project." *Lancet* 367: 1193–1208.

Levine, Ruth. 2004. *Millions Saved: Proven Successes in Public Health.* Washington, DC: Center for Global Development, 129–36.

Pelletier, David. 1994. "The Potentiating Effects of Malnutrition on Child Mortality: Epidemiologic Evidence and Policy Implications." *Nutrition Reviews* 52: 409–15.

People's Health Movement. 2006. In *Global Health Watch 2005–2006: An Alternative Health Report,* ed. Global Health Watch Staff. London: Zed Books.

Rosenberg, T. 2006. "The Scandal of 'Poor People's Diseases.'" New York Times, 29 March.

Sachs, Jeffrey D. 2005. *The End of Poverty.* New York: Penguin Books.

Sanchez, Pedro, M. S. Swaminathan, P. Dobie, and N. Yuksel. 2005. *Halving Hunger: It Can Be Done.* London: Earthscan Millennium Project.

Sinuon, M., R. Tsuyuoka, D. Socheat, A. Montresor and K. Palmer. 2005. "Financial Costs of Deworming Children in All Schools in Cambodia." *Transactions of the Royal Society of Tropical Medicine and Hygiene* 99: 664–68.

Stephenson, Lani S., and Celia V. Holland. 1987. *The Impact of Helminth Infections on Human Nutrition.* London: Taylor and Frances.

Stephenson, Lani S., Michael C. Latham, and Eric Otteson. 2000. "Malnutrition and Parasitic Helminth Infections." *Parasitology* 121: S23–S38.

WHO (World Health Organization). 2002. *State of the World's Vaccines and Immunization.* Geneva: World Health Organization.

World Bank. 2003. *Combating Malnutrition: A Time to Act.* Washington, DC: World Bank.

7

Public Access to Seeds and the Human Right to Adequate Food

Marc J. Cohen and Anitha Ramanna

The human right to adequate food cannot effectively be realized without measures to ensure public access to plant genetic resources that are embodied in seeds. Plant genetic resources contain vital information that determines the characteristics of plants. Farmers and plant breeders require access to these resources, as they form the building blocks of agricultural innovations upon which continued food supplies depend. The world needs to continuously increase crop productivity and to develop new varieties to face current and future biological, environmental, and sociopolitical stresses. Plant genetic resources are crucial for sustainable food security: they form the basis of farmers' livelihoods, and consumers in both rich and poor countries indirectly depend on farmers' and breeders' access to these resources. Conserving plant genetic diversity is also important for effective response to humanitarian emergencies, which can destroy local seed systems.

Plant genetic resources are material of plant origin, including seeds and other vegetative propagating material (shoots, tubers, tissue), that contain plant genes (FAO 2001, Art. 2; see also Odek 1994). These resources include genetic material from agricultural and forage crops, trees, medicinal and ornamental plants, unexploited plants, and wild relatives (Keystone Center 1991). Sustainable agricultural growth requires a large pool of genetic resources. Genetic diversity is found in farmers' crop varieties, which are traditional varieties that have evolved and are cultivated by farmers. Farmers' crop varieties are therefore important for both traditional and industrial agriculture, as they contain genetic diversity used for improving existing varieties and developing new ones.

Public access to seeds refers to the need for some seeds to be easily available at affordable prices or no cost to all stakeholders. The ability to easily access seeds is under threat due to an increasingly proprietary agricultural research environment and to conflicts among relevant international agreements. Intellectual property rights (IPR), that is, limited property rights over information resources, are being extended to agriculture internationally through such instruments as the Agreement on Trade Related Aspects of Intellectual Property Rights (TRIPS) of the World Trade Organization (WTO) (WTO 2006a, 2006b). Developing-country governments are also attempting to establish ownership rights over genetic resources through agreements such as the Convention on Biological Diversity (CBD). In addition, some of these governments are attempting to preserve the rights of farmers to save, reuse, exchange, and sell seed (a key aspect of "Farmers' Rights," see below) through the International Treaty on Plant Genetic Resources for Food and Agriculture (ITPGRFA). The tensions among these global agreements and their implementation at the national level is resulting in competing claims over genetic resources. This is leading to the greater privatization of genetic resources that have been in the public domain.

In principle, patents and other forms of IPR protection are socially useful and can contribute to food security. Intellectual property rights protection can stimulate innovation, but food crop innovation also requires access to plant genetic resources, as plant breeders and farmers continuously mix and recombine those resources to create new varieties. Thus, there is a need for ensuring an appropriate balance between resources that are privately owned and those in the public domain. This balance between seeds in the public and private domain is undergoing significant changes due to the extension of IPR to plant varieties and seeds and the interpretation of Farmers' Rights as ownership-type rights. The existence of IPR is not, in itself, a risk to the progressive realization of the human right to adequate food. Rather, it is the lack of attention to achieving a balance between IPR and public access to seeds that seriously threatens the human right to adequate food.

A significant lacuna exists today as global obligations to promote public access to plant genetic resources are not effectively articulated. International obligations for providing public access to seeds can be derived from international agreements that recognize the importance of agriculture and conservation of genetic resources in realizing the human right to adequate food. The International Covenant on Economic, Social, and Cultural Rights (ICESCR), one of the core international human rights instruments, explicitly recognizes the importance of agriculture in realizing the right to adequate food. Guideline 8.12 of the right-to-food guidelines mentions agricultural research and the conservation and sustainable use of genetic resources for food and agriculture as part of a strategy for implementing the right to food (FAO 2006b).

This chapter seeks to clarify the global community's obligations with respect to public access to plant genetic resources as a basis for the progressive realization of the right to adequate food. It explains how conflicts over IPR and Farmers' Rights pose serious threats to such public access, and the need for international measures to overcome these tensions. Restrictions on access to seeds could potentially limit food supplies in terms of both quantity and quality, and could threaten the livelihoods of a vast number of farmers across the globe. Conflicts over IPR and Farmers' Rights are resulting in a battle for ownership rights over agricultural resources that could lead to underutilization of crop genetic resources by both professional crop scientists and farmer-breeders. This could have negative consequences for sustaining crop productivity and for the welfare of farming communities and consumers alike.

To illustrate the difficulties that arise from reliance on national solutions, the chapter examines India's attempt to balance competing claims. The chapter then outlines recommendations for action by the global community to fulfill the obligation of promoting public access to seeds.

IMPORTANCE OF PUBLIC ACCESS TO PLANT GENETIC RESOURCES IN REALIZING THE HUMAN RIGHT TO ADEQUATE FOOD

The shift from chiefly public to increasingly private regimes governing plant genetic resources is interrelated with the human right to adequate food on several levels. Restrictions on access to genetic resources would affect *breeders*, who require plant genetic resources to sustain productivity and create more nutritious crops; *farmers*, who require access to meet their own food needs, earn income to buy food and other necessities, and cope with difficult environments; *consumers*, who would lose out on the benefits of lower costs, greater availability of food, and improved nutrition without such access for farmers and breeders; and humanitarian assistance agencies that provide seeds to communities affected by disasters.

Traditionally, agricultural resources were considered to be in the public domain. The U.S. Patent and Trademark Office ruled in 1899 that allowing patents "upon the trees of the forests and plants of the earth . . . would be unreasonable and impossible" (Doyle 1985, 51). Large transnational "life sciences" firms are now using molecular biology to manipulate genes and identify important traits in traditional or farmers' crop varieties, and are seeking ownership rights over both new and farmers' varieties. The global seed industry is highly concentrated, with the top ten corporations controlling half of the $21 billion world market. Moreover, these firms overlap with the top ten pesticide companies, which control 84 percent of the closely related $30 billion global market (ETC Group 2005).

Governments of developing countries are trying to protect farmers' varieties and genetic resources by asserting their sovereignty over them. Falcon and Fowler (2002, 198) quote analysts who compare this enclosure of the "genetic commons" to the earlier closing of land commons in England. In the meantime, the quantity of land suitable for growing food crops is shrinking, due to degradation and conversion to nonagricultural uses. Drastic shifts in climatic conditions have serious implications for food production in both the South and the North. Overuse of pesticides complicates crop protection, as pests develop resistance to an ever wider range of chemicals. New crop varieties, traditional varieties, and the genetic resources that they contain are all important, as they have useful traits. Ensuring food security requires adequate availability of plant genetic resources to cope with these challenges.

Restrictions on public access to seeds could threaten food supplies by limiting the creation of new crop varieties. There is much debate over whether food supplies will be adequate in the future to meet population growth (Anonymous 2006; von Braun et al. 2005). In addition, rapid urbanization and income growth in the developing world is boosting demand for meat, meaning that additional grain is needed for feed (von Braun et al. 2005). Even if agricultural growth is sufficient to meet rising demand, it will be essential to devote adequate resources to producing new varieties to cope with ecological, economic, demographic, and social stresses.

Access to genetic resources is also important for farmers' livelihoods. According to the UN Millennium Project, half the world's hungry people live in smallholder farming households that are unable to grow or buy enough food to meet their needs. Another 30 percent of the hungry are low-income pastoralists, fisher folk, people who depend on forests for their livelihoods, or landless rural laborers (United Nations Millennium Project Taskforce on Hunger 2005, 3–4; IFAD 2001, 16–18). In Bangladesh, agriculture accounts for 53 percent of male employment and 77 percent of female employment. The figures are about 50 percent each in Thailand, and about 90 percent each in Uganda, but only 24 percent and 6 percent in Mexico (World Bank 2005). Even in India, with its high-tech industry and growing middle class, the food-insecure population is concentrated in the rain-fed, resource-poor farming areas. These areas have received less government support generally and less public agricultural research support than the well-endowed and irrigated areas. Hence, to a very large and real extent, states will meet their obligation to fulfill (facilitate) the human right to adequate food when food-insecure people have agriculture-related opportunities that allow them to grow or buy the food they need. State action to facilitate creation of off-farm opportunities is also important, but productivity gains in small-farm staple food production play the main role in reducing poverty and fostering food security in most low-income countries (Lipton 2005). Continued public access to plant genetic resources must underpin efforts to create agriculture-related opportunities.

Nonfarming consumers depend indirectly on plant genetic resources. When consumers buy cereals, vegetables, and fruits, they usually are not aware of the enormous efforts of breeders and farmers that provide them with the variety available. Productivity gains also lower prices for consumers. In both China and India, for example, agricultural research has helped reduce poverty through increased agricultural productivity, which not only led to direct on-farm benefits (such as reduced unit costs), but also to lower food prices, higher wages, greater rural employment on and off the farm, and cheaper food in urban areas. Because urban poor people spend half or more of their income on food, this meant less poverty in both urban and rural areas (Meinzen-Dick et al. 2004). In principle, consumers could realize these benefits from either public or private sector research and development (R&D), but in practice, the private sector carries out very little research on the staple food crops that poor people consume, as the returns are not likely to cover the investment costs (Pardey et al. 2006).

Access to seeds is also important for coping with humanitarian emergencies. Natural and human-induced disasters often have devastating impacts on seed systems. Since the 1990s, the gene banks of the international agricultural research centers (IARCs) supported by the Consultative Group on International Agricultural Research (CGIAR) have played an increasingly important role in restoring disaster-affected seed systems. The IARCs' efforts in Rwanda, through the "Seeds of Hope" project following the 1994 genocide, and in Honduras and Nicaragua following Hurricane Mitch in 1998 ("Seeds of Hope II"), are among the best-known examples (Varma and Winslow 2005; Louka 2002). Today, Sub-Saharan Africa has derived as much as 25 percent of its improved crop germplasm from IARC seeds originally provided in response to humanitarian emergencies (Natsios 2006).

The Rwandan civil war and genocide did not merely take an appalling toll on human life; the conflict also obliterated the country's seed system and the highly regarded public agricultural research establishment. In 1995, eight IARCs worked closely with public agricultural research institutes in eastern, central, and southern Africa to find appropriate seeds. Importantly, the IARCs carried their efforts out in close consultation with Rwandan farming communities. The centers also assisted with multiplication of surviving Rwandan varieties, and stored these as a hedge against future destruction. The latter effort involved work at Ugandan and Tanzanian research centers, in collaboration with Rwandan farmers who had engaged in on-farm conservation at their own behest. Seeds of Hope became the model for CGIAR system emergency seed relief efforts elsewhere (Varma and Winslow 2005).

AGRICULTURE, SEEDS, AND THE
HUMAN RIGHT TO ADEQUATE FOOD

The ICESCR, which is binding on states parties, stresses the important role of agriculture in realizing the right to adequate food. It calls for state action to:

> improve methods of production, conservation and distribution of food by making full use of technical and scientific knowledge, by disseminating knowledge of the principles of nutrition and by developing or reforming agrarian systems in such a way as to achieve the most efficient development and utilization of natural resources. (UN OHCHR 1966, Art. 11.2a)

The Covenant emphasizes the use of maximum available resources for achieving the realization of rights (Art. 2.1). Although the term "available resources" is generally interpreted to mean financial resources, it could also be read to include plant genetic resources and technologies important for food security.

Efforts to clarify the content of the human right to adequate food further emphasize the connection between access to plant genetic resources and realizing this right. According to General Comment 12 (GC 12) of the UN Committee on Economic, Social, and Cultural Rights (CESCR), "The right to adequate food is realized when every man, woman and child, alone or in community with others, has physical and economic access at all times to adequate food or means for its procurement" (UN CESCR 1999, para. 6).

Economic access to food cannot be achieved unless breeders and farmers have adequate availability of seeds to produce food. Moreover, the concept of "adequate" food includes the notion of sustainability, in both the environmental and intergenerational sense (UN CESCR 1999, para. 7). GC 12 interprets states' obligation to fulfill (facilitate) this right as requiring them to "pro-actively engage in activities intended to strengthen people's access to and utilization of resources and means to ensure their livelihoods, including food security" (UN CESCR 1999, para. 15). GC 12 also stresses that states must not take any measures that impede existing access to food and must also ensure that individuals or corporations do not deprive individuals of their access to food. In addition, states parties must identify vulnerable groups and frame policies to help them (see chapter 3 of this volume). States cannot meet these obligations unless they take measures to ensure that individuals or entities do not deny access to seeds to those who require it, particularly small and marginalized farmers who may have limited or no access to formal seed markets.

Like the ICESCR, GC 12 stresses the important role of food production in national implementation of the right to adequate food, calling upon states parties to the covenant to adopt "a national strategy to ensure food and nutrition security for all" (UN CESCR 1999, para. 21).

The strategy should address critical issues and measures in regard to *all* aspects of the food system, including the production, processing, distribution, marketing and consumption of safe food, as well as parallel measures in the fields of health, education, employment and social security. Care should be taken to ensure the most sustainable management and use of natural and other resources for food at the national, regional, local and household levels. (UN CESCR 1999, para. 25; emphasis in original)

The right-to-food guidelines, which go into much greater detail than GC 12 on possible steps to realize the right to adequate food, emphasize in particular the importance of agricultural research for poor farmers and consumers, encouraging states to:

- promote agricultural research and development, in particular to promote basic food production with its positive effects on basic incomes and its benefits to small and women farmers, as well as poor consumers (FAO 2006b, Guideline 8.4); and
- within the framework of relevant international agreements, including those on intellectual property, promote access by medium- and small-scale farmers to research results enhancing food security (FAO 2006b, Guideline 8.5).

As already indicated, continued agricultural research presupposes adequate access to plant genetic resources. Guideline 8.12 explicitly addresses conservation and sustainable use of those resources:

States, taking into account the importance of biodiversity and consistent with their obligations under relevant international agreements should consider specific national policies, legal instruments and supporting mechanisms to prevent the erosion of and ensure the conservation and sustainable use of genetic resources for food and agriculture, including, as appropriate, for the protection of relevant traditional knowledge and equitable participation in sharing benefits arising from the use of these resources, and by encouraging, as appropriate, the participation of local and indigenous communities and farmers in making national decisions on matters related to the conservation and sustainable use of genetic resources for food and agriculture. (FAO 2006b)

Conservation and sustainable use of genetic resources are of importance for sustaining rural livelihoods and continued plant breeding needed to assure adequate global food supplies. Food production and efficient development of agrarian systems—which are stressed in the covenant—both depend upon farmers' continued access to genetic resources. Poor farmers in developing countries usually achieve access through saving, reusing, and informally exchanging and selling seed, rather than through formal seed markets. In Southern Africa, for example, smallholders obtain only about 10 percent of their seed from formal markets (Zerbe 2002). Indeed, in many poorer developing countries, formal, state-regulated seed markets barely exist, and where they do, state regulation is often quite minimal. Even in India, which has a large formal agricultural sector, some 80 percent of the farmers rely on farm-saved seed (Government of India 2005). At the January 2007 World Social Forum in Nairobi, seventy African nongovernmental organizations (NGOs) from twelve countries reaffirmed the importance of farmer-saved seed in Africa for agricultural knowledge, biodiversity, and innovation that has benefited the whole world (World Food Policy 2007).

A 1999 study by the UN Human Rights Commission's special rapporteur on the right to food urged promotion of Farmers' Rights (see the section below on the conflict between TRIPS and Farmers' Rights) as part of the right to food:

> Farmers' rights should be given attention by the human rights community and promoted in the continued promotion of the right to food, since our future food supply and its sustainability may depend on such rights being established on a firm footing. (UN CHR 1999, para. 121)

The CESCR, the United Nations' body overseeing implementation of the ICESCR, has commented on potential conflicts between the human right of scientific innovators to benefit from the protection of the moral and material interests arising from their innovations, on the one hand, and the human right to adequate food on the other. The committee considers that states parties' efforts to realize the former right must "constitute no impediment to their ability to comply with their core obligations *in relation to the [right] to food. . . .*" Moreover, the CESCR stresses states parties' "duty to prevent unreasonably high costs for *access to . . . plant seeds* or other means of food production" (UN CESCR 2005, para. 35, emphasis added). Clearly, in the committee's view, IPR should not raise the price of plant genetic resources so as to put them beyond the reach of poor farmers.

NEED TO CLARIFY INTERNATIONAL OBLIGATIONS

The ICESCR calls in Article 2 for international cooperation to attain the progressive realization of all economic, social, and cultural rights. GC 12 elaborates on this obligation, characterizing the role of international cooperation as "essential," and calls for "joint and separate action" by states parties to achieve the realization of the right to adequate food at home and abroad (UN CESCR 1999, para. 36). Furthermore, GC 12 specifies:

> States have a joint and individual responsibility, in accordance with the Charter of the United Nations, to cooperate in providing disaster relief and humanitarian assistance in times of emergency, including assistance to refugees and internally displaced persons. (UN CESCR 1999, para. 38)

International practice falls far short of these norms. Developed countries continue to fail to deliver on their decades of pledges to provide at least 0.7 percent of their gross national income in aid (OECD 2006). Official development assistance (ODA) to agricultural and rural development at present is below the level of the early 1980s in real terms (FAO 2005), despite the importance of agriculture to realizing the right to adequate food and reducing poverty. According to the UN Office for the Coordination of Humanitarian Affairs, donors provided just 66 percent of the amount requested in its 2006 emergency appeals. By sector of assistance, the figures were 92 percent for food, 41 percent for protection, human rights, and rule of law, and just 26 percent for agriculture (including seeds) (UN OCHA 2007).

In relation to the issue of public access to seeds, not only are international obligations missing in practice, but also in theory. There are no clear conceptual or practical guidelines for resolving IPR conflicts or incentives to promote the sharing of seeds. At the same time, the institutions that conserve and maintain crops, seeds, and genetic resources are facing severe financial shortages (Imperial College of Science, Technology and Medicine 2006).

Created in 1971, the CGIAR is an association of public and private, nonprofit members that support a large network of gene banks. These collections are essential for sustaining biodiversity, as they collectively represent one of the world's largest efforts at off-farm conservation of plant genetic resources. They contain over 600,000 samples of crop, forage, and agroforestry genetic resources. Of these, almost 533,000 are designated "in trust" for the global community under agreements with the Food and Agriculture Organization of the United Nations (FAO). The terms of these agreements provide that the germplasm within the in-trust collections will be made available without restriction to researchers around the world, on the understanding that no patents can be applied to the material without the expressed consent of the IARC that provides the material (SGRP 2003).

With the changing laws on intellectual property and restrictions on use and sharing of genetic resources, this system of open access is under threat. There are disagreements about whether patents can be granted on innovations derived from material accessed from the CGIAR-supported gene banks. The gene banks are struggling to set in place a framework for dealing with contentious intellectual property issues.

Since the late 1980s, ODA to the CGIAR-supported IARCS has stagnated (Pardey et al. 2006). Beyond the CGIAR system, as of 2000, some 28 percent of developing countries, 33 percent of countries in transition, and 13 percent of developed countries had reduced gene bank budgets (Imperial College of Science, Technology and Medicine 2006).

TRIPS AND PUBLIC ACCESS TO SEEDS

Two forms of IPR relevant to agriculture are patents and plant breeder's rights (PBR). Patents restrict others from making, using, or selling an invention for twenty years. To obtain a patent, the claimant must demonstrate that her or his product or process is novel, embodies an inventive step, and has industrial applicability (Haugen 2005). PBR are less stringent than patents in terms of scope and coverage. Both forms of protection are national; those seeking IPR must apply separately in each country where they wish to have protection.

Developed countries are attempting to promote IPR through TRIPS. Its Article 27.3 (b) requires all WTO members to provide IPR protection for plant varieties, either by patents, an effective sui generis system (that is, a system created specially for this purpose), or any combination of the two (WTO 2006b). The agreement does not specify the nature of the sui generis system, and its Article 8 (1) explicitly permits WTO members to "adopt measures necessary to promote public health *and nutrition*, and to promote the public interest in sectors of vital importance to their socioeconomic and technological development," consistent with other provisions of TRIPS (Gray 2003, emphasis added). This is sometimes referred to as the "compulsory licensing" provision, because it permits states to compel IPR holders to make their intellectual property available in order to advance public health and nutrition.

Developed countries and the seed industry have pressed developing nations to model sui generis systems of IPR protection for plant varieties on the existing systems of PBR, also known as Plant Variety Protection (PVP), found in developed countries and some developing countries (GRAIN 1999). Since 1961, governments have extended PVP under the terms of an international agreement called the International Union for the Protection of New Varieties of Plants (known by its French acronym, UPOV). The 1961 UPOV agreement provided PVP to novel, distinct, uniform, and stable plant varieties, and gave breeders exclusive marketing rights to varieties they have developed. As genetically modified crops have only come onto the market since the mid-1990s, UPOV focused exclusively on the products of conventional plant breeding until then. UPOV 1961 included a breeders' exemption and a farmers' exemption. These allowed breeders other than the PVP holder to carry out further research, and permitted farmers to save, reuse, and exchange seed. UPOV was revised in 1972, 1978, and 1991. Under the 1991 version, which all new UPOV members have to accept, member states can forbid farmers to save or reuse protected variety seeds (although states *may* allow this), and farmers cannot exchange them. UPOV 1991 also strengthens the rights of PVP holders to restrict further research by other breeders (Barton 1999; Kameri-Mbote 2003; Manzella 2006). Governments of developing countries have resisted this more restrictive version of UPOV as providing insufficient exemptions for farmers and researchers. There are fears that systems that provide broader rights to PVP holders would undermine food security and biodiversity, confer monopoly rights on seed firms, and undermine the CBD's concept of equitable sharing of resource benefits.

IPR protection can stimulate innovations that provide broad social benefits, including better health and nutrition and enhanced farm productivity. For example, the University of Wisconsin patented the process for fortifying milk with vitamin D. Consumption of fortified milk has greatly reduced the incidence of rickets, a crippling vitamin D deficiency disorder. The university established the Wisconsin Alumni Research Foundation to hold this and other patents. The foundation has contributed $750 million from royalties back to the university for further research, including graduate student fellowships (thereby benefiting one of the authors of this chapter).

At least in theory, new IPR-protected crop varieties might offer agronomic advantages to farmers, nutrition advantages to consumers, and, through productivity gains, price advantages to consumers. However, in order to use patented varieties, farmers would most likely have to purchase seed every season, and this might prove extremely difficult for low-income farmers in developing countries, who rely heavily on seed saving and informal exchange. Patent holders have obtained legal judgments against North American farmers who replanted the seeds of protected varieties (CBC News 2004). At present, patent law related to agriculture is in its infancy or as yet unborn in many developing countries. As it develops, the advantages of patented plant varieties are likely to be out of reach for the poorest farmers in developing countries, while the productivity gains that better-off farmers achieve may reduce prices, to the further detriment of those who plant traditional varieties (Marlin-Bennett 1997).

A more proprietary research environment likewise impinges on the ability of public sector and nonprofit plant breeders to obtain access to both products and processes for research oriented toward poor farmers and consumers. They may have to obtain often costly licenses or spend considerable time negotiating free licenses that may restrict the dissemination of research results (Gray 2003; Pardey and Beintema 2001).

Also, there is an inherent inequity in seed patents. Farmers have selected and developed crop varieties for millennia, but such farmer varieties belong to no one in particular. The actions of individual farmers and farming communities across generations are not patentable. Moreover, in most countries, it is time consuming and expensive to seek a patent, so even if a poor but innovative present-day developing-country smallholder wanted to do so, it is unlikely that she could afford the necessary time and legal representation (Marlin-Bennett 1997). Therefore, it is important for developing countries to choose the right form of IPR protection and frame limits within which public access to seeds can also be ensured.

CONFLICT BETWEEN TRIPS AND FARMERS' RIGHTS AND IMPLICATIONS FOR PUBLIC ACCESS TO SEEDS

Along with the access and benefit sharing provisions of CBD, Farmers' Rights are increasingly being used by some developing nations to restrict access to once-public materials as a way of countering TRIPS. The controversy between TRIPS and Farmers' Rights affects public access to seeds because it leads states into a battle over agricultural resources. As developed countries promote greater scope of patents and PBR over agricultural innovations, developing countries push for ownership rights over plant genetic resources that have been in the public domain. The result is an interstate North-South tit-for-tat game that takes resources out of the public sphere (Fowler 1994; Bjørnstad 2004).

Developing-country governments are interpreting the sui generis clause in TRIPS in ways that enable them to establish Farmers' Rights. Farmers' Rights are an attempt to counter breeders' rights. Farmers' Rights have had a long and difficult history, emerging as a topic of intense conflict in FAO meetings during the 1980s, and continuing today to be a source of global controversy. The concept originated in the writings of Pat Roy Mooney and Cary Fowler (now the executive secretary of the Global Crop Diversity Trust), activists with the Rural Advancement Foundation International (now the ETC Group), who pointed out that farmers' significant contributions to plant breeding and conservation of plant genetic resources remain unrecognized and unrewarded. In 1989, Farmers' Rights were for the first time formally recognized by the intergovernmental FAO Conference as:

> rights arising from the past, present and future contributions of farmers in conserving, using and making available plant genetic resources, particularly those in the centers of origin/diversity. These rights are vested in the international community, as trustees for present and future generations. (FAO 1989, para. 108)

The concept includes the right of farmers to select, save, reuse, exchange, and sell seeds, but goes well beyond that, emphasizing farmers' role in conserving biodiversity for the benefit of the larger global community. In addition to this "open access" aspect, Farmers' Rights are also sometimes understood to include IPR protection for farmer-developed crop varieties (discussed further below). More generally, the term is used by advocates of small-scale, traditional farming (Manzella 2006). In this chapter we focus mainly on seed saving and related aspects, as well as on the extension of IPR protection to farmers' crop varieties.

Governments of developing countries have pressed for recognition of farmers' contributions to plant breeding and equitable benefit sharing. They have criticized TRIPS for recognizing only formal breeders' rights. Industrialized-country governments and the global seed industry, while agreeing to recognize the contribution of farmers, have opposed measures that restrict IPR.

The ITPGRFA focuses on ensuring access, conservation, and sustainable use of plant genetic resources as a basis for food security. It was adopted by the FAO Conference in 2001 and entered into force in 2004, with the required 40 states (including the European Union) having ratified the treaty. As of June 2006, there were 104 states parties to the treaty, and another 22 that had signed but not yet ratified it. The ITPGRFA emerged from over seven years of FAO-sponsored negotiations. Farmers' Rights are mentioned in the Preamble, which stresses that these rights are to be implemented at both the national and international level:

> *Affirming* that the past, present and future contributions of farmers in all regions of the world, particularly those in centres of origin and diversity, in conserving, improving and making available these resources, is the basis of Farmers' Rights;
>
> Affirming also that the rights recognized in this Treaty to save, use, exchange and sell farm-saved seed and other propagating material, and to participate in decision-making regarding, and in the fair and equitable sharing of the benefits arising from, the use of plant genetic resources for food and agriculture, are fundamental to the realization of Farmers' Rights, as well as the promotion of Farmers' Rights at national and international levels. (FAO 2001, 1)

Article 9, the main part of the treaty focusing on Farmers' Rights, reads as follows:

> 9.2 The Contracting Parties agree that the responsibility for realizing Farmers' Rights, as they relate to plant genetic resources for food and agriculture, rests with national governments. In accordance with their needs and priorities, each Contracting Party should, as appropriate, and subject to its national legislation, take measures to protect and promote Farmers' Rights, including:
>
> (a) protection of traditional knowledge relevant to plant genetic resources for food and agriculture;
>
> (b) the right to equitably participate in sharing benefits arising from the utilization of plant genetic resources for food and agriculture; and
>
> (c) the right to participate in making decisions, at the national level, on matters related to the conservation and sustainable use of plant genetic resources for food and agriculture.
>
> 9.3 Nothing in this Article shall be interpreted to limit any rights that farmers have to save, use, exchange and sell farm-saved seed/propagating material, subject to national law and as appropriate. (FAO 2001, 5)

In contrast to the Preamble, Article 9 gives national governments sole responsibility for Farmers' Rights. The treaty makes suggestions on implementing Farmers' Rights, including protection of traditional knowledge, equitable benefit sharing, participation in decision making, and rights to save and sell seed, but these are not legally binding.

During the negotiations, developing and developed countries differed over whether Farmers' Rights should be promoted at the international level as well as nationally. The United States and the European Union insisted on leaving the question to national law and policy. Developing countries, pressed by civil society organizations, had sought to include an international obligation that would, in effect, have elevated Farmers' Rights to the status of an internationally recognized human right. The Preamble references this in weak, hortatory terms (Bjørnstad 2004; ETC Group 2001).

The relationship among various aspects of the CBD, ITPGRFA, and TRIPS is a source of enormous controversy between developing and developed nations. Countries trying to implement these agreements are faced with dilemmas regarding how to resolve the tensions. It is not unusual for different international institutions to take contradictory positions on an issue. For example, in the 1980s, the World Bank and the UN Children's Fund engaged in considerable debate over the extent to which structural adjustment programs should shield government-funded social programs from fiscal cutbacks. In this case, the disagreement ultimately led to greater attention to social protection issues on the part of the international financial institutions.

In spite of several years of negotiations, however, no accepted solution has thus far emerged to resolve the tensions between Farmers' Rights and TRIPS, and at present, few substantive attempts are being made to evolve a global solution. This lacuna has serious implications for ensuring the realization of the human right to adequate food, as it could lead to restrictions on access to plant genetic resources for farmers, breeders, and public and private institutions. It could also reduce incentives for conservation of biodiversity, thereby further undermining plant breeding.

The conflict between TRIPS and Farmers' Rights must be seen in the context of the traditional common heritage regime, which asserts, "The major food plants of the world are not owned by any one people and are quite literally a part of our human heritage from the past" (Kloppenburg 1988, 152). In other words, such resources should be in the public domain. Farmers' Rights initially emerged under this principle, with the global community designated as trustee for current and future generations. However, with the increasing extension of IPR over plant varieties, seeds, and genes, developing countries began to demand changes that transformed the concept of Farmers' Rights. They voiced their opposition to the asymmetric extension of IPR to breeders' varieties, while leaving farmers' varieties and Southern genetic resources freely available as "common heritage." Developing countries were unwilling to grant breeders' rights until Farmers' Rights were protected and mechanisms were established to share benefits from exploitation of genetic resources. Developed countries and the seed industry remained staunchly unwilling to agree to restrictions on IPR.

In the negotiations over the CBD, which concluded in 1992, developing countries rejected the principle of common heritage. The convention instead focuses on access and benefit sharing with regard to plant genetic resources, subjecting them to the sovereign rights of nations. Already in 1991, the FAO Conference had stated that genetic resources are subject to state sovereignty and called for creation of an International Fund for Farmers' Rights whereby farmers, as well as their governments, would share in the benefits. This fund did not materialize. Without such a fund, sovereign national rights over plant genetic resources are vested in states, which may or may not provide direct benefits to farmers. Critics argue that some interpretations of the CBD have actually served to hasten the "commodification" of resources once in the public domain, rather than their conservation, by effectively offering states benefits from deals with enterprises that are interested in those resources (GRAIN 2005).

Another aspect of conflict between TRIPS and Farmers' Rights is the right of farmers to save, use, exchange, and sell seed. Restrictions on this right would be a threat to many poor farmers' livelihoods. Under plant patent legislation, reproducing, exchanging, or selling seed is illegal without the consent of the patent holder, who can obtain compensation for violations. PBR have in the past exempted farm-saved seed, but it is not clear, even under the TRIPS sui generis provision, whether such activities will still be allowed. The ITPGRFA is neutral on this thorny issue, leaving its resolution to further debate, legislation, and policy at the national level (Moore and Tymowski 2005).

In 2000, in an attempt to address the TRIPS-Farmers' Rights conflict, the Council of Ministers of the Organization of African Unity (the predecessor of the African Union) endorsed the Model Law for the Protection of the Rights of Local Communities, Farmers, and Breeders, and for the Regulation of Access to Biological Resources. Though not binding on member states, it offers them guidance in devising a sui generis system for implementing the TRIPS provision on plant varieties. The model law recognizes Farmers' Rights, and requires prior informed consent from both the state and local communities before commercial breeders can gain access to biological resources. The provision on Plant Breeders' Rights gives them exclusive rights to produce and sell the varieties they have developed, but farmers can save and resell the seeds of these varieties and can further adapt them. The model law explicitly prohibits patents on life forms. It is consistent with UPOV 1978, rather than the more restrictive UPOV 1991 (Ekpere 2000).

India has enacted ambitious legislation that goes beyond any other existing statutes in trying to balance the rights of farmers and breeders. We will examine this in some detail.

INDIA'S ATTEMPT TO RESOLVE THE CONFLICTS

India is a party to all the conflicting agreements we have discussed—the ICESCR, CBD, TRIPS, and ITPGRFA. It has thus faced the problem of resolving the tensions in establishing national laws to implement these agreements. India has attempted to evolve a balance by framing laws that adhere to the main aspects of all the agreements, with policies aiming to implement both Breeders' Rights and Farmers' Rights.

India's Protection of Plant Varieties and Farmers' Rights Act (Government of India 2001) is unique in that it is not only one of the first national laws to establish Farmers' Rights, but also one of the first to attempt to implement both TRIPS and Farmers' Rights. The act provides PBR not only to new varieties developed by breeders working at private and public research institutions, but also to varieties developed by farmers or NGOs. Thus it enables farmers to assert ownership rights over their varieties. India has also tried to ensure that farmers have the right to save, use, and exchange seed, while limiting their right to sell seed covered by PBR.

India long accepted the common heritage principle, with no system of PBR or Farmers' Rights. The public sector has always accounted for most agricultural research in India, and the country is home to one of the CGIAR-supported IARCs and a UN biotechnology research institute (ASTI 2005). Indian policy underwent substantial change due to both domestic and international factors. The Seed Association of India, formed in 1985, actively lobbied for PBR, and the industry is increasingly involved in agricultural research. Adoption of the TRIPS agreement added external pressure to establish such rights.

Enormous protest against implementing TRIPS and introducing plant breeders' rights arose from NGOs and farmers' lobbies in India. They asserted that TRIPS and "western IPR systems . . . negate the contribution of Third World farmers as breeders and hence undermine farmers' rights," while patents "allow the usurpation of indigenous knowledge as a western invention through minor tinkering or trivial translation" (Shiva and Radha undated). NGOs in India pointed to the need for protecting traditional knowledge. They argued that the sui generis clause in TRIPS could be utilized to formulate a unique system in India that upheld Farmers' Rights. NGOs developed alternate systems such as "Community Intellectual Rights" (Shiva and Radha undated) and demanded that India must be paid for use of genetic resources and that there must be formal recognition of farmers' varieties (Sahai 2001).

Following this debate, India's parliament attempted to conform to TRIPS by using the sui generis clause to establish rights for both breeders and farmers. As Madhav Gadgil of the Indian Institute of Science observes,

> It is necessary that India accepts the broad framework of IPRs prevalent in the industrial countries to function efficiently in the emerging global framework. . . . They (industrial countries) can impose on us an intellectual property rights regime of their own design. It is best to accept this reality and then actively work towards modifying the IPR regime to serve our interests better. (Gadgil 1997, 9–10)

India's law attempts to balance farmers' and breeders' rights by allowing stakeholders to claim intellectual property rights over four types of varieties. These include varieties covered under existing intellectual property laws for breeders, namely, new varieties and essentially derived varieties. The latter have genetic content or a pedigree that is not fundamentally distinct from that of the protected new variety. Protection of essentially derived varieties extends the scope of the initial PBR. In India's legislation, the concept seems to have been adopted with the view that it could provide some protection to publicly bred varieties that have been only slightly modified (Seshia 2001). NGOs that have the capacity to modify varieties could perhaps utilize the provision, and it could also be used to make claims for varieties that are used as progenitors in breeding programs.

In addition, the law creates novel systems not found in other existing intellectual property laws for protecting the innovations of farmers and public sector institutions. It protects both new varieties and extant varieties. "New varieties" refers to those protected under existing PBR systems such as UPOV. The provision for granting protection to extant varieties has no historical parallel, nor does it fit into the theoretical framework governing intellectual property protection (UN ESCAP 2001). It is an attempt to extend protection to existing varieties, with the objective of granting rewards for past innovation (Srinivasan 2003). The law defines as extant varieties those notified under the Seeds Act as well as farmers' varieties, varieties in the public domain, and varieties about which there is common knowledge. India's 1966 Seeds Act provides for the registration and certification of varieties as an attempt to check the quality of seeds. This provision expands the concept of Farmers' Rights considerably, permitting "any farmer or group of farmers or community of farmers claiming to be a breeder of the variety" to apply to register their varieties.

India's Protection of Plant Varieties and Farmers' Rights Act resembles pre-1991 versions of UPOV in terms of protection for breeders, with a crucial provision allowing farmers to save, reuse, exchange, and sell seeds of a protected variety but not under the breeder's registered name:

> A farmer shall be deemed to be entitled to save, use, sow, resow, exchange, share or sell his farm produce including seed of a variety protected under this

Act in the same manner as he was entitled before the coming into force of this Act: Provided that the farmer shall not be entitled to sell branded seed of a variety protected under this Act. Explanation: For the purposes of clause (iv), "branded seed" means any seed put in a package or any other container and labeled in a manner indicating that such seed is of a variety protected under this Act. (Government of India 2001, Chapter VI, Clause 39, 1 [iv])

Most analysts agree that this provision permits farmers to sell seeds in a generic form without a label, but prevents them from competing with breeders and seed companies by selling under a brand name. However, some authors express concern that granting IPR will lead to further privatization of the seed sector, and India's pending membership in UPOV might also affect the interpretation of this provision. Seed companies appear to have compromised during the framing of the legislation, but their positions may not be as accommodating during the implementation stage (Gopalakrishnan 2001; Ghose 2003).

India's policy has significant implications for ensuring the right to adequate food. The first is the possibility of an "anticommons tragedy." This arises when too many parties independently possess the right to exclude others from utilizing a resource (Aoki 1998). It results in resource underutilization rather than overuse (Buchanan and Yoon 2000). Heller and Eisenberg (1998) point out the potential for an anticommons situation with respect to patents in biomedical research due to the existence of too many owners holding rights to previous discoveries, which could constitute obstacles to future research and lead to fewer useful products for improving public health.

India's legislation is an attempt to evolve a multiple rights system. While the act is based on the important principle of fair and equitable distribution of ownership rights, by assigning multiple rights, it may actually pose obstacles to utilization and exchange of resources, as multiple stakeholders assert claims over a crop variety. If a breeder applies to register a new variety that uses material over which other stakeholders hold rights, this would require negotiations and compensation. In many cases, new varieties contain multiple protected materials subject to IPR. Some actors are also less capable of asserting their rights and will be left out—and these are likely to be poor farmers and their communities. For these stakeholders, the cost of asserting claims may be too high. This situation could lead to lack of investment and underutilization of crop genetic resources as inputs.

The new regime may also alter relations of exchange. If it becomes possible for farmers to register their varieties under the act, they may have an incentive to charge for their use rather than sharing resources freely with other farmers. Historically, public research institutions in India provided seed varieties to individual farmers, but under the new regime they may seek to charge for use of their materials by private companies rather than giving them away to farmers. Research institutes would also have greater incentive to transfer materials to actors who would pay for their use rather than giving them away to the international agricultural centers. Any disruption or impediment to these flows caused by property rights claims could be detrimental to the very biodiversity the law is intended to protect and to the livelihoods of smallholder farmers in India's rain-fed environments, who maintain that biodiversity. If all this happens, the act will have negative consequences for sustaining crop productivity and for the welfare of the farming communities it seeks to compensate. India and other developing countries need to evolve mechanisms to ensure continued flows of agricultural resources as part of Farmers' Rights.

So far, India's active Right to Food Campaign has not addressed these issues specifically. Instead, it has concentrated its attention on food provisioning programs and access to employment (Right to Food Campaign 2006).

The introduction of genetically modified crops has also led to debates over the right to food in India and other countries, raising questions about the economic, political, and social impact of genetic engineering. Proponents of agricultural biotechnology argue that it has the potential to solve India's agricultural problems by raising productivity and the quality of crops. Opponents point to the negative implications of biotechnology on the environment and farmer's livelihoods. Indian activist Vandana Shiva asserts that biotechnology enables corporate control and monopoly power over seeds (Shiva, Emani, and Jafri 1999).

The extent to which India and other WTO member states that are also states parties to the ICESCR can balance their obligations, and also balance breeders' and Farmers' Rights, so far remains untested through the WTO dispute resolution system. With the Doha Round WTO negotiations at an impasse, there is, temporarily, some room for creativity on the part of governments of developing countries. But those governments are under considerable pressure from developed countries (the major source of ODA and key trading partners) and the seed industry, often including their own domestic firms, as in India. A related concern, however, is that efforts to comply with TRIPS obligations will drain governmental resources, energy, and attention needed to progressively realize the right to adequate food (Haugen 2005).

NEED FOR A GLOBAL RESPONSE

The need to find the appropriate balance between private and public interests in relation to plant genetic resources is being neglected in the battle for ownership rights. While developed countries and industry seek to assert rights through IPR laws, developing countries are also trying to establish ownership rights though mechanisms such as Farmers' Rights and the CBD. In effect, this privatizes both breeders' new crop varieties and "traditional" farmers' varieties.

Food security is under threat due to the increasing barriers to accessing plant genetic resources. The free flow of these resources, which existed for centuries, enabled farmers and plant breeders alike to introduce crops to new areas and to improve crops through selection and breeding. No nation has ever fabricated or maintained a prosperous food system based solely on genetic resources found in its own territory (Falcon and Fowler 2002, 198). Given looming climatic, ecological, social, and economic challenges to food security, access to plant genetic resources remains crucial. As noted earlier, access to these resources is also essential for addressing humanitarian emergencies. Relying on IPR for crop innovations is not adequate if material is not available for innovations. Indeed, as Graff and colleagues point out,

> Uncertainty over the total amount of IP transaction costs scares off investment in R&D projects, unless the expected returns are particularly attractive. This will continue as long as there is uncertainty in the IP landscape for plant biotechnologies and genetic materials. (Graff et al. 2004, 123)

Failure to resolve the tensions between TRIPS and Farmers' Rights inhibits public plant breeding and farmers' ability to access genetic resources. Both are important for the realization of the right to adequate food, as emphasized in the right-to-food guidelines (FAO 2006b), as is international cooperation.

Yet, at present, international cooperation does not match up to calls for aid for agricultural development and research, conservation of genetic resources in gene banks, or humanitarian assistance. There is no clear articulation of the global obligation to protect public access to seeds. Nevertheless, international action is required to ensure public access to seeds as a means of realizing the human right to adequate food.

Seen in terms of the rings of responsibility (see chapter 1 of this volume), national governments have a crucial role to play. However, national policies may not resolve the conflicts discussed above. National governments, acting on their own, will frequently have a strong incentive to seek rents from their "sovereign rights" over genetic resources under the CBD, and so may well become players in the anticommons tragedy. If each country sets up barriers to accessing genetic resources—a plausible scenario without international action—limits exchange of resources, and competes to stake claims over innovations, the implications would be severely negative for poor farmers, plant breeders, and consumers.

Global cooperation to assure continued public access to seeds, including adequate levels of financial and technical assistance from the governments of wealthy countries to support agricultural research and biodiversity conservation (both on-farm and in gene banks), can change the incentive structures that poorer states presently face. Furthermore, as discussed below, the ITPGRFA's Multilateral System requires a *global* governance mechanism to keep the affected germplasm in the public domain.

In this book, the global community is seen as a loose coalition of actors at the international, national, and local levels. The governing body of the ITPGRFA could provide the lead within this global community for stronger cooperation to ensure public access to seeds, but it would also require the involvement of additional actors, including farmers and their organizations, NGOs, business groups, national governments, and other international organizations. The private sector and NGOs could, in particular, expand current limited efforts to make IPR-protected crop technologies available to developing countries on a royalty-free basis, particularly where the resulting products are unlikely to be reintroduced into developed-country markets.

TOWARD SOLUTIONS: THE INTERNATIONAL TREATY ON PLANT GENETIC RESOURCES FOR FOOD AND AGRICULTURE

The ITPGRFA does offer a path toward solutions. Its "Multilateral System" seeks to promote "facilitated access" to substantial staple crop germplasm for all stakeholders. Although a clear interpretation of the term "facilitated access" would emerge only when applied in practice, its basic aim is to preserve a part of the genetic commons free from enclosure. A key purpose of the system, therefore, is to ensure that adequate germplasm remains available for research and breeding (Moore and Tymowski 2005). The Multilateral System consists of a specified list of crops with agreed utilization rules. The negotiations resulted in agreement to include thirty-five food crops and twenty-nine forage plants considered important for food security, with the possibility of further additions. The Multilateral System applies to varieties of listed crops under the management and control of states parties, in the public domain, and in the in-trust collections of the CGIAR-supported IARCs.

The treaty aims to strike a balance among varied interests. It creates a mixed system in which plant genetic resources are neither completely freely available (as under the common heritage approach) nor completely subject to private IPR or sovereign national rights. In principle, even very poor farmers could access the Multilateral System's material, for example through cooperatives or farmers' associations. The treaty requires that recipients of material who commercialize a product pay "an equitable sharing of the benefits" back to the Multilateral System.

The treaty is ambiguous on the nature of Farmers' Rights and their relationship to TRIPS, however, and this question remains extremely contentious. NGOs have criticized the treaty because it lacks international obligations with respect to Farmers' Rights (GRAIN 2001). Other analysts—including Gerald Moore, FAO's chief legal counsel for most of the period of the treaty negotiations—argue that the Multilateral System to some extent constitutes Farmers' Rights at the international level by preserving open access to a significant amount of germplasm (Moore and Tymowski 2005). During the negotiations over the treaty, developed and developing nations clashed over whether crops accessed from the Multilateral System could be subject to IPR. The final text states that IPR cannot be claimed on material "in the form received"; a similar provision is found in the "in trust" agreements between FAO and the CGIAR IARCs (Moore and Tymowski 2005). This means that varieties accessed from the Multilateral System cannot be subject to IPR, but genes, genetic material, and improvements on the material could be claimed as intellectual property subject to protection. There is still enormous uncertainty and debate over the meaning of this provision. This issue is of extreme importance, as it affects access to materials held by the IARCs.

While the ITPGRFA provides some direction on developing measures to ensure public access to seeds, several problems remain. The treaty, like the CBD, recognizes state sovereignty over plant genetic resources. To a large degree, the Multilateral System represents a voluntary delegation of that sovereignty, which states could later undo. However, the inclusion of the IARC in-trust collections in the system (formally signed on World Food Day, October 16, 2006) is important, given their unique global public-goods character. Maintaining these collections in the public domain will require an appropriate *global* governance mechanism, as they are held on behalf of the global community. The treaty places the burden on the IARCs to assure that varieties derived from their germplasm remain free from IPR protection that would restrict further access, but this is expensive and time consuming for the centers. FAO is considered a "third-party beneficiary" under the Multilateral System, and therefore has the right to assist the centers in monitoring compliance with this provision. The standard Material Transfer Agreement agreed to by the treaty's governing body provides for settlement of disputes by binding arbitration, but in some legal systems, such as that of the United States, such a mechanism does not preclude further expensive litigation.

Finally, the issue of resources for maintaining the world's public access gene banks remains to be addressed. The Global Crop Diversity Trust, established in 2003, seeks to raise an endowment of $260 million to preserve 1,500 gene banks, including those at the IARCs, in perpetuity. At present, most of the banks lack adequate funding, and few meet global standards.

So far, the trust has received $42 million out of $61 million pledged, mainly from developed countries, with modest contributions from developing countries, foundations, and private seed companies (Croptrust 2006). At its first meeting, held in 2006, the ITPGRFA governing body formally recognized the Crop Trust as an "essential element" of the treaty's funding strategy (FAO 2006a). The trust also is facilitating development of a gene bank of last resort, capable of withstanding catastrophic natural disasters or nuclear war, located above the Arctic Circle in Svalbard, Norway (Weiss 2006). It has joined with the International Rice Research Institute, a CGIAR-supported IARC, to help support a disaster-proof gene bank in the Philippines that will contain germplasm from all known varieties of rice, the main food of nearly half the human race (BBC 2007).

RECOMMENDATIONS

The ITPGRFA governing body—an intergovernmental institution—should become the global community's principal forum with the responsibility to focus on public access to seeds as a means of realizing the human right to adequate food. Mechanisms must be evolved for making plant genetic resources, seeds, crops, and technologies essential for food security easily available. The governing body of the treaty should take the conceptual lead in discussions of such mechanisms. Realistically, coordination and harmonization of the various relevant international agreements to ensure that IPR and Farmers' Rights do not restrict food security will involve lengthy and difficult negotiations among the states parties. But discussion should be transparent and should involve input from a wider array of nonstate stakeholders, with the treaty governing body accorded a prominent role.

The ITPGRFA's Multilateral System represents a positive start in this direction, but additional measures are needed in the short term to assure that this system operates effectively. It is important that it remain possible to add additional germplasm and crops to the system, since genetic engineering permits the use of traits from different species in breeding, and many non-staple crops have traits with useful agronomic or nutritional properties.

There are two options for addressing the question of IPR and the Multilateral System's materials. One approach is to ensure that this material and any derived innovations remain free from IPR, with adequate resources provided to the treaty governing body to allow it to challenge IPR claims. Alternatively, in implementing the treaty's provision requiring payments to the Multilateral System when breeders commercialize derived innovations, the treaty body could charge a substantially higher fee when breeders seek IPR. The resulting royalty revenue could fund gene bank maintenance and provide benefits to the farm communities that originally developed parent crop varieties. The treaty governing body would again need resources to monitor commercialization and royalty payments. A variation on this option would prohibit IPR protection of derived varieties in developing countries. Adoption of a particular approach would have to emerge from negotiations among states parties, but again, the process should be transparent and involve input from a wider range of stakeholders.

Such negotiations should also facilitate the treaty governing body becoming a vehicle to promote cooperation among gene banks, firms, NGOs, farmers, and governments to utilize germplasm effectively to advance food security. The governing body could also promote collaboration and sharing of information resources, perhaps even including trading of patents (patent swaps) between parties, to produce crops and varieties useful for food security.

In addition, the governing body would need to develop models on how to effectively implement IPR and Farmers' Rights. It is important to find ways to resolve the tensions arising from various international agreements that are leading to resources being taken out of the public domain. Case studies of how various countries are attempting to implement these treaties, and the lessons learned, could be disseminated globally.

The parties to the ITPGRFA are nation-states, so obligations would ultimately also rest with national governments. Member states would have the responsibility to ensure that the treaty's Multilateral System works effectively and also to promote national mechanisms for public access to seeds domestically. Business groups and NGOs must be involved in the governments' efforts and must also be vested with obligations to provide access to technologies and crops important for food security.

The path to long-term, sustainable food security lies not only in obligations to provide food, but also in measures to ensure that seeds, crops, and plant genetic resources are easily available to those who produce and sustain food supplies. The global community must maintain a fair, equitable, and reasonable balance between public and private interests, and ensure public access to seeds, in order to realize the human right to adequate food.

ACKNOWLEDGMENTS

The authors wish to thank the following for their helpful comments on earlier drafts of this chapter: participants in the June 2006 Human Security and Global Governance 2 (HUGG 2) Conference, held in Vancouver, Canada, and sponsored by the Toda Institute for Global Peace and Policy Research; Professor George Kent, University of Hawai'i; Professor Ellen Messer, Tufts University; Dr. Melinda Smale, International Food Policy Research Institute; and Mr. Daniele Manzella, consultant, FAO Legal Office. We are also grateful to Hans Morten Haugen for sharing a copy of his University of Oslo PhD thesis.

REFERENCES

Anonymous. 2006. "Double Whammy in Store for India?" *Times of India*, 16 June, 11.

Aoki, Keith. 1998. "Neocolonialism, Anticommons Property, and Biopiracy in the Not-so Brave New World Order of International Intellectual Property Protection." *Indiana Journal of Global Legal Studies* 6: 11–58.

ASTI (Agricultural Science and Technology Indicators). 2005. "Country Profile: India." www.asti.cgiar.org/profiles/india.cfm?arow=86.

Barton, John. 1999. "Intellectual Property Management." *Biotechnology for Developing-Country Agriculture: Problems and Opportunities*. IFPRI 2020, Focus 2, Brief 7 of 10. Washington, DC: IFPRI. www.ifpri.org/2020/focus/focus02/focus02.pdf.

BBC. 2007. "Deal Gives Rice Diversity a Boost." 12 March. http://news.bbc.co.uk/2/hi/science/nature/6441689.stm.

Bjørnstad, Svanhild-Isabelle Batta. 2004. "Breakthrough for 'the South'? An Analysis of the Recognition of Farmers' Rights in the International Treaty on Plant Genetic Resources for Food and Agriculture." *FNI Report* 13/2004. Lysaker, Norway: The Fridtjof Nansen Institute. www.fni.no/doc&pdf/FNI-R1304.pdf.

Buchanan, James, and Yong Yoon. 2000. "Symmetric Tragedies: Commons and Anticommons." *Journal of Law and Economics* 43 (1): 1–13.

CBC (Canadian Broadcasting Company) News. 2004. "Percy Schmeiser's Battle." www.cbc.ca/news/background/genetics_modification/percyschmeiser.html.

Croptrust (The Global Crop Diversity Trust). 2006. Data posted at www.croptrust.org.

Doyle, Jack. 1985. *Altered Harvest: Agriculture, Genetics and the Fate of the World's Food Supply*. New York: Viking Press.

Ekpere, J. A. 2000. *The OAU's Model Law for the Protection of the Rights of Local Communities, Farmers, and Breeders, and for the Regulation of Access to Biological Resources: An Explanatory Booklet*. Lagos: Organization of African Unity Scientific, Technical, and Research Commission. www.grain.org/brl_files/oau-booklet.pdf.

ETC Group (Action Group on Erosion, Technology, and Concentration). 2001. "The Law of the Seed!" *ETC Group Translator* 3 (1). www.etcgroup.org/documents/trans_treaty_dec2001.pdf.

———. 2005. "Oligopoly, Inc. 2005: Concentration in Corporate Power." *Communique* No. 91 (November/December). www.etcgroup.org/upload/publication/44/01/oligopoly2005_16dec.05.pdf.

Falcon, Walter P., and Cary Fowler. 2002. "Carving Up the Commons: Emergence of a New International Regime for Germplasm Development and Transfer." *Food Policy* 27 (3): 197–222.

FAO (Food and Agriculture Organization of the United Nations). 1989. *Report of the Conference of FAO, 25th Session, Rome, 11–29 November 1989*. Rome: FAO. www.fao.org/docrep/x5588E/x5588E00.htm.

———. 2001. *International Treaty on Plant Genetic Resources for Food and Agriculture* (Official English version). Rome: FAO. ftp://ftp.fao.org/ag/cgrfa/it/ITPGRe.pdf.

———. 2005. *The State of Food and Agriculture 2005*. Rome: FAO. ftp://ftp.fao.org/docrep/fao/008/a0050e/a0050e_full.pdf.

———. 2006a. *Report of the Governing Body of the International Treaty on Plant Genetic Resources for Food and Agriculture, First Session*. Madrid, Spain, 12–16 June. Rome: FAO. ftp://ftp.fao.org/ag/cgrfa/gb1/gb1repe.pdf.

————. 2006b. *The Right to Food Guidelines: Information Papers and Case Studies.* Rome: FAO. www.fao.org/docs/eims/upload/214344/RtFG_Eng_draft_03.pdf.

Fowler, Cary. 1994. *Unnatural Selection: Technology, Politics and Plant Evolution.* Yverdon, Switzerland: Gordon and Breach.

Gadgil, Madhav. 1997. "A Framework for Managing India's Biodiversity Resources in the Context of CBD and GATT." *RIS Biotechnology and Development Review* 1 (1): 1–14.

Ghose, Janak Rana. 2003. "The Right to Save Seed." Paper presented at the 2004 biannual global meeting of the International Association for the Study of Common Property. www.iascp2004.org.mx/downloads/paper_509.pdf.

Gopalakrishnan, N. S. 2001. "An 'Effective' *Sui Generis* Law to Protect Plant Varieties and Farmers' Right in India—A Critique." *Journal of World Intellectual Property* 4 (January): 157–72.

Government of India. 2001. *Protection of Plant Varieties and Farmers' Rights Act.* www.agricoop.nic.in/PPV&FR Act, 2001.pdf.

————. 2005. *Economic Survey 2005–2006.* http://indiabudget.nic.in/es2005-06/esmain.htm.

Graff, Gregory D., Brian D. Wright, Alan B. Bennett, and David Zilberman. 2004. "Access to Intellectual Property: A Major Obstacle to Developing Transgenic Horticultural Crops." *California Agriculture* 58 (2): 120–26.

GRAIN (Genetic Resources Action International). 1999. "Beyond UPOV: Examples of Developing Countries Preparing Non-UPOV Sui Generis Plant Variety Protection Schemes for Compliance with TRIPS." www.grain.org/briefings/?id=127.

————. 2001. "A Disappointing Compromise." *Seedling* (December). www.grain.org/seedling/?id=174.

————. 2005. "The FAO Seed Treaty: From Farmers' Rights to Breeders' Privileges." *Seedling* (October). www.grain.org/seedling/?id=411.

Gray, Kevin R. 2003. "Right to Food Principles Vis-à-vis Rules Governing International Trade." Center for International Development at Harvard University www.cid.harvard.edu/cidtrade/Papers/gray.pdf.

Haugen, Hans Morten. 2005. *The Right to Food and the TRIPS Agreement.* PhD thesis, University of Oslo.

Heller, Michael A., and Rebecca S. Eisenberg. 1998. "Can Patents Deter Innovation? The Anticommons in Biomedical Research." *Science* 280 (5364): 698–701.

IFAD (International Fund for Agricultural Development). 2001. *Rural Poverty Report 2001.* New York. Oxford University Press. www.ifad.org/poverty/index.htm.

Imperial College of Science, Technology and Medicine. 2006. *Crop Diversity At Risk: The Case for Sustaining Crop Collections.* London: Imperial College of Science, Technology and Medicine. www.croptrust.org/documents/wyereport.pdf.

Kameri-Mbote, Patricia. 2003. "Community, Farmers' and Breeders' Rights in Africa: Towards a Legal Framework for Sui Generis Legislation." *University of Nairobi Law Journal.* www.ielrc.org/content/a0302.pdf.

Keystone Center. 1991. *Oslo Plenary Session. Final Consensus Report: Global Initiative for the Security and Sustainable Use of Plant Genetic Resources. Third Plenary Session, 31 May–4 June 1991, Oslo, Norway.* Keystone, CO: Keystone Center.

Kloppenburg, Jack Jr. 1988. *First the Seed: The Political Economy of Plant Biotechnology, 1492–2000.* New York: Cambridge University Press.

Lipton, Michael. 2005. *The Family Farm in a Globalizing World: The Role of Crop Science in Alleviating Poverty.* 2020 Vision for Food, Agriculture and the Environment. Discussion Paper No. 40. Washington, DC: IFPRI. www.ifpri.org/2020/dp/vp40 .pdf.

Louka, Elli. 2002. *Biodiversity and Human Rights: The International Rules for the Protection of Biodiversity.* Ardsley, NY: Transnational Publishers.

Manzella, Daniele. 2006. Personal communication to the authors, 9 October.

Marlin-Bennett, Renée. 1997. "Agricultural Trade and Food Security." In *Hunger in a Global Economy,* ed. M. J. Cohen, 46–53. Silver Spring, MD: Bread for the World Institute.

Meinzen-Dick, Ruth, Michelle Adato, Lawrence Haddad, and Peter Hazell. 2004. "Science and Poverty: An Interdisciplinary Assessment of the Impact of Agricultural Research." *Food Policy Report.* Washington, DC: IFPRI. www.ifpri.org/pubs/fpr/ pr16.pdf.

Moore, Gerald, and Witold Tymowski. 2005. "Explanatory Guide to the International Treaty on Plant Genetic Resources for Food and Agriculture." *IUCN Environmental Law and Policy Paper* No. 57. Gland, Switzerland, and Cambridge, UK: IUCN. www.iucn.org/themes/law/pdfdocuments/EPLP57EN.pdf.

Natsios, Andrew. 2006. "Keynote Address." Presented at the Conference on Poverty Reduction in Conflict and Fragile States: Perspectives from the Household Level, sponsored by the U.S. Agency for International Development Office of Poverty Reduction, the Households in Conflict Network, and the German Institute for Economic Research, Washington, DC, 8 November.

Odek, James O. 1994. "Bio-Piracy: Creating Proprietary Rights in Plant Genetic Resources." *Journal of Intellectual Property Law* 2 (Fall):141–81.

OECD (Organization for Economic Cooperation and Development). 2006. "Aid Flows Top USD 100 Billion in 2005." www.oecd.org/document/40/0,2340,en _2649_34447_36418344_1_1_1_1,00.html.

Pardey, Philip G., and Nienke Beintema. 2001. "Slow Magic: Agricultural R&D in the Century Since Mendel." *Food Policy Report.* Washington, DC: IFPRI. www.ifpri.org/ pubs/fpr/fpr31.pdf.

Pardey, Philip G., Nienke Beintema, Steven Dehmer, and Stanley Wood. 2006. "Agricultural Research: A Growing Global Divide?" *Food Policy Report.* Washington, DC: IFPRI. www.ifpri.org/pubs/fpr/pr17.pdf.

Right to Food Campaign. 2006. Homepage. www.righttofoodindia.org/index.html.

Sahai, S. 2001. "India's Plant Variety Protection and Farmers' Rights Act." www.iprs online.org/ictsd/docs/SahaiBridgesYear5N8Oct2001.pdf.

Seshia, Shaila. 2001. *Plant Variety Protection and Farmers' Rights in India: Law-making and the Cultivation of Varietal Control.* M.Phil. dissertation, Institute of Development Studies, University of Sussex.

SGRP (System-wide Genetic Resources Programme). 2003. *Booklet of CGIAR Centre Policy Instruments, Guidelines and Statements on Genetic Resources, Biotechnology and Intellectual Property Rights, Version II.* Rome: International Plant Genetic Resources Institute. www.cgiar.org/corecollection/docs/sgrp_policy_booklet_2003.pdf.

Shiva, Vandana, and Holla-Brar Radha. Undated. *Protection of Plants, People and Intellectual Rights: Proposed Amendments to the Draft Plant Varieties Act, 1993.* New Delhi: Research Foundation for Science, Technology, and Natural Resource Policy.

Shiva, Vandana, A. Emani, and A. Jafri. 1999. "Globalisation and Threat to Seed Security: Case of Transgenic Cotton Trials in India." *Economic and Political Weekly* 34: 601–13.

Srinivasan, C. S. 2003. "Exploring the Feasibility of Farmers' Rights." *Development Policy Review* 21 (4): 419–47.

UN CESCR (United Nations Committee on Economic, Social, and Cultural Rights). 1999. *Substantive Issues Arising in the Implementation of the International Covenant on Economic, Social and Cultural Rights*. General Comment 12 (Twentieth Session, 1999): "The Right to Adequate Food" (art. 11). Geneva: ECOSOC E/C.12/1999/5. www.unhchr.ch/tbs/doc.nsf/MasterFrameView/3d02758c707031d58025677f003 b73b9?Opendocument.

———. 2005. General Comment 17 (Twenty-fifth Session, 2005): "The Right of Everyone to Benefit from the Protection of the Moral and Material Interests Resulting from Any Scientific, Literary or Artistic Production of which He or She is the Author" (art. 15, paragraph 1 [c] of the *International Covenant on Economic, Social and Cultural Rights*). Geneva: ECOSOC E/C. 12/GC/17. www.unhchr.ch/tbs/doc.nsf/(Symbol)/E.C.12.GC.17.En?OpenDocument.

UN CHR (United Nations Commission on Human Rights), Sub-Commission on Prevention of Discrimination and Protection of Minorities. 1999. *The Realization of Economic, Social, and Cultural Rights: The Right to Adequate Food and to Be Free from Hunger, Updated Study on the Right to Food Submitted by Mr. Asbjørn Eide in Accordance with Sub-Commission Decision 1998/106*. Geneva: ECOSOC E/CN.4/Sub .2/1999/12. http://daccessdds.un.org/doc/UNDOC/GEN/G99/138/13/PDF/G99 13813.pdf?OpenElement.

UN ESCAP (United Nations Economic and Social Co mmission for Asia and the Pacific). 2001. *Institutional Capacity-Building to Deal with the Implications of TRIPS for Industrial and Technological Development: Case Study of India*. Bangkok: ESCAP.

UN Millennium Project Taskforce on Hunger. 2005. *Halving Hunger: It Can Be Done*. London: Earthscan. www.unmillenniumproject.org/documents/HTF-SumVers _FINAL.pdf.

UN OCHA (United Nations Office for the Coordination of Humanitarian Affairs). 2007. "Consolidated & Flash Appeals 2006: Global Requirements & Funding per Sector, as of 4 January 2007." http://ocha.unog.ch/fts/reports/daily/ocha_R30_ y2006___07010321.pdf.

UN OHCHR (United Nations Office of the High Commissioner for Human Rights). 1966. *International Covenant on Economic, Social, and Cultural Rights*. Geneva: OHCHR . www.ohchr.org/english/law/cescr.htm.

Varma, Surendra, and Mark Winslow. 2005. *Healing Wounds: How the International Centers of the CGIAR Help Rebuild Agriculture in Countries Affected by Conflicts and Natural Disasters*. Washington, DC: CGIAR. www.cgiar.org/pdf/healingwounds.pdf.

Von Braun, Joachim, Mark W. Rosegrant, Rajul Pandya-Lorch, Marc J. Cohen, Sarah A. Cline, Mary Ashby Brown, and María Soledad Bos. 2005. *New Risks and Opportunities for Food Security: Scenario Analyses for 2015 and 2050*. 2020 Vision for Food, Agriculture, and the Environment Discussion Paper No. 39. Washington, DC: IFPRI. www.ifpri.org/2020/dp/dp39/2020dp39.pdf.

Weiss, Rick. 2006. "The World's Agricultural Legacy Gets a Safe Home." *Washington Post*, 19 June, A1.

World Bank. 2005. *World Development Indicators 2005*. CD-ROM. Washington, DC: World Bank.

World Food Policy. 2007. "World Social Forum 2007—Kenya: African Seed Diversity." www.worldfoodpolicy.org/html/wsf/wsf.htm.

WTO (World Trade Organization). 2006a. "Intellectual Property: Protection and Enforcement." www.wto.org/english/thewto_e/whatis_e/tif_e/agrm7_e.htm.

———. 2006b. "Intellectual Property (TRIPS)—Frequently-Asked Questions." www.wto.org/english/tratop_e/trips_e/tripfq_e.htm.

Zerbe, Noah. 2002. "Contested Ownership: TRIPS, CBD, and Implications for Southern African Biodiversity." *Perspectives on Global Development and Technology* 1 (3–4): 294–321.

8

Global Support for School Feeding

S. Vivek

In the early 1980s the chief minister of Tamil Nadu in India sought to introduce school feeding across the state. Objections came from all quarters: some said it would not be administratively feasible, others feared food poisoning, financial difficulties were cited, and the litany of objections accumulated. The chief minister reputedly bulldozed all objections and the scheme was started. The coverage of the scheme was gradually increased to include children up to class ten, covering children from roughly ages six to sixteen. Today the scheme is hailed as one of the most important developmental programs in the world. School feeding not only protected children from hunger during the day, but also increased enrollment and attendance in school. Today Tamil Nadu boasts of very high completion of primary schooling, and is moving fast toward universal completion of class ten. School feeding is not just about protecting children from hunger—it is an important tool to assist children to reach full physical, mental, and emotional development.

This book examines the obligations of the global society in assuring the realization of the right to food. I am convinced that if there is one obligation that we cannot neglect, it is school feeding. School feeding is the most widely implemented food program across the world. It has been implemented in many countries, from the richest, including the United States, to the poorest. The benefits of school feeding are well established, and we know that it is well within the administrative capacity of all governments to implement it. School feeding is surprisingly cheap. For example, the World Food Programme (WFP) spends an average of just nineteen cents per child per day (WFP 2005, 1). In India the cost is almost half that of WFP, and it is likely to be lower in other countries where school feeding is most needed.

191

The promise and possibility of school feeding should be argument enough to extend it to every child in need. It is both a legal and a moral obligation of the global society to provide school feeding as a matter of right to children across the world. The next section deliberates on issues relating to the legal obligations of the global society.

SCHOOL FEEDING AS A LEGAL RIGHT

The right to food is recognized as a legal right in an assortment of international covenants and national constitutions (FAO 1998). But until the 1980s the right to food and other socioeconomic rights (such as housing, education, etc.) were considered as "soft rights" that were not legally binding on governments (for a discussion see Eide, Krause, and Rosas 2001). This came partly from a belief that it might not be financially feasible for governments to implement these rights. Governments were viewed as having an obligation in principle to implement these rights, but they were not actually pressed to do so. This approach to socioeconomic rights has gradually changed over the years. It is now more commonly agreed that socioeconomic rights are concrete rights, like civil and political rights, and the corresponding obligations are binding as well. As a result, there is an increasing jurisprudence on these issues across the world.

The most far-reaching litigation internationally on the right to food so far is *PUCL vs UoI and Ors.* in the Supreme Court of India (Guha-Khasnobis and Vivek 2005; Right to Food Campaign 2006). This litigation is among the few examples of courts taking a strong stand in protecting the right to food. One reason why courts have been reluctant to take up issues relating to the right to food is that the obligations of governments and societies are not yet clearly specified with respect to this right. Though this litigation in the Supreme Court of India refers to national laws by domestic courts, it points to the complexity in making right to food justiciable and the importance of clarifying obligations arising out of right to food.

The right to food can be addressed in many ways, including cash transfers, employment, direct feeding programs, subsidized food, land reforms, and many protective measures (for discussions of various large-scale interventions see Drèze and Sen 1989 and World Bank 2006). General Comment 12 rightly says:

> The most appropriate ways and means of implementing the right to adequate food will inevitably vary significantly from one State party to another. . . . The strategy should be based on a systematic identification of policy measures and activities relevant to the situation and context, as derived from the normative content of the right to adequate food. (UN CESCR 1999, para. 21–22)

Any practical approach to the right to food has to include a basket of measures since no single measure can address the food needs of every individual in the society. The needs of children under six, adolescent children, working adults, school children, aged people, and others are all different. In other words, a food program may be able to address the needs of one section of the population, but any conception of the right to food needs to involve an array of measures.

It can be reasonably agreed that the right to food of children deserves special attention from the society. But "children" is too large and complex a group in itself to be addressed in one go. The right to be breastfed is a key concern for the infant—but is irrelevant for a child of six. Social arrangements to enable all children to receive breastfeeding would be completely different from measures to address the right to food of school children. Other chapters in this book, including that by Arun Gupta, look at early childhood. I wish to concentrate on another important group: school-age children.

In today's increasingly complex world, a lengthy period of preparation is crucial for children to develop and be able to participate in society. This period of preparation does not come to an end at the age of six. Children pick up some of their most crucial skills, including literacy, numeracy, and the ability to use a wide range of modern institutions, when they are of school age. Society has an obligation to offer the basic minimum services to the child, including school feeding, because hunger in these formative years is unacceptable in itself and also because hunger has serious detrimental effects on the education of children. School feeding programs improve school attendance dramatically, protect children from hunger in the classroom, and have a strong impact on educational achievement.

Of late there is an argument that school-age children do not deserve our priority since most clear malnutrition is in preschool-age children. This argument is problematic in two broad ways. First, the notion stems from the idea of scarcity of resources. Without doubt the world's resources are finite and thus scarce in some sense, but there is no reason to believe that school feeding programs will significantly strain the resources of the society or governments. Further, it is not clear why school feeding should be pitted against child care and not against a vast array of other categories of government expenditure.

Second, it is a mistake to understand food only in terms of nutrition. Food has biological, social, and cultural functions. Each of these is important in determining our well-being and also in developing capacities to navigate in this complex world. To understand the importance of school feeding, we have to evaluate it in terms of protecting children from hunger, its positive impact on education, and on other social and cultural rights that school feeding programs affect. Equally important, even a simple school feeding program is popular with children. To understand the impact of school feeding we should consider its links with education, gender equality, and many other domains. In human rights language this can be understood as the interdependence of rights. The following section looks at the nature of a rights-based school feeding program, which will subsequently enable me to discuss possible ways of international cooperation in implementing this entitlement.

A VISION FOR GLOBAL SCHOOL FEEDING PROGRAMS

School feeding programs (SFP) are important for *intrinsic* as well as *instrumental* reasons (see Sen 2000, 366). It is intrinsically important for every child to have an appropriate meal of good quality and to be free from hunger. Food also serves many instrumental roles, such as enabling the child to reach full physical and mental development. Further, school feeding has important effects on gender equality. Since school feeding stands at the intersection of several rights, I look at a few key human rights and examine their significance for SFPs.

The rights-based approach to food indicates that no effort should be spared to reach every child in need. Consider the following statement from WFP:

> When available funds are not enough, as in recent years, projects and food rations have to be downsized. Children are forced to leave school, and momentum towards rebuilding a stable tomorrow is lost. A clear commitment to global school feeding is a commitment to a safer future. This is a commitment that we cannot fail to make. (WFP 2005, 1)

Making school meals a concrete legal entitlement would help in building momentum to reach all children. This involves creating clear eligibility norms, specifying the benefits, and extending the benefits to all eligible beneficiaries. Though the last point looks obvious to some, the most important bone of contention in public policy often relates to extending the program to cover the universe of beneficiaries. The rights-based approach means that no child should be left behind due to financial reasons.

SFPs should be implemented not by merely giving any edible substance, but should be oriented toward full physical and mental development of the child, as emphasized in Article 27, paragraph 1, of the Convention on the Rights of the Child (CRC). It says, "States Parties recognize the right of every child to a standard of living adequate for the child's physical, mental, spiritual, moral and social development." In other words, the meal should be nutritious, appropriate for the age, and should take into consideration the developmental needs of the child. This should be done after taking into consideration the local nutritional deficiencies and ways of addressing them.

Supplementing food with micronutrients is a low cost way of addressing severe nutritional deficiencies in children. Many school feeding programs include weekly administration of iron tablets, periodic deworming, and other interventions to enhance the nutritional value of the SFP. According to the WFP an "essential package" of interventions includes "basic education, school meals, clean drinking water, separate sanitary latrines, micronutrient supplementation, de-worming treatment, school gardens as well as basic skills education (health, hygiene and life skills, including the prevention of malaria and HIV)." In other words, an SFP should not be viewed merely as a lunch program, but as an integrated program that addresses the full development of the child.

Education should be an important goal of the program. Article 28 of CRC says, "States Parties recognize the right of the child to education, and with a view to achieving this right progressively and on the basis of equal opportunity, they shall, in particular . . . (d) Take measures to encourage regular attendance at schools and the reduction of drop-out rates." SFPs play several important roles in education: protecting children from classroom hunger, enabling them to concentrate in the class; enabling the full cognitive development of the child; acting as an incentive for the parents to send children to school and making school a more welcome place, especially for children vulnerable to hunger; and improving school attendance, in particular in the post-lunch sessions (Drèze and Goyal 2003, 4673). The best means of providing this is to give children a tasty, filling, and nutritious meal every day in school.

The program should seek to address discrimination in all forms. In most cultures food plays an important role in identity and could be used creatively to promote various rights of marginalized communities (Atkins and Bowler 2001; for the role of food in culture see Witt 1999, xii, 292). For example, in India SFPs seek to have an impact against caste discrimination (on caste and school feeding see Drèze and Goyal 2003, 4673; Thorat and Lee 2005). School feeding also has a great potential to eliminate school discrimination against girl children. The biggest success story of SFPs has been their ability to increase school enrollment and attendance. Enrollment of girl children in particular tends to shoot up, paving the way for more equity in education among boys and girls. The widespread social benefits of this cannot be overemphasized.

Going beyond this, Article 29 (d) of CRC talks of "the preparation of the child for responsible life in a free society, in the spirit of understanding, peace, tolerance, equality of sexes, and friendship among all peoples, ethnic, national and religious groups and persons of indigenous origin." Given the importance of food in most cultures, SFPs should be designed creatively to tackle local discrimination in all forms, where it can. Emphasis should be placed on all children sharing the meal equitably, and there should be no symbolic or actual discrimination in the process of preparing, serving, and eating the meal. What meal is prepared and who prepares it also has symbolic significance in many cultures, which could be creatively utilized in SFPs.

According to General Comment 12 (GC 12) of the Committee on Economic, Social and Cultural Rights: "The core content of the right to adequate food implies the availability of food in a quantity and quality sufficient to satisfy the dietary needs of individuals, free from adverse substances, and acceptable within a given culture; the accessibility of such food in ways that are sustainable and that do not interfere with the enjoyment of other Human Rights" (UN CESCR 1999, para. 8). In some contexts this could be interpreted as meaning that local foods should be given the first priority in deciding the menu. They should be local in the sense of being favored by the culture and familiar to children. Many have argued in favor of fortified biscuits and other processed snacks. However, it is usually possible to prepare nutritious food without using highly processed products (for a discussion of such highly processed foods, see Nestle 2002). Given that school feeding takes place at a highly impressionable age, school feeding provides an excellent opportunity for delivering nutrition education, which would be missed by providing highly processed foods. Further, these processed foods generally do not give children a filling, wholesome meal.

Some observers have pointed out that school-based feeding programs discriminate against children who are not in school. This is an important point, especially because children who are not attending school may be especially vulnerable to malnutrition. One possible solution would be to enable children who are not enrolled in school to nevertheless participate in the school feeding program. This could be an attractive way of drawing out-of-school children into schooling. However, to the extent necessary, separate feeding programs should be arranged for children who cannot access school-based feeding programs.

To summarize, a rights-based SFP should address every child at risk of hunger and malnutrition, defined in the broadest of terms. Food should be culturally suitable and nutritious. Since nutrition is a key concern of SFPs, nonfood aspects of malnutrition should be addressed where possible. In particular, this should involve preparation of meals in a hygienic environment, periodic deworming, and nutrition education to children (for a detailed discussion on deworming see chapter 6 of this book). The best of the programs combine school feeding with a basic school health program. Emphasis should be given to children sharing the meal in a cordial and nondiscriminatory fashion. Where possible, symbolic and substantial measures should be adopted to eliminate all forms of discrimination.

The specific nature of the program will depend on various local issues, including the extent and distribution of children at risk of hunger and malnutrition, existing administrative systems, school timings, specific forms and causes of malnutrition in the region, and so on. Imposing a universal blueprint for SFPs is likely to be counterproductive and would be incapable of creatively addressing closely related issues. Though it may look complex at an abstract level to think of a flexible program, I feel that it is possible to respect local considerations and develop suitable systems creatively.

MODELS OF INTERNATIONAL COOPERATION

There is a scope for international cooperation at different levels for a rights-based global SFP. Three key domains for cooperation are cost sharing, program design, and quality enhancement.

Inadequacy of budgets has been the most constraining factor in universalizing SFP. Universalization will mean different things in different contexts. In India, for example, it stands for covering all children in government schools. In some other context it could mean all school-age children. At the minimum, I understand universalization as calling for the coverage of all children selected, using broad criteria that are not compromised by financial considerations. India's experience of converting school feeding into a rights-based program following a direction by the Supreme Court clearly indicates that a universal SFP is feasible. Due to the low cost of the program, India was able to cover over 130 million children without a telling impact in the overall budget. I am not claiming that there are no budgetary difficulties in implementing the scheme, but that resources can be found and are available if there is sufficient political will to implement it. Given the low costs of the program, it is my contention that every country is capable of offering a basic program to every child.

While I contend that it is possible for any government to offer a basic SFP, it may be beyond the capacity of many governments to afford a good-quality program that can meet the potential of SFP. This is where the international community should step in.

In India, state governments struggled at the beginning of the program to meet the setup costs of the midday meal scheme. School feeding programs in developing countries often operate with the most basic of infrastructure, such as simple kitchen and storage, stoves or firewood, water provisions, and a handful of vessels. In the most underfunded conditions, the cook prepares the meal in the open with just one vessel using firewood. Functional infrastructure can greatly improve the quality of food and ensure that the classroom routine is not disrupted by cooking activities (Drèze and Goyal 2003, 4673). Commitment from the international community to enhance the quality of SFPs initiated by local governments could go a long way in helping governments implement SFPs of an adequate quality. Providing part of the infrastructure and equipment costs can do this.

The daily costs of providing the meal and wages for the workers are two big expenses, apart from infrastructure required for running the program. Where a basic SFP exists, a little additional resource can often ensure a reasonably nutritious meal. A partnership between governments and the international community could ensure nutrition, variety, and a tasty meal for the child. One particular area of cooperation could be in the provision of micronutrient supplements, deworming, and other components that address health or nutritional needs of children. Similarly, the international community could take responsibility to provide some component of the meal. For example, regular provision of milk, eggs, or fruits could dramatically improve the nutritional quality of an otherwise basic meal. Another imaginative intervention could be funding the kitchen garden for the school. This would involve very little expense in the form of labor compensation and provision of raw materials. All of these have precedents in modes of international cooperation.

Further international expertise and experience could be used in improving the design of the school feeding programs. This is a relationship that should be done not just between developed and developing countries, but among developing countries as well. There is a lot of valuable experience and resources that developing countries could share among themselves. International organizations such as the WFP and UNICEF have much to contribute in this regard.

Where national and local governments take the initiative to set up a reasonably good program, the international community should give a hand to develop a functional school health program that goes with the school feeding program. Some of the most successful SFPs have been offered along with good school health programs. Schools provide a good institutional basis for offering a large number of basic health services. This would become more significant as schooling reaches more marginalized people. School health programs would assist in providing deworming, micronutrient supplementation, and other basic health services that are essential to children's nutrition.

States should be understood to be obligated to offer at least a basic SFP. The role of the international community should be to strengthen those programs. International support can come in the form of resources, expertise, joint monitoring, and in contributing specific components of the program to improve its effectiveness.

That still leaves the question of how many and which children should be chosen as beneficiaries. The choice depends on the incidence of hunger and malnutrition and the nature of the school system, among other things. Some paradigms for assistance seek to target resources by selecting the most "responsive" children or by having complex anthropometric systems for choosing "deserving" children (Sen 1995, 619). One important problem with such measures is that they calculate returns to the program in individual terms, whereas school feeding has important interpersonal and social goals as well. For example, socialization among children of all castes cannot be measured on an individual basis.

Without doubt, resources should be used judiciously. Cost-benefit analysis should be done after taking into account a full range of benefits of the program, and not by merely looking at individual responses to a narrow range of indicators. Social goals cannot be attained in short time spans and they would be missed if organizations are expected to show results within six months. In other words, SFPs should be broadly conceived and designed in a way that can deliver social as well as individual goals. Further, care should be taken to ensure that targeting children does not lead to stigmatization, which would have adverse consequences for the child.

Within these considerations, it is possible to use resources judiciously and develop sound interventions. Tamil Nadu, for example, has a simple self-selection process in which parents are asked to enroll their children if they wish to. This provides a simple method for excluding richer children who may not need the program. A scheme like this may have some errors of inclusion from the perspective of targeting, but it will be far superior in avoiding errors of exclusion that are more serious for SFPs. It is important to recognize that this scheme is based on the fact that wealthier parents overwhelmingly enroll their children in private schools in India, and so including a few children who are not in need may not be of much financial consequence to the SFP. In most parts of India, private schools are not a part of the government program. In a rights-based system, care should be taken to make it possible for excluded children to contest it and be considered for the program.

RECOMMENDATIONS AND CONCLUSION

School feeding should be recognized as an essential component of the right to food and should be made an entitlement of every child in need. The SFP thus created should assist the full physical, mental, emotional, and social development of the child in consonance with the overall vision created by human rights law and principles. Specifically, the SFP should be designed to (1) eliminate classroom hunger, (2) provide adequate nutrition, (3) encourage school participation, and (4) promote social and gender equality.

This should be implemented through a global school feeding program offered in partnership among nations. Efforts of national and local governments should be complemented by the global society in order to create a far-reaching SFP. Depending on the capacity of local governments, global support can be in the form of capital costs; a part of operating costs; sharing of expertise; or provision of specific components of the program such as deworming tablets, micronutrient supplements, water treatment plants, food grains, and so on.

The need to clarify global obligations has been discussed across all chapters in this book. A global treaty on school feeding would enable the mobilization of financial resources. At the same time an international treaty on an issue like this has the potential to foster political will and public participation that could make the crucial difference between success and failure. For the international community and in most countries, the right to food now has a merely symbolic existence. To avoid cynicism about these rights, it is time to give them a concrete content and to take bold measures toward ensuring the realization of the right. A rights-based global school feeding program would make a major contribution to the realization of the human right to adequate food for all.

REFERENCES

Atkins, P. J., and Ian R. Bowler. 2001. *Food in Society: Economy, Culture, Geography.* New York: Hodder Arnold.

Drèze, Jean, and Amartya Kumar Sen. 1989. *Hunger and Public Action.* Oxford: Clarendon Press.

Drèze, Jean, and Aparajita Goyal. 2003. "The Future of Mid-day Meals." *Economic and Political Weekly* (1 November): 4673. www.epw.org.in/articles/2003/11/6447 .pdf.

Eide, Asbjørn, Catarina Krause, and Allan Rosas. 2001. *Economic, Social and Cultural Rights: A Textbook.* 2nd rev. ed. Dordrecht and London: M. Nijhoff.

FAO (Food and Agriculture Organization of the United Nations). 1998. "Implementing the Right to Food in National Legislation." In *The Right to Food in Theory and Practice*, ed. FAO Legal Office. Rome: FAO. www.fao.org/docrep/w9990e/w9990e00 .htm.

Guha-Khasnobis, Basudeb, and S. Vivek. 2005. *Rights-based Approach to Development: Lessons from the Right to Food Movement.* Paper presented at Conference on Hunger and Food Security, Jaipur.

Nestle, Marion. 2002. *Food Politics: How the Food Industry Influences Nutrition and Health.* California Studies in Food and Culture. Berkeley: University of California Press.

Right to Food Campaign. 2006. "Legal Action: Introduction." www.righttofoodindia
.org/case/case.html.

Sen, Amartya. 1995. "The Political Economy of Targeting." In *Public Spending and the Poor: Theory and Evidence*, eds. Dominique Van de Walle and Kimberly Nead, Baltimore: Johns Hopkins University Press.

Sen, Amartya. 2000. *Development as Freedom*. New York: Knopf.

Thorat, Sukhdeo, and Joel Lee. 2005. "Caste Discrimination and Food Security Programs." *Economic and Political Weekly* (24 September).

UN CESCR (United Nations Committee on Economic, Social and Cultural Rights). 1999. *Substantive Issues Arising in the Implementation of the International Covenant on Economic, Social and Cultural Rights*. General Comment 12. Geneva: ECOSOC. E/C.12/1999/5. www.unhchr.ch/tbs/doc.nsf/(Symbol)/3d02758c707031d58025 677f003b73b9?Opendocument.

WFP (World Food Programme). 2005. *Global School Feeding Report 2005*. Rome: WFP.

Witt, Doris. 1999. *Black Hunger: Food and the Politics of U.S. Identity*. Race and American Culture. New York: Oxford University Press.

World Bank. 2006. *Repositioning Nutrition as Central to Development: A Strategy for Large-scale Action*. Directions in development. Washington DC: World Bank.

9

Reflections

George Kent

We have been exploring global obligations relating to the human right to adequate food. The underlying motivation has been to find a way to get the global community to be more responsive to the major forms of malnutrition throughout the world. We have no breakthrough solutions, but we can offer some reflections on the issue.

LEGAL OBLIGATIONS

The world has gone through many phases and fashions in addressing problems of malnutrition (Jonsson 2007). Early on, the answer was simple: more food. Soon we got more sophisticated and differentiated among types of food: the answer became more protein or more calories or more micronutrients. Then we began to see that handout programs had disadvantages, and we promoted livelihood programs, teaching people to fish instead of handing them a fish. Then we discovered that many poor people did not have a place to fish, and we began to analyze the political economy of hunger, seeing that it was at its root a matter of poverty and power differentials.

We now see that the problem is not simply one of unconnected units such as families or nations, but rather that the problems of poverty and hunger have a lot to do with the social systems and the quality of relationships. Trade, for example, may lift some people, but often it leaves others behind.

The level of concern that people show for the well-being of others, especially distant others, is low. They are others, not part of "us." The rhetoric may sound promising, but the level of action tells us that the rhetoric is misleading. The goals set at frequent global summits are not taken seriously. It is not that global strategies have failed, but rather that there never has been a global strategy that could seriously be expected to achieve the goal of ending hunger and other major forms of malnutrition.

Many agree that we all have some moral responsibility to the distant needy. However, there is great reluctance to make a solid commitment to care for them. The consequences are evident: the charity approach has great value, but it is has not been sufficient to keep large numbers of people from misery. Some moral responsibilities to assist ought to be raised to legal obligations. To offer an analogy, at an early stage a village might have no established ambulance service, and simply deal with emergencies on an ad hoc basis, as they arise. At an intermediate stage they might have a volunteer ambulance service funded by donations. At an advanced stage they will see the need to levy taxes in order to regularize the ambulance service that is provided. At this stage the people recognize and accept these taxes as an obligation.

Some responsibilities can be clarified by turning them into legal obligations, whether locally, nationally, or globally. Human rights law says that states have the primary obligation for ensuring the realization of the human right to adequate food for people living under their jurisdiction. The obligations of states to people living outside their jurisdictions are not entirely clear.

Moreover, international law has not plainly established the "legal personality" of the entity we describe as the global-community-taken-as-a-whole. Global obligations can be clarified through international legal deliberations of the sort used in negotiating international treaties or in the process leading up to the right-to-food guidelines (FAO 2006). Through such a process, the global community should be recognized, and it should be assigned specific legal obligations. It should be acknowledged that the global community has an obligation to ensure the realization of all human rights for all people, by supporting the efforts of the primary parties that carry this responsibility, the states, and also by providing some kinds of support directly to the people of those states whose governments fail them. The exact character and extent of this obligatory support remains to be worked out.

In clarifying the obligations of the global community, it is necessary to speak about the obligations of all parties that act globally, including states, international agencies, and business enterprises. Illustrating this point, in chapter 4 Mike Brady examines the obligations of corporations, and in chapter 7 Marc Cohen and Anitha Ramanna consider the obligations of seed companies, research organizations, and other bodies. Each international actor has distinct obligations, depending on the particular role it plays.

As explained in chapter 3 by Federica Donati and Margret Vidar, apart from the requirement to provide assistance there are also other types of obligations, such as the obligation to not discriminate in the provision of assistance. At times international assistance relating to food and nutrition appears to be provided in discriminatory ways, a situation that needs to be corrected. There is also the obligation to do no harm, based on the obligation to respect. No global actors should do anything that interferes with the capacity of states to ensure the realization of their people's right to food or any other human rights. The World Bank's structural adjustment agreements have been shown to contribute to the violation of human rights (Abouharb and Cingranelli 2006), and its policies have interfered with the human right to free primary education (Tomaševski 2006). Many feel that structural adjustment programs have resulted in the violation of the human right to adequate food.

In chapter 3, Donati and Vidar highlight the distinction between the law as it currently exists, *de lege lata,* and the law as we might wish it to be, *de lege ferenda.* This book is mainly about the law as we might wish it to be. There is a gray area in between that results from the fact that we tend to interpret *de lege lata* in ways we would like it to be. Where there is widespread agreement on the interpretation, often it can be described as an elaboration of existing law. Where there are serious disagreements about what the law means, there is a need for new law to resolve the differences. This book is motivated by a sense that we need new and better law regarding the human rights obligations of the global community.

Current international human rights law says that states parties to the major treaties are obligated to cooperate with other states and to provide assistance to states that are needy. However, the law is not yet clear on the extent to which any particular state, or the collectivity of states, or the collectivity of all global actors, is obligated to provide assistance. Presently, the prevailing view appears to be that providing some assistance is sufficient to meet the requirements. Broadly, the argument here (as in chapter 1) is that the global community should be seen as obligated to provide assistance either up to the point that the right is realized everywhere or until the effort reaches the limits of the global community's capacity to provide assistance. It is not yet clear how those limits should be specified, but it is evident that no human rights should be realized in ways that violate other human rights, whether for the same person or for other people. There should be clear obligations to assist the needy, and also clear limits to those obligations. There is as yet no consensus on this as a point of principle, and much work remains to be done in defining the key terms in practical ways.

The exploration of what human rights law ought to say about the obligations of the global community with regard to the right to food and with regard to human rights generally should be carried further, in various settings.

A good place to start would be for the United Nations Committee on Economic, Social and Cultural Rights to conduct a Day of Discussion on Obligations of the Global Community, and follow that with a General Comment on the theme. Perhaps an Optional Protocol on Global Obligations could be prepared to clarify those aspects of the International Covenant on Economic, Social and Cultural Rights.

THE SOURCES OF OBLIGATION

Of the many things the global community *could* do about malnutrition, what *must* it do? Where does obligation come from? Setting aside the legalisms, the view taken here is that generally, if you have the capacity to protect someone from great harm, or you can deliver great benefits, and you can do that at small cost or risk to yourself, then you are obligated to do so. Obligations to others derive partly from having the capacity to produce large benefits for others at little cost to oneself. In chapters 5 and 6, for example, Arun Gupta and Michael Latham show that the programs they advocate would produce large gains in health status at little monetary cost.

In some cases these are recurrent costs, but in others—such as the case of measles, as described by Latham—it is conceivable that a large surge of effort could bring the problem to a permanent end, comparable to the global victory over smallpox. Effective assistance for economic development is supposed to be of this character. A surge of investment should be able to launch self-sustaining vigorous economic activity, so that further assistance becomes unnecessary. We could use many more successes of this sort.

Many of the obligations we face—such as taxes and military service and obeying traffic rules—have been formulated by our societies and our governments. In principle we get to participate in their formulation, especially in democracies, but when we come right down to it, many of our daily obligations, such as speed limits and tax bills, feel like they are imposed on us from outside. In some cases we have made clear choices to accept obligations, as in our marriage vows or our mortgage contracts, for example.

For powerful people and powerful countries, the practical truth is that obligations cannot be imposed. The powerful are obligated to the extent that they agree to be obligated. Indeed, the basic principle of international law is that a country becomes obligated in accordance with a particular international treaty if and when it ratifies that treaty. There are conditions under which countries are said to be obligated even when they have not ratified, but as a practical matter, on important issues, countries—especially powerful countries—usually must agree to be obligated.

Thus there are major global summits and extended international negotiations to work out treaties. It is in these contexts that nations work out what commitments they are willing to make. Thus, one should not think of obligations as something imposed by outside agents. Paradoxically, the question is, what do countries *agree to be obligated* to do?

We can agree with analysts who insist that large corporations ought to be held accountable by independent and strong governments (e.g., Richter 2001), but in the end we have to recognize the limits of possibility. When nations or corporations or international agencies are so powerful as to be literally out of the control of others, we have to ask what commitments are such bodies, and others, willing to make? And we have to ask who will hold them accountable to these standards?

This submission to the realities of politics means shifting from the idea that there are fundamental moral principles that ought to bind people and nations to the idea that commitments can be worked out as a matter of negotiations, in a social contract approach to the ordering of society. However, there is a difference. Ordinary contracts are about offering benefits to others in exchange for benefits to oneself. In contrast, in the sense the term is used here, commitments are made to take up global obligations in relation to human rights not so much because of anticipation of reciprocal benefits but mainly out of a sense of moral responsibility, based on compassion and concern for the well-being of others. Of course in practice the two kinds of motivations are often mixed.

CAPACITY AND WILL

Much attention is now being given to capacity building in development and human rights work. In one example, the International Food Policy Research Institute (IFPRI) addresses the issue in their article "Building Local Skills and Knowledge for Food Security" (IFPRI 2005). Capacity building generally refers to strengthening the skills and other resources needed to reach goals, whether in governments, local communities, or individuals. Moral philosophers such as Amartya Sen and Martha Nussbaum take it to a deeper level, arguing that poverty is not about money so much as it is about the deprivation of basic capabilities. Thus capacity building is crucial to development and to the realization of human rights (Nussbaum 2006; Sen 2000).

Global agencies tend to assume that national leaders and others down the line are anxious to address nutrition issues and only need a bit of help. Social programs often fail because they naively assume that all of the intended actors share the authors' motivations and goals and are only waiting to be shown the way. However, the fact is that not everyone really wants to do what needs to be done to achieve development or the ending of hunger, poverty, or particular diseases. Sometimes the will is not there.

Some national governments may place great emphasis on building capacity in local communities as a way of evading their own responsibilities. It may be argued that, similarly, the global community has been evading its responsibilities by focusing on deficiencies at local and national levels.

The world as a whole has plenty of capacity in terms of material resources and knowledge, but it shows little interest in really addressing the global malnutrition problem. Whether at local, national, or global levels, concern about capacity should be matched by a comparable concern for the adequacy of the motivation to address the issues.

When it is not handled well, capacity building can in effect turn into a blame-the-victim exercise, finding the deficiencies only in the needy themselves and not in the larger social system in which they are embedded. Often there is a failure to recognize that the poor lack decent opportunities in which to apply their skills. In fact the conditions of the needy may be largely due to the failures of others, especially the more powerful, to do what they should be doing. The powerful need to build the capacity to critically assess their own actions as well as the actions of others.

In "The $10 Solution" in the January 15, 2007, issue of *Time* magazine, Jeffrey Sachs, director of the Earth Institute at Columbia University and leading advocate of the Millennium Development Project, wrote calling on the rich people of the world to each give about three dollars a year to buy malaria-preventing bed nets for Africans. Most people would have read his article as being about Africa's poverty. It can also be read as being about the poverty of global governance. What sort of world is this that cannot organize itself well enough and commit itself deeply enough to buy ten-dollar bed nets to save the lives of its poorest people?

BUILDING GLOBAL CAPACITY

When international agencies press for increasing capacity at the national level, they often seem to avoid the question: What are the responsibilities of the global community in development and in ensuring the realization of human rights? No one doubts that, viewed globally, the primary responsibility for these things lies at the national level, and work should be undertaken to strengthen capacity at the national level. At the same time we must recognize that some nations either cannot or will not do what needs to be done, and the global level itself has distinct responsibilities.

Ultimately, our collective moral responsibility is not to nations but to people. This means that we must not write off people who live in nations whose governments, for whatever reason, lack the capacity or the will to ensure their own people's development and the realization of all their human rights. What then are the responsibilities of the global community? Those responsibilities should be plainly articulated and acknowledged. This book has attempted to clarify global obligations relating to the human right to adequate food.

If we agree that there are global obligations, then just as there is a need for building capacity at the local and national levels, there is also a need for building capacity among policy makers in the global community. IFPRI's article on capacity building opens by saying:

> Experts are increasingly aware that efforts to promote development and improve food security in poor countries cannot succeed in the long run without well-qualified local individuals and institutions. (IFPRI 2005)

We should consider the mirror-image sentence as well:

> Experts in local communities are increasingly aware that efforts to promote development and improve food security in poor countries cannot succeed in the long run without well-qualified individuals and institutions at regional and global levels.

We normally think of the major international organizations as sources of knowledge and skills that are deployed by them to facilitate development of the poor countries of the world. However, these institutions can themselves be sites of development, places in which people at the high end work at improving their capacities and their understandings of how the world works. To illustrate, the title of a recent book, *The Search for Empowerment: Social Capital as Idea and Practice at the World Bank*, at first appears to be just another one of those manuals through which the bank tries to fix the world around it, but on closer examination we see that it is really about how to fix the bank itself (Bebbington et al. 2006).

The Office of the United Nations High Commissioner for Human Rights has published the *Handbook on National Human Rights Plans of Action* (UN OHCHR 2002). Why is there no counterpart *Handbook on Global Human Rights Plans of Action*?

Similarly, there is an *Economic, Social and Cultural Rights: Handbook for National Human Rights Institutions* (UN OHCHR 2005). Why is there no corresponding handbook for global human rights institutions?

The World Health Organization (WHO) has been preparing its *Planning Guide for National Implementation of the Global Strategy for Infant and Young Child Feeding* (WHO 2006). Where is the planning guide for global implementation?

The United Nations Children's Fund (UNICEF) calls for the establishment of a nutrition "safety net" as a central component of national policies (UNICEF 2006). Why not have a global nutrition safety net as well?

The work of building capacity is sometimes viewed as the need for those with knowledge and skills to share them with those who need those things.

We should move toward more of a partnership model, based on learning and planning together about how to deal with the problems in which we are embedded together. We should recall the comment attributed to an aboriginal Australian woman, Lila Watson, upon greeting a visitor, probably dressed in a suit: "If you have come to help me, you are wasting your time, but if you have come because your liberation is bound up with mine, then let us work together."

Capacity building, like other forms of teaching/learning, should be a mutual exercise. Similarly, strategic planning activity should engage not only high-level officials but also people from civil society and nongovernmental organizations. It should include representatives of the people for whom these plans are made. In human rights work, as in development work, there is a need for partnership between policy makers at the top and the intended beneficiaries, ordinary people at ground level. This does not mean having people at the top point to deficiencies at the bottom so that they can instruct people how to perform. After all, local people also can point to deficiencies in others and highlight the need for *them* to do things differently.

The present global system does not produce good results in relation to many human rights. This is explained in part by the simple fact that there is no effective system of global governance in place that would be capable of dealing with the problems. There is a lack of institutional capacity. This means that there is a positive obligation to create the forms of global governance that would be required if all human rights of all people are to be realized.

BUILDING GLOBAL WILL: WHY END HUNGER?

The contributors to this book are realistic and know that nation-states and international agencies will not make more vigorous commitments to addressing global malnutrition simply because some analysts have made arguments for why they should do that. It is only when people and agencies themselves see clear and compelling reasons for doing something that they will make strong commitments to it. We come then to the crucial question: *Why* end hunger and other forms of malnutrition?

Most people will want to prevent or remedy their own serious malnutrition or that of their family members. The puzzle raised here is why any of us should want to deal with the malnutrition problems of others, especially distant others whom we don't know and will never meet.

Many view the alleviation of malnutrition as a kind of economic investment. The World Bank identifies three major reasons for intervening to reduce malnutrition:

- high economic returns
- high impact on economic growth
- poverty reduction (World Bank 2006, 1)

The World Bank, being a bank, says, "the returns to investing in nutrition are very high." It shows that, indeed, in many cases, small inputs yield large outputs. However, there is little discussion about who is to do the investing and who is to get the returns. If I am told that if I invest a thousand dollars in some project, you will get fantastic returns from it, I don't really have much incentive to make that investment. If you were my brother or my uncle, I might consider the investment, but if you were a complete stranger, I would walk away from this so-called opportunity.

The World Bank says that countries have not invested enough, but at the same time it acknowledges that for the bank itself, "between 2000 and 2004 its investments in the short route interventions that improve nutrition fastest amounted to not more than 3.8 percent of its lending for human development—and less than 0.7 percent of total World Bank lending" (World Bank 2006, 16, 128). Surely, if the global community wants individual countries to devote more of their scarce resources to addressing problems of malnutrition, the global agencies and the donors of official development assistance should follow the same advice.

The World Bank believes that calculations of the benefits from improving nutrition would help to persuade national governments to increase their commitments to nutrition programs (World Bank 2006, 107–9). If that can be expected to work at the national level, why doesn't this approach work globally, convincing the global community to invest more in nutrition? As the bank observes, "The development community, and the world as a whole, has consistently failed to address malnutrition over the past decades" (World Bank 2006, 128).

Some say there are good instrumental reasons for ending hunger. We are told people who are not malnourished can become more productive workers. This seems to imply that when people live in places of high unemployment and there is little opportunity to do productive work, we might as well ignore their hunger. It also suggests that we should ignore those who are disabled. Arguably, in "realistic" economic terms, we should recognize that many people who are hungry are liabilities, not assets. Why not just abandon them?

Perhaps one good reason to end hunger is to reduce threats to our security:

At the international level, there appears to be a growing recognition of the threat to peace and security posed by hunger and extreme deprivation. Local conflicts over scarce resources can quickly spread into regional conflicts with massive destabilising impacts, preventing any serious consideration of long-term food security issues in the affected countries. It is in the self-interest of all countries to avoid such situations. (FAO Committee on World Food Security 2001, para. 42)

The Millennium Development Project also has expressed concern that people who are poor and hungry might eventually rise up and threaten those who are well off (UN Millennium Project 2005b, 6–8).

Another argument for reducing malnutrition in poorer countries is that it would help to stem the flow of migrants from those countries.

Some argue that reducing hunger in the world would help to reduce environmental damage by reducing population growth rates (Eckholm 1982).

In chapter 6, Michael Latham makes the argument that ending measles everywhere would be of considerable economic benefit to the north. He says:

As long as measles has not been eradicated worldwide, it remains necessary for people in industrialized countries (where measles transmission has been largely eliminated) to continue measles vaccination and surveillance. This is very costly, and these costs would end if measles were eradicated worldwide. . . . With worldwide measles eradication, U.S. savings could be close to $800 million a year.

This is convincing. However, Latham does not offer comparable arguments about benefits to the north from eradication of intestinal worms and malaria. This does not mean that the north should ignore worms and malaria, but the reality is that they probably get less attention precisely because they don't threaten northerners. One observer argues, "As fatal illnesses go, AIDS is the best one for a poor person to catch because rich people get it too" (Rosenberg 2006).

It is useful to point out that improving people's nutrition status can lead to other good things, whether for "them" or for "us." However, the benefits to "us" of ending hunger for "them" may not be sufficiently compelling. Moreover, emphasizing the instrumental value may lead to neglect of the core intrinsic value, the idea that improving people's nutrition status is a good thing in itself. Most of us feed our children because it is the right thing to do, not because it will lead to something else. Having healthy, well-nourished children and adults is good in itself. We should not have to explain why.

There are reasons to not end hunger. In his *A Dissertation on the Poor Laws* in England of 1786, Joseph Townsend observed that for many, hunger provides the motivation to work:

Hunger is not only a peaceable, silent, unremitted pressure, but, as the most natural motive to industry and labour, it calls forth the most powerful exertions; and, when satisfied by the free bounty of another, lays a lasting and sure foundation for good will and gratitude. (Townsend 1786)

The hunger "problem" helps to ensure that many people will not only work, but will work cheaply. That is surely a blessing to those who benefit from the fruits of their labor.

Allowing hunger to persist may yield other benefits as well. Some believe that hunger helps to protect the world from runaway population growth. Ending hunger through assistance programs can be very costly, and there are always other good ways in which we could employ our limited resources. Some believe that generous social welfare programs produce waves of migration to the areas with the most generous handouts.

Why should I invest in ending your malnutrition? Perhaps I might get some economic returns from the investment. For example, if I was your employer, better meals might allow you to work more productively. Or perhaps I have reason to believe that if you were healthier, you would purchase more of the products I produce. However, as suggested above, often the prospects for such direct returns are slim. It may be that if you get better food you will be less motivated to work hard.

Some of the arguments for and against working to address malnutrition in all its forms are based on questionable claims of fact. More importantly, much of the reasoning is morally defective because it is based mainly on consideration of effects on our own welfare, our own interests. Some of the arguments show little concern for the well-being of the hungry themselves. If we all act simply as narrowly self-interested *homo economicus*, there is no really convincing reason to work to end hunger in the world.

Another possible reason for me to "invest" in ending your malnutrition is that I care about you. If you were my child or my spouse or my uncle, I might go to considerable lengths to improve your nutrition status. Of course if you were my second cousin twice removed, I might not be so eager to help.

What if you were not a relative but a member of my community? We can define *community* as a group of people with a particularly high level of concern for one another's well-being. On that basis, I would be willing to help out others in my community who were in need, by definition. My community is a cluster of people whom I regard as part of "us." Many people draw sharp lines between "us" and "them," or between "my people" and "those others." For some, it is a more gradual thing, with the level of caring generally diminishing with greater distance.

Earlier I said that fundamentally the hunger problem is the poverty problem. However, poverty alone is not a sufficient explanation. After all, the world as a whole is not poor. Even more fundamentally, malnutrition exists and persists because of the powerlessness of the poor and the indifference of the rich. There are three key points:

- *Disjunction.* Hunger and other major forms of malnutrition persist largely because the people who have the power to solve the problem are not the ones who have the problem.

- *Material interests.* The powerful serve mainly the powerful, not the powerless, because the powerless cannot do much for the benefit of the powerful.
- *Compassion.* On the whole, the people who have the power do not have much compassion for the powerless.

The powerful have the capacity but not the will to address the problem adequately, while the powerless have the will but not the capacity. The lack of capacity comes through with brutal clarity when we see many small farmers in India committing suicide because they cannot keep up with their debts (Chu 2006; Frontline/World 2006; Shiva 2004).

Former U.S. senator George McGovern believes that ending hunger would be a good deal:

> Anyone who looks honestly at world hunger and measures the cost of ending it for all time will conclude that this is a bargain well worth seizing. More often than not, those who look at the problem and the cost of its solution will wonder why humanity didn't resolve it long ago. (McGovern 2001, 15)

The explanation for the failure to act should now be clear. While we may wish it were otherwise, it is factually a mistake to view humanity as one. We are divided, so it matters that the costs of ending hunger would go to one group while the benefits would go to another.

Hunger could be ended if the people who have the power cared more about the people who have the problem, but the evidence is clear: they don't care enough. The problem is evident in the forlorn appeals of the World Food Programme (WFP) for money to feed the hungry. In May 2006, for example, the WFP actually had to cut in half the meager rations for displaced people in Darfur, Sudan. On average, since 1992, the global Consolidated Appeals Process for humanitarian assistance has received only about two-thirds of what it has requested (UN OCHA 2006).

Overall, the level of concern in rich countries for development in poor countries is indicated by the fact that (as pointed out in chapter 1) in 2005 official development assistance reached an all-time high that amounted to only 0.33 percent of the combined gross national income of the donor countries (UN ECOSOC 2006, para. 2). Much of the increase has been in terms of debt relief rather than new funds. Remarkably, the fifty least-developed countries receive only about one-third of all aid flows (UN Department of Economic and Social Affairs 2006, 22). The largest amount for any single country was for Iraq, over $3 billion (OECD 2006). ActionAid International, a nongovernmental organization, has shown that much of international assistance is "phantom aid." Much of what is pledged is not delivered. About a quarter of what is delivered goes to consultants (ActionAid

2006). CARE found that much of the more than $5 billion a year that goes to help Africa deal with its food situation is wasted (CARE 2006).

On the whole, the rich really don't care much about the poor. The consequences are captured succinctly in the title of a 2004 study: *Fatal Indifference: The G8, Africa and Global Health* (Labonte et al. 2004). The chapter on "Nutrition, Food Security and Biotechnology" concludes with the understated observation, "The lack of explicit commitments, goals and strategies related to enhanced food security, especially in the regions of the world where undernourishment is most prevalent, is disturbing" (p. 15).

International agencies have suggested ways to strengthen commitments of poor countries' governments for dealing with malnutrition (FAO Committee on World Food Security 2001; Heaver 2005; World Bank 2006, 121–22). Perhaps we should turn the question around, and ask how the commitment of the global community itself might be strengthened.

Many argue that we ought to care more, but the argument has not been compelling. We do not yet have a strong community at the global level. Many poor people, and even entire countries, are abandoned to their fate. A great deal of research has been done on *how* the different forms of malnutrition could be addressed. Now we need more attention to the question of *why* they should be addressed. What would induce the global community to embrace the obligation to end hunger and other major forms of malnutrition in the world?

The disjunction between those who have the problems and those who have the power to solve them is seen both within countries and globally. The lack of caring within countries is evident when we see widespread malnutrition side-by-side with widespread wealth.

There are good signs when it comes to short-term disaster relief and other sorts of humanitarian assistance, but the levels of international assistance remain low in relation to the levels of need. In a genuinely caring global community, people would not be left to live and die in intolerable conditions in any part of the globe.

The point is not simply that our sharing the planet intertwines our separate fates. That is only a mechanical connection. Rather, the issue is shared feeling, the feeling that your joy is my joy and that even if I am safe, any harm that comes to you hurts me. In the end, there is only one good reason to end hunger: we care about each other. Ending hunger is the right thing to do. As former World Bank president James Wolfensohn said, "It is not a matter of return on investment, but how we act in the world" (Vesely 2006).

We should be concerned with ending serious malnutrition worldwide for its own sake, and not only because it might somehow produce benefits for us. People should be able to live in dignity because they are people. No other reasons should be necessary. The main reason for ending hunger in the world is that it is not right for people to remain hungry. No other reason should be necessary. Any other reason is inadequate.

STRATEGIZING TO BUILD GLOBAL COMMITMENT

Normally the commitment comes first, and then the action plan is worked out. After all, there is no point in working out the details about how to build that bridge across the river if the town council has not yet committed the funding to do the job. However, it may be that if you formulate a clear and convincing action plan first, you could use that to get the commitment. The town council and everyone else might be more receptive to the bridge proposal if they were presented with a detailed plan, and not just a vague idea.

Thus, strategizing may be a feasible alternative to the commitment-first approach. People and nations are more likely to make commitments to addressing global malnutrition if it can be shown convincingly that it would be possible to produce large benefits to others at little cost.

The primary responsibility for ensuring the realization of human rights lies with states, and thus the national governments that represent them. Strategic planning at the global level is not a substitute for planning at the national level; rather, global planning should complement and support planning at the national level.

The *Planning Guide for National Implementation of the Global Strategy for Infant and Young Child Feeding* (WHO 2006) suggests an approach. The guide proposes a seven-step process, comparable to many other similar guides to planning:

Step 1. Identify and orient key stakeholders and prepare for developing a comprehensive strategy.
Step 2. Assess and analyze the local situation.
Step 3. Define preliminary national objectives.
Step 4. Identify and prioritize actions.
Step 5. Develop a national strategy.
Step 6. Develop a national plan of action.
Step 7. Implement and monitor.

Each of these steps could be adapted to guide the planning of actions to be taken by the global community. The major purpose of the planning at the global level would be to support efforts at the national level. However, the global effort also should look after the interests of those people whose national governments either cannot or choose not to do what needs to be done for them.

Planning at the regional level can make an important contribution by serving as a bridge between national level and global level strategic planning.

The global planners would have to address many difficult issues. As in any other situation in which assistance is offered (e.g., social welfare programs), means must be found to ensure that those who receive assistance do not exaggerate their needs in order to obtain more assistance. Assistance must be provided in ways that are empowering, not disempowering.

It would be useful to focus the strategic thinking initially on an area in which there is a high level of need, high level of knowledge, and low cost for the delivery of services that would have a high positive impact. For example, one could start with the focus established for the Millennium Development Project's Goal 1, centering on the achievement of a sharp reduction in the number of underweight children throughout the world (UN Millennium Project 2005a). Or some other initial focus might be chosen, such as working for the promotion of better methods of infant feeding, as proposed by Arun Gupta in chapter 5 of this book, or for the elimination of malaria, measles, and worms, as suggested by Michael Latham in chapter 6. There are many forms of malnutrition that constitute major public health problems and should be addressed globally as well as locally.

The Copenhagen Consensus group did a careful study of which global problems should be addressed with highest priority (Lomborg 2004; Copenhagen Consensus Center 2006). It is useful to have the group's guidance in formulating priorities. Undoubtedly, more good could be done if global resources were allocated differently. However, the group's analysis was based on the concept that there is a single pool of resources to be allocated among different possible programs. The current reality is that different issues have different potentials for attracting funding. There is no central decision-making body with the power to allocate a global pool of resources.

There are several different nutrition problems of global importance. Different projects would draw on different pools of resources. If funds are made available for, say, the fortification of foods or the iodization of salt, and those funds are not fungible in the sense that they might be allocated to some other project, then one should go ahead with the planning for those projects and look elsewhere for funds for other projects.

Thus, it would be sensible to undertake strategic planning to deal simultaneously with several different nutrition problems of global importance. The planning and the implementation for each of them could be carried out separately, but with coordination among them. The approach could be comparable to that used for addressing the eight goals of the Millennium Development Project, except that there would be well-designed, goal-directed global programs of action, and not just national programs of action.

No matter what particular goal is selected, the key point here is that it is important to formulate a serious strategy to ensure its achievement. As argued in chapter 1, the strategy should be driven by a clear vision of the sort of world that would ensure that the problem would not endlessly reappear. There would be a need for systematic monitoring of progress to ensure that the effort is on target, and there would have to be methods for redirecting the action if and when it falters. There must be a clear commitment of material and other resources, and a management body would have to be established to oversee and direct the action.

. A strategy is not simply a collection of activities; it is an organized program of action designed to reach a goal. A serious strategy is one that is expected to lead to the achievement of the goal. By this standard, few of what have been claimed to be global strategies for dealing with global problems can really be regarded as serious.

The major parties that would need to work together should plan together. The process should lead to a clear division of responsibilities among them. In negotiating this division of responsibilities, the major parties, at all levels, would work out their commitments.

For each goal, the final plan should include effective mechanisms for calling all the parties to account, to make sure they honor their commitments. In chapter 1, I pointed out that several annual reports say whether or not we are on track to achieve the various Millennium Development Goals. However, they do not link that movement to the efforts made toward those ends, whether by the developing countries or by the global community. All parties with relevant responsibilities should be held accountable. Specific monitoring and evaluation mechanisms need to be established for that purpose.

Each plan should also include effective procedures for dealing with failures of particular parties to honor their commitments. When you are building a bridge, you don't call off the project just because an electrician does not show up one morning. If you are committed to the project, you find some way to work around the obstacles. Similarly, if some agents do not do what they are supposed to do to keep children from going hungry, you find some way around that problem.

Each plan should establish that many of the jobs are to be based on performance contracting. This means that when people do not produce the results they are supposed to produce, they don't get paid, or they get fired. Their contracts should explain that.

We have spoken about the need for global resources to deal with malnutrition in terms of money, and also the need for better skills and better planning. However, planning is normally undertaken with the assumption that the proposed action program is to be embedded within the existing institutional structure. That structure also needs to be critically reviewed and changed as necessary. A recent study shows that

> today more money is being directed toward the world's poor and sick than ever before. But unless these efforts start tackling public health in general instead of narrow, disease-specific problems—and unless the brain drain from the developing world can be stopped—poor countries could be pushed even further into trouble, in yet another tale of well-intended foreign meddling gone awry. (Garrett 2007)

Vicente Navarro has sketched out his views of the ideal national health system (Navarro 2007). He is concerned not simply with the delivery of medical care, but also with the political, economic, social, and cultural determinants of health, the lifestyle determinants, and the socializing and empowering determinants. While he focuses on national systems, his approach could help us to think about the ideal global health and nutrition system. Clarifying that design would help us to appreciate the extent to which our present global health system falls short. There is a need for comprehensive institutional arrangements—local, national, regional, and global—to ensure the realization of the right to adequate food, nutrition, health, and other related rights for all.

MULTIPARTY OBLIGATIONS; MULTIPARTY PLANNING

We have argued that there is a need for clear recognition of obligations on the part of the global community in relation to nation-states, but that two-level analysis is too simple. Even the multilevel rings-of-responsibility image introduced in chapter 1 is too simple. The reality is that there are many different types of actors, intertwined in many ways, that should play a part in ensuring the realization of the human right to adequate food for all people.

There are several mechanisms for coordination at the country level, including the United Nations Development Assistance Framework (UNDAF), the Common Country Assessments (CCA), and the Poverty Reduction Strategy Papers (PRSP) (UN OHRLLS 2007). There are also many agencies that deal with nutrition issues at regional and global levels, including agencies of national governments such as foreign ministries and agencies that provide foreign aid, academic and research institutions, nongovernmental organizations, the private sector in various forms, multilateral agencies outside the United Nations, and the various agencies associated with the United Nations. Agencies that function at the global level are coordinated through several bodies, some focused on specific nutrition issues. Many of the global actors concerned with nutrition issues come together regularly under the auspices of the United Nations System Standing Committee on Nutrition (SCN).

To the extent that its members are willing, SCN could serve as the major global forum for working out a sensible division of responsibilities among all the parties:

> The mandate of the SCN is to promote cooperation among UN agencies and partner organizations in support of community, national, regional, and international efforts to end malnutrition in all of its forms in this generation. It will do this by refining the direction, increasing the scale and strengthening the coherence and impact of actions against malnutrition world wide, and raise awareness of nutrition problems and mobilize commitment to solve them at global, regional and national levels. (UN SCN 2006a)

The SCN's Strategic Framework, available at its website, is about the functioning of the SCN itself, not about the action plans to be carried out in the field. More relevant here is the Action Plan 2006–2010 and Biennium Budget 2006–2007, also available on the SCN's website. The Action Plan is organized in terms of five areas of activity, three objectives, and four targets. They speak mainly about what sort of plans and communications strategies should be formulated by a specific date, not about what nutrition outcomes should be achieved. Thus they are process oriented rather than outcome oriented. Attention should be given to both.

The SCN Action Plan says, in paragraph 10:

> The SCN is not in itself an implementing agency. It is a forum in which the relevant UN agencies come together to harmonize their nutrition policies and programmes, coordinate activities, and promote *joint action*, in partnership and common cause with representatives of national governments (the Bilateral Partners) and of non-government organizations (the NGOs/CSOs). (UN SCN 2006b)

That is certainly needed. The question, then, is what would be the best way to organize this work?

The present approach is based on strengthening the country-level planning processes, with the UN agencies acting through the resident UN coordinator. Each of the UN agencies involved uses small amounts of donor funds to help steer national resources into national programs on issues such as salt iodization or breastfeeding promotion. The SCN's approach emphasizes the building of national capacities for planning and for carrying out these programs.

Many poor countries have serious problems of malnutrition because they are lacking in capacity and/or will. Their capacities can be increased to some degree, but in many cases the local resources are simply inadequate to do the job that is needed within a reasonable time frame. The approach that focuses on capacity building in poor countries should not become a method by which the global community as a whole avoids carrying its share of the burden.

The Strategic Framework and Action Plan cover a broad variety of SCN activities, perhaps too broad. It might be useful for the SCN to focus more decisively on facilitating strategic planning by its affiliated agencies to address malnutrition worldwide in all its forms, in order to ensure realization of the human right to adequate food for all people. This would mean helping to set the agenda, and finding funds, space, and technical advice to support the joint strategic planning process.

Many key actors concerned with food and nutrition issues come together regularly under the auspices of the SCN. However, the SCN works mainly with high-level players from national governments, global agencies, and civil society; it does not reach to the inner rings of responsibility. Strategic planning to deal with any particular nutrition problem should be not only multiparty but also multilevel. The inclusion of representatives from all levels can help to ensure that the strategic planning exercise is also a significant educational and capacity building exercise for all who are involved. Multilevel planning can help to overcome the massive disjunction between rich and poor, and it can facilitate capacity building through mutual learning.

Such efforts should formulate concrete plans of action. This should include clarifying the division of tasks among the different parties, and clarifying the means for financing. Much can be learned from experience in dealing with other problems of global scale. For example, the idea of assessments of "fair shares" of the costs of addressing HIV/AIDS might be adapted to programs for dealing with specific nutrition issues (Kates and Lief 2006). The fair share concept does not go so far as imposing obligatory taxlike assessments, but it moves in that direction.

As indicated earlier, the SCN's action areas presently are defined mainly in process terms. The SCN's work might be funded more readily if it were defined explicitly in terms of nutrition goals. For example, a compelling strategy for sharply reducing the proportion of underweight young children in the world by 2015 probably would attract more funds than would goals that were described broadly in terms of advocacy, communication, assessment, and so on. The goal of the work should emphasize the ends in mind, not the means.

To illustrate, reducing the proportion of underweight young children could be a sensible focus, particularly since it was the core of Millennium Project's Goal 1 and its Hunger Task Force. Paragraph 28 of SCN's Action Plan recognizes that SCN provided a good deal of input to that task force, and says that turning the Millennium Project's proposal for halving hunger into reality should be one of the main aims of the new SCN Task Force on Development of Integrated Approaches. It would be useful if SCN organized a joint planning effort to carry forward the work started by the Hunger Task Force, in coordination with the WFP and UNICEF's End Childhood Hunger and Undernutrition Initiative (ECHUI) (UNICEF 2007). As Paragraph 28 of the SCN Action Plan suggests, if it is handled well, work on reducing underweight among young children could serve as a model for dealing with other major nutrition problems.

On the basis of this book's explorations, we can say that at the very least there is a moral obligation on the part of the global community to undertake serious planning to address the major forms of malnutrition. If the human right to adequate food means anything at the global level, surely it must mean this.

Planning is a useful thing to pursue, but we have to acknowledge that impact of this effort is likely to be limited. Powerful people do things because they want to do them, not because some law or some analyst says they should. When it comes to looking after the well-being of others, people do not care because they have obligations. They accept obligations because they care.

The major conclusion is straightforward and inescapable: All of us should act decisively to end hunger and other forms of malnutrition in the world for one major reason—it is the right thing to do.

EMPHASIZING RIGHTS AND DUTIES

In planning effective nutrition programs, whether locally, nationally, or globally, it is important to be clear about the rights of the rights holders and the duties of the duty bearers. One of the basic arguments of the rights approach to planning is that beyond having good intentions to deliver particular kinds of services, the duty bearers should explicitly recognize that people have, or should have, specific rights. There should also be mechanisms of accountability that ensure that the duty bearers do what they are supposed to do. To illustrate, in a *Breastfeeding Mothers' Bill of Rights* proposed in the state of New York, mothers would have very specific entitlements:

Before You Deliver:
The right to information free from commercial interests, which provides the nutritional, medical and psychological benefits of breastfeeding; An explanation of some of the problems a mother may encounter, and how to avoid or solve them.

In the Maternal Healthcare Facility:
The mothers' right for her baby to stay with her after delivery to facilitate beginning breastfeeding immediately; to insist the baby not receive bottle feeding; to be informed about and refuse any drugs that may dry up breastmilk; 24 hour access to the baby with the right to breastfeed at any time.

When You Leave the Maternal Healthcare Facility:
The right to refuse any gifts or take-home packets, distributed by the maternal healthcare facility, that contain commercial advertising or product samples; access to breastfeeding resources in one's community. (*Amherst Times* 2006)

Similarly, where Arun Gupta proposes, in chapter 5, a Minimum Essential Program to support breastfeeding, this should be understood as meaning not only that it would be nice if women had these services, but that they should have a right to them. Following Vivek's argument in chapter 8, global standards could be set out for school feeding programs, and the global community could accept the obligation to ensure that those standards are met (Kent 2006). Some intergovernmental organizations such as the World Food Programme and the World Bank could help with planning and other support services, while others, such as the Office of the High Commissioner for Human Rights, could ensure that they carried out their duties in relation to the human right to adequate food.

Just as there are national safety nets regarding children's nutrition and health in some countries, there could be a global safety net as well. Standards could be set for feeding programs in extreme emergency situations, with the global community ensuring that all who need it would get at least some minimum level of service. The legislation of rights would mean that specific duty bearers would have to have clear mandates to ensure that these entitlements were fulfilled. And it would mean that they could be held accountable if the rights were not realized. In this way, the assertion of rights would be empowering for the rights holders.

We normally think of rights-based social systems as operating at local or national levels, but the concept can be extended to the global level. For example, it is possible to imagine a global nutritional safety net for children, one that is designed to ensure that no child's nutritional status falls below some particular level. There could be a layered system of safety nets, with the outer ones designed to catch communities in distress, rather than individual children. The world could, for example, make a commitment that says any area in which the child mortality rate is above, say, 100, is *entitled* to whatever services are required to reduce the level to below that number. If the world wanted to do this, it could do it. There are no insurmountable technical obstacles.

This entitlement could include not only material assistance but also the services of skilled public health planners. These planners could work with local officials to make better use of locally available resources.

In a rights-based plan, the will of the duty bearers to do what needs to be done is reinforced by the creation of a strong legal mandate for the duty bearers. The rights holders must have an institutionalized capacity to call the duty bearers to account if they should falter. This can go a long way in helping to ensure that the duty bearers have the will to do the right thing.

RECOMMENDATIONS

This chapter has reviewed the nature of global obligations related to the human right to adequate food. The major recommendations for concrete action that come out of these reflections are as follows:

- The United Nations Committee on Economic, Social and Cultural Rights should clarify the external obligations of states parties to the covenant by conducting a Day of Discussion on Obligations of the Global Community and preparing a corresponding General Comment.

- The United Nations Committee on Economic, Social and Cultural Rights should monitor the global community through the states parties to the International Covenant on Economic, Social and Cultural Rights. The committee should ensure that the global obligations of the reporting nations are carried out through their foreign assistance programs, through the global agencies in which they participate, and through specific action plans that they help to formulate and implement.
- The United Nations System Standing Committee on Nutrition should facilitate multiparty, multilevel planning to formulate joint strategies for dealing with specific problems of large-scale malnutrition.
- Governmental and nongovernmental organizations concerned with food and nutrition should promote multiparty, multilevel planning to formulate joint strategies for dealing with nutrition problems of interest to them, whether on the local, national, regional, or global scale.

REFERENCES

Abouharb, M. Rodwan, and David L. Cingranelli. 2006. "The Human Rights Effects of World Bank Structural Adjustment, 1981–2000." *International Studies Quarterly* 50 (June): 233–62.

ActionAid International. 2006. *Real Aid 2: Making Technical Assistance Work.* Johannesburg, South Africa: ActionAid International. www.actionaid.org/index.asp?page_id =1120.

Amherst Times. 2006. "Krueger Introduces Breastfeeding Mothers Bill of Rights." www.lizkrueger.com/news/news214.html.

Bebbington, Anthony J., Michael Woolcock, Scott E. Guggenheim, and Elizabeth Olson. 2006. *The Search for Empowerment: Social Capital as Idea and Practice at the World Bank.* Bloomfield, CT: Kumarian Press, 2006.

CARE International UK. 2006. *Living on the Edge of Emergency—An Agenda for Change.* www.reliefweb.int/library/documents/2006/care-africa-01oct.pdf.

Chu, Henry. 2006. "Hope Has Withered for India's Farmers: As the Nation Touts Its High Growth Economy, the Poor Who Work the Land Commit Suicide." *Los Angeles Times,* 11 August. www.latimes.com/news/nationworld/world/la-fg-farmers 11aug11,0,203873.story?track=tothtml.

Copenhagen Consensus Center. 2006. Copenhagen Consensus. www.copenhagencon sensus.com/Default.aspx?ID=675.

Eckholm, Erik P. 1982. *Down to Earth: Environment and Human Needs.* New York: W.W. Norton.

FAO (Food and Agriculture Organization of the United Nations). 2006. *The Right to Food Guidelines: Information Papers and Case Studies.* Rome: FAO. www.fao.org/ docs/eims/upload/214344/RtFG_Eng_draft_03.pdf.

FAO Committee on World Food Security. 2001. *Fostering the Political Will to Fight Hunger.* Rome: FAO CFS. www.fao.org/docrep/meeting/003/Y0024E.htm.

Frontline/World. 2006. *Seeds of Suicide* (film). "Behind the Lens: Interview with Chad Heeter." www.pbs.org/frontlineworld/rough/2005/07/seeds_of_suicidlinks .html.

Garrett, Laurie. 2007. "The Challenge of Global Health." *Foreign Affairs,* January– February. www.foreignaffairs.org/20070101faessay86103/laurie-garrett/the-chal lenge-of-global-health.html.

Heaver, Richard. 2005. *Strengthening Country Commitment to Human Development: Lessons from Nutrition.* Washington, DC: World Bank Directions in Development Series. www-wds.worldbank.org/external/default/main?pagePK=64193027&pi PK=64187937&theSitePK=523679&menuPK=64154159&searchMenu PK=64187552&theSitePK=523679&entityID=000090341_20050228153225&sea rchMenuPK=64187552&theSitePK=523679.

IFPRI (International Food Policy Research Institute). 2005. "Building Local Skills and Knowledge for Food Security." *IFPRI Forum,* December. www.ifpri.org/pubs/ newsletters/ifpriforum/if200512.asp.

Jonsson, Urban. 2007. "Child Malnutrition: From the Global Protein Crisis to a Violation of Human Rights." In *Sustainable Development in a Globalized World: Studies in Development, Security and Culture,* ed. Björn Hettne. London: Palgrave Macmillan.

Kates, Jennifer, and Eric Lief. 2006. *International Assistance for HIV/AIDS in the Developing World: Taking Stock of the G8, Other Donor Governments and the European Commission.* Oakland, CA: Kaiser Family Foundation. www.synergyaids.com/doc uments/Int%20AsstHivAidsDevlpWrld.pdf.

Kelly, Erin. 2004. "Human Rights as Foreign Policy Imperatives." In *The Ethics of Assistance: Morality and the Distant Needy,* ed. Deen K. Chatterjee. Cambridge: Cambridge University Press.

Kent, George. 2006. "School Meals as Entitlements." In *Food for Education: Experts Seminar, Reviewing the Evidence.* World Food Programme, Rome, 8–9 May 2006. Rome: WFP, 46–57. www.schoolsandhealth.org/download-docs/FoodforEducation/ SF%20Research%20Seminar%20Report.pdf.

Labonte, Ronald, Ted Schrecker, David Sanders, and Wilma Meeus. 2004. *Fatal Indifference: The G8, Africa and Global Health.* Landsdowne, South Africa: University of Cape Town Press. www.idrc.ca/en/ev-45682-201-1-DO_TOPIC.html.

Lomborg, Bjørn, ed. 2004. *Global Crises, Global Solutions.* Cambridge: Cambridge University Press.

McGovern, George. 2001. *The Third Freedom: Ending Hunger in Our Time.* New York: Simon & Schuster.

Navarro, Vicente. 2007. "What Is a National Health Policy?" *International Journal of Health Services* 37: 1–14.

Nussbaum, Martha. 2006. "Capabilities, Human Rights and the Universal Declaration." In *Human Rights in the World Community: Issues and Action,* third edition, ed. Richard P. Claude and Burns H. Weston, 27–37. Philadelphia: University of Pennsylvania Press.

OECD (Organization for Economic Cooperation and Development). 2006. Graph. www.oecd.org/dataoecd/17/39/23664717.gif.

Reuters Foundation. 2006. "World Bank Sees Health Aid Needs at Least $25 Bln/yr." 25 May. http://today.reuters.com/news/newsarticle.aspx?type=healthNews& storyid=2006-05-25T195234Z_01_N25332576_RTRUKOC_0_US-ECONOMY-HEALTH-WORLDBANK.xml&src=rss.

Richter, Judith. 2001. *Holding Corporations Accountable: Corporate Conduct, International Codes, and Citizen Action.* London and New York, Zed Books.

Rosenberg, Tina. 2006. "The Scandal of 'Poor People's Diseases.'" *New York Times,* 29 March.

Sen, Amartya. 2000. *Development as Freedom.* New York: Alfred A. Knopf.

Shiva, Vandana. 2004. "The Suicide Economy of Corporate Globalization." *Znet.* www.countercurrents.org/glo-shiva050404.htm.

Tomaševski, Katarina. 2006. *The State of the Right to Education Worldwide—Free or Fee: 2006 Global Report.* Copenhagen. www.katarinatomasevski.com/.

Townsend, Joseph. 1786. *A Dissertation on the Poor Laws.* http://socserv2.socsci.mc master.ca/~econ/ugcm/3ll3/townsend/poorlaw.html.

UN Department of Economic and Social Affairs. 2006. *The Millennium Development Goals Report 2006.* New York: DESA. http://mdgs.un.org/unsd/mdg/Resources/Static/ Products/Progress2006/MDGReport2006.pdf.

UN ECOSOC. (United Nations Economic and Social Council). 1999. *Substantive Issues Arising in the Implementation of the International Covenant on Economic, Social and Cultural Rights:* General Comment 12 (Twentieth Session, 1999) The Right to Adequate Food (art. 11). Geneva: ECOSOC E/C.12/1999/5. www.unhchr.ch/tbs/doc.nsf/ MasterFrameView/3d02758c707031d58025677f003b73b9?Opendocument.

———. 2006. *Review of Trends and Perspectives in Funding for Development Cooperation: Note by the Secretary General.* Geneva: ECOSOC E/2006/60. 8 May. http://daccess dds.un.org/doc/UNDOC/GEN/N06/341/56/PDF/N0634156.pdf?OpenElement.

UNICEF (United Nations Children's Fund). 2006. *Progress for Children: A Report Card on Nutrition* 4 (May). New York: UNICEF. www.unicef.org/progressforchildren/ 2006n4/.

———. 2007. End Childhood Hunger and Undernutrition Initiative. http://endingchild hunger.blogspot.com/.

UN Millennium Project. 2005a. *Halving Hunger: It Can Be Done.* Task Force on Hunger. London: Earthscan/Millennium Project. www.unmillenniumproject.org/reports/tf _hunger.htm.

———. 2005b. *Investing in Development: A Practical Plan to Achieve the Millennium Development Goals.* London: Earthscan/Millennium Project. www.unmillenniumproject .org/reports/.

UN OCHA. (United Nations Office for the Coordination of Humanitarian Affairs). 2006. *The Consolidated Appeals Process (CAP).* http://ochaonline.un.org/cap2005/ webpage.asp?Nav=_about_en&Site=_about&Lang=en.

UN OHCHR. (United Nations Office of the High Commissioner for Human Rights). 2002. *Handbook on National Human Rights Plans of Actions. Professional Training Series No. 10.* New York and Geneva: OHCHR. 29 August. www.unhchr.ch/pdf/nhrap .pdf.

———. 2005. *Economic, Social and Cultural Rights: Handbook for National Human Rights Institutions. Professional Training Series No. 12.* New York and Geneva: UNHCHR www.ohchr.org/english/about/publications/docs/train12_e.pdf.

UN OHRLLS (UN Office of the High Representative for the Least Developed Countries, Landlocked Developing Countries and the Small Island Developing States). 2007. "CCA/UNDAF/PRSP." www.un.org/special-rep/ohrlls/ohrlls/ohrlls%20man date.htm.

UN SCN (United Nations System Standing Committee on Nutrition). 2006a. Home page. www.unsystem.org/scn/.

———. 2006b. *Action Plan 2006–2010.* www.unsystem.org/scn/Publications/html/man date.html.

Vesely, James. 2006. "The President, the Billionaire and the War against Poverty." *Seattle Times*, 18 June. http://seattletimes.nwsource.com/html/opinion/2003066785 _vesely18.html.

WHO (World Health Organization). 2006. *Planning Guide for National Implementation of the Global Strategy for Infant and Young Child Feeding (Draft)*. Geneva: WHO. www.who.int/child-adolescent-health/publications/NUTRITION/Planning _guide.htm.

World Bank. 2006. *Repositioning Nutrition as Central to Development: A Strategy for Large-Scale Action*. Washington, DC: World Bank. http://web.worldbank.org/WBSITE/ EXTERNAL/TOPICS/EXTHEALTHNUTRITIONANDPOPULATION/EXTNUTRI TION/0,,contentMDK:20613959~menuPK:282591~pagePK:210058~piPK:210062 ~theSitePK:282575,00.html.

10

Recommendations

*Mike Brady, Marc J. Cohen, Federica Donati, Arun Gupta,
George Kent, Rolf Künnemann, Michael C. Latham, Anitha
Ramanna, Sandra Ratjen, Margret Vidar, and S. Vivek*

In this book we have sought to clarify the obligations of the global community in relation to the human right to adequate food and nutrition and other related human rights. We have done so in order to improve the effectiveness of efforts to address all major forms of malnutrition. The book is a project of the Task Force on International Dimensions of the Right to Food of the Working Group on Nutrition, Ethics, and Human Rights of the United Nations System Standing Committee on Nutrition (SCN). SCN is a multistakeholder body, bringing together representatives of UN agencies and other intergovernmental organizations that focus on nutrition, national governments from both developed and developing countries, and a broad range of civil society organizations.

Many of us work for agencies or organizations that participate actively in SCN. However, we write here in our personal capacities, and are not expressing the views of our respective agencies or organizations.

When we refer to the *global community*, we mean all people of the world. That community has clear moral responsibilities and legal obligations to ensure the realization of the human right to adequate food and related human rights. To date, however, actions have not matched rhetoric about cutting hunger in half by 2015; indeed major forms of malnutrition have increased in much of the developing world over the last few years.

Malnutrition is clearly a global problem that does not recognize national boundaries, as when poor and hungry people flee across borders to escape violence or natural disasters. Global problems require global solutions, but the current system of international relations, put in place over 350 years ago, continues to vest all authority in the sovereign nation-state. In today's world, more than half of the 100 largest economies are those of transnational firms, global civil society networks play an increasingly important role in shaping policy, and international nongovernmental organizations (NGOs) are major actors in relief and development.

A new approach to the hunger problem is emerging, based on the premise that there is a human right to adequate food, and that it must be taken seriously. The SCN and its members have facilitated this new thinking, and several countries have been showing how this right can be recognized and realized.

We have a number of specific recommendations with respect to the role that the global community should play in implementing rights-based plans to eradicate malnutrition in all its forms. We believe that these will lead to significant action toward the realization of the human right to adequate food and a world free from hunger. We focus these recommendations on seven broad areas:

- Global-level state obligations
- Intergovernmental organizations
- Nonstate transnational actors
- Humanitarian assistance
- Nutrition of mothers, infants, and preschool children
- Nutrition of school-age children
- Access to plant genetic resources for food and agriculture
- Food sovereignty

GLOBAL-LEVEL STATE OBLIGATIONS

Our global food system is just that, *global*. We need to focus on how to manage this global system, and establish new institutional arrangements that are needed for the global governance of food and agriculture, particularly as it relates to the human right to adequate food.

It is up to all people, acting collectively through their states, to devise elements of global governance of food and agriculture, especially as they relate to the human right to adequate food. It is now primarily the United Nations and its associated agencies that serve these functions. Action is frequently taken in the name of the global community, particularly on matters of security and trade, and, to some extent, human rights. If the global community can take responsibility for issues relating to security, there is no reason why it cannot take comparable responsibility for issues such as health and nutrition.

Moreover, the International Covenant on Economic, Social, and Cultural Rights (ICESCR), a core instrument of international human rights law that is binding upon states parties, creates global obligations alongside national duties. In Article 2, it calls upon states to act individually and "through international assistance and co-operation, especially economic and technical" to achieve the progressive realization of the rights that it specifies. Article 11 on the right to an adequate standard of living, including the right to adequate food, reiterates the call for international cooperation; this is the only right for which the ICESCR reiterates its general point regarding global obligations.

The duty of richer states to assist poorer states in the progressive realization of the right to adequate food and other economic, social, and cultural rights is widely recognized. However, the covenant does not define any particular level of cooperation necessary to fulfill this obligation. States can argue that any participation in bilateral cooperation or multilateral development agencies does this.

Nevertheless, many experts on international human rights law argue that the obligation to devote the "maximum of available resources" specified in Article 2 of the ICESCR applies not only to states acting within their own territory, but also with regard to international cooperation. Based on this interpretation, the global community has an obligation to devote a greater share of its resources to international development and direct a larger proportion of those resources to promoting economic, social, and cultural rights.

Since 1970, the global community has repeatedly reaffirmed the principle that wealthy nations should devote at least 0.7 percent of their national income to development assistance, a figure cited in Guideline 19.12 of the right-to-food guidelines. However, this pledge is not considered binding, and most donor states have strongly resisted the creation of a firm target for the level of assistance. In any event, the member states of the Organization for Economic Cooperation and Development, which account for over 90 percent of all development assistance resources, have never collectively provided more than half of the 0.7 percent figure in any given year. A few individual states regularly meet or exceed the target, notably the Scandinavian countries and the Netherlands.

It is desirable to have greater consensus on the meaning of the duty to assist and how the requirement to expend the maximum of available resources relates to it. Just as states' obligations are calibrated to their capacities, the expectations placed on donor countries and on the global community as a whole also should be calibrated to their capacities.

There does seem to be a movement toward greater recognition of general and specific obligations of states to cooperate for the furtherance of human rights everywhere and at least a general obligation of those states that can afford to do so to provide technical and material assistance to other states. Based on this emerging understanding, the special rapporteur on the right to food of the UN Human Rights Council argues that in order for states to fully comply with their obligations on the right to food, they must respect, protect, and support the fulfillment of the right to food of people living in other territories.

The obligation to respect is a minimum obligation that requires states to ensure that their policies and practices do not lead to violations of the right to food or undermine nutrition status in other countries. This obligation does not require any resources to be provided; it is simply the principle to do no harm. For example, states should refrain from trade-related practices such as trade barriers and the dumping of foodstuffs that undermine the right to food elsewhere. It is estimated that up to 15 million Mexican farmers and their families, many from indigenous communities, may lose their livelihoods as a result of the North American Free Trade Agreement and unfettered competition with subsidized U.S. corn. Their income has fallen to such an extent that it jeopardizes their nutrition security.

At the 2005 World Summit marking the sixtieth anniversary of the founding of the United Nations, the global community asserted its right to provide protection to people suffering violations of their human rights. The UN Security Council reaffirmed this right in 2006. Thus, at least under some circumstances, the international community has a responsibility to protect human rights, including the right to adequate food, even if this means intervening in the territory of a sovereign state.

The obligation to support the fulfillment of the right to food requires states, depending on the availability of resources, to facilitate the realization of the right to food in other countries and to provide the necessary aid when required. Developing states that do not possess the necessary resources for the full realization of the right to food should actively seek international assistance, and wealthier states have a responsibility to respond.

We recommend the following steps to further clarify and solidify emerging understandings:

- The UN Committee on Economic, Social and Cultural Rights (CESCR) should clarify the external obligations of states parties to the International Covenant on Economic, Social and Cultural Rights (ICESCR) by conducting a Day of Discussion on Obligations of the Global Community and preparing a corresponding General Comment.
- The Committee should then monitor the global community through the states parties to the ICESCR. The committee should ensure that the global obligations of reporting nations are carried out through their bilateral development assistance programs, through their participation in global agencies, and through specific action plans that they help to formulate and implement.
- Civil society organizations should deliver parallel reports to the CESCR on the extraterritorial obligations of states with respect to the right to food.

- The special rapporteur on the right to food should increasingly scrutinize states parties' obligations to cooperate in realizing the right to food at the global level.
- Relevant international forums should be called upon to discuss and negotiate extraterritorial state obligations to provide firmer content to the obligation to cooperate internationally in the realization of the right to food under the ICESCR, including the obligations to expend the maximum resources and to respect, protect, and fulfill.
- States parties to the ICESCR should adopt an Optional Protocol that provides a complaint mechanism at the international level.
- Governments and NGOs concerned with food and nutrition should promote multiparty, multilevel planning to formulate joint strategies for dealing with nutrition problems, whether on a local, national, regional, or global scale; the SCN should play a catalytic and facilitating role in this process.
- The SCN should promote implementation of existing international obligations to respect, protect, and fulfill the right to food and support further standard setting to clarify obligations and further develop international law.

INTERGOVERNMENTAL ORGANIZATIONS

We insist that international governmental organizations should be understood to represent the global community—that is, all the world's people, and not just their governments—and act on its behalf. States also should act to protect the global community by ensuring that international organizations do no harm with respect to the right to adequate food.

States have the same human rights obligations in whatever context they are working, whether voting in the UN General Assembly, the Security Council, or the governing bodies of the World Bank, the International Monetary Fund (IMF), the Food and Agriculture Organization of the United Nations (FAO), the World Health Organization (WHO), or the World Trade Organization (WTO). Similarly, states should bear in mind their human rights obligations during bilateral and multilateral trade and other negotiations. It can be argued that intergovernmental bodies as such and their secretariats have independent human rights obligations on the basis that human rights are generally universally recognized and that most members of the UN and other intergovernmental organizations have extensive human rights obligations.

The obligation to respect implies that states should refrain from making decisions within the WTO, IMF, World Bank, or any other international agencies that can lead to violations of the right to food in other states. Similarly, the duty to protect requires states to inhibit international agencies from taking actions that result in violations. This suggests that structural adjustment programs and other forms of cooperation promoted by the World Bank, IMF, and other international and regional financial institutions should contribute to creating an enabling environment for the realization of human rights, including the right to food, and should not undermine those rights.

If trade dispute mechanisms were empowered and instructed to take global human rights obligations into account, such obligations could be effectively enforced on a par with international trade rules. Human rights obligations should be regarded as UN Charter rules and therefore of higher rank than other international rules.

We recommend that:

- States should explicitly recognize human rights law as having higher status than other rules of international law, such as global and regional trade agreements.
- The rules of the WTO should be amended so that dispute settlement mechanisms are obliged to take the human right to adequate food into account in the settlement of trade disputes.
- All relevant intergovernmental organizations, including the United Nations, its specialized agencies, and the WTO, should adopt human rights provisions and establish recourse mechanisms to enable complaints of violations of the right to food to be addressed by an independent body, with adequate redress provided in case a violation is found.
- Scholars should continue to research and clarify what obligations intergovernmental organizations have and should have, and how they could be held to account for nonfulfillment of their obligations.
- Civil society organizations should encourage the UN human rights system to mainstream the right to adequate food and the related extraterritorial obligations.
- Civil society organizations should press all intergovernmental organizations involved with food and nutrition to respect, protect, and fulfill the right to food.

NONSTATE TRANSNATIONAL ACTORS

Experts on economic, social, and cultural rights increasingly agree that states have obligations to respect and protect the right to food in other countries that extend to the regulation of all agents under the states. This extends to the regulation of all agents under the state's jurisdiction—such as transnational corporations and international NGOs—so as to prevent them from abusing the human rights of individuals in other states. Globalization increasingly means that some of these nonstate actors are more powerful than at least some states.

A separate legal question is whether nonstate actors such as corporations and NGOs can be held to have independent human rights obligations. There is a minority school of thought that argues that they do have such obligations. Some say that in light of the failure of both the home states and the states in which they operate to adequately hold such parties to account, NGOs and corporations must be viewed as having independent human rights obligations.

Corporations rival the power of governments in terms of their economic power and often infringe on the right to food and other human rights. The case of the marketing practices of infant formula firms is well known, as is the role of aggressive marketing of energy-dense, nutrient-poor foods to children and adolescents in creating the global pandemic of obesity. For their own legitimacy in a globalized world, corporations may sooner or later have to accept *global* regulation.

A poor state may be tempted not to regulate corporate and individual conduct that infringes on individuals' right to food. If it did, it might suffer losses of foreign exchange. Other countries may suffer from such high levels of corruption as to make them both unwilling and unable to take action.

The obligation to protect requires states to ensure that their own citizens and companies, as well as other third parties subject to their jurisdiction, including transnational corporations and international NGOs, do not interfere with the realization of the right to food in other states. This puts a duty on the sending state to regulate its corporations and other nonstate actors in order to protect the people of receiving states. This obligation of the state to control its constituents complements the obligations of receiving states to protect their people from outside agents. The obligation to protect should be understood to hold not only within states but extraterritorially.

National governments have a duty to protect their people and people living in other countries against negative impacts on the right to food of third parties. From this perspective, governments are responsible for regulating and proscribing the activities of corporations that abuse human rights.

There is a need for a global regulatory system capable of holding transnational corporations to account through new or reformed international institutions. UN bodies with a food and health mandate should set global standards in consultation with relevant parties, not through negotiation with business interests where the right to food might be traded off against financial concerns. Experience with the International Code of Marketing of Breastmilk Substitutes, and subsequent, relevant resolutions of the World Health Assembly (WHA), provide a useful model as to how to develop standards.

The global community should introduce effective monitoring systems, but these are unlikely to ensure compliance in the absence of an enforcement capacity. This would require global incorporation, where transnational firms with sales above a certain level and of a certain territorial extent would register with a global body and abide by and report on certain terms of reference, such as respect for the right to adequate food. Only through the global community's collective action will it be possible to establish checks and balances to protect the right to adequate food, such as external auditing and legal obligations on named company directors to ensure the accuracy of data. The global regulatory authority could also accept complaints from other stakeholders, including NGOs, and conduct investigations, bringing cases before an international court if breaches are found. Global incorporation would permit various actors, such as company insurers, to hold the corporation accountable by means other than legal action.

It is appropriate that business interests express their views during the process of developing global standards. But it is essential that regulations are developed under the auspices of bodies whose primary concern is the right to food, rather than trade and company profits, so that effective global regulations are put into place and enforced, even if companies object to them.

The global community should take responsibility for introducing monitoring mechanisms at the global level to ensure that company self-monitoring and national measures are effective, and to provide protection when they are not. Doing so does not usurp the power of the nation-state, but recognizes that the transnational nature of certain business interests requires global, as well as national, regulation.

The global community could also ensure that states take action to hold their corporations to account. Punitive tariffs could be levied on imports from a country found to allow its corporations to violate agreed standards. This would serve to transfer the wealth that is unfairly gained.

We recommend that:

- The WHO, FAO, the special rapporteur on the right to food, and other UN bodies with a focus on food or health should develop proposals for systems to regulate companies' impact on the right to food. These should include the creation of a UN global authority for regulating transnational corporations, to be tasked with implementing the proposals. The proposals should be determined through a process of *consultation* with health experts, NGOs, and business interests, not a process of *negotiation*. Endorsement of the proposals should be sought from the World Health Assembly as the world's highest health policy–setting body.

- The newly created UN global regulatory authority should specify the information required from corporations to enable reporting on their impact. It should develop criteria to specify the corporations subject to its regulations based on turnover and territorial extent and compile a list of corporations meeting the criteria.
- The global authority should accept complaints from NGOs and government authorities about breaches of human rights norms relating to the right to food, and it should conduct transparent investigations, publishing the results of its findings.
- National governments, acting individually and also through the proposed global authority, should examine the basis of incorporation of businesses within their territories, and consider introducing a legal requirement to respect the right to food and other human rights. Responsibilities for reporting and the duties of directors in this regard should be considered. Present standards used should be shared through the global authority with a view to identifying core provisions for a globally incorporated company to be registered with and monitored by the global authority. These provisions can also form the basis for minimum national standards.
- NGOs should continue to monitor the impact of corporations on the right to food and call for action at the global level for meaningful monitoring and enforcement of standards to ensure that the right to food is respected. NGOs should also continue to compile case studies and to register complaints with appropriate national, regional, and global bodies.
- The special representative of the secretary-general on the issue of human rights and transnational corporations and other business enterprises should pay particular attention to questions of production, processing, and marketing of food, with a view to further clarifying the responsibilities of corporations with regard to the right to adequate food and the right to the highest attainable standard of health.
- The special representative should also focus on the impact of the merchandising strategies of the food industry on food safety, food quality, and the nutritional status of children and adolescents.
- States and international organizations should act to protect consumers from harmful practices of food enterprises, and ensure food safety through systems such as the WHO-FAO Codex Alimentarius Commission. International initiatives to control obesity and to control the marketing of food to children fall into this category.
- Academics and scholars should continue to research and clarify what obligations transnational corporations have and how they should be held to account for nonfulfillment of these obligations.

- The SCN should endorse the above recommendations, and it should facilitate the development of proposals for the UN global authority for regulating transnational corporations.

HUMANITARIAN ASSISTANCE

In principle, there is broad consensus that the global community must come to the aid of people in need of assistance due to humanitarian emergencies. There have been some important developments aimed at basing humanitarian assistance on impartial needs assessment rather than politics. It may be argued that the global "responsibility to protect" agreed to at the 2005 World Summit includes protection from violations of the right to food, particularly when the result is gross, systematic, and large-scale hunger. But practice falls far short of principle, as the global community has repeatedly failed to respond adequately to UN Consolidated and Flash Appeals for humanitarian assistance. While appeals for food aid usually do better than those for health, agricultural, human rights, and protection assistance, the humanitarian aid system is not based on the principle of the right to assistance and a global duty to provide that assistance. Instead, it relies on the willingness of donors to provide resources on a case-by-case basis, with politics and media attention strongly influencing outcomes.

According to the CESCR in its General Comment 12, states parties to the ICESCR have a joint and individual responsibility to cooperate in providing disaster relief and humanitarian assistance in times of emergency, including assistance to refugees and internally displaced persons. Each state should contribute to this task in accordance with its ability. Priority in food aid should be given to the most vulnerable populations. Food aid should be provided in ways that do not adversely affect local producers and local markets and should be organized in ways that facilitate the return to self-reliance of the beneficiaries through production or procurement. Food aid commodities must be safe and culturally acceptable to the recipient population. States parties should refrain from embargoes and other measures that endanger conditions for food production and access to food in other states. They should also refrain from the use of food as an instrument of political and economic pressure.

We recommend that:

- The global community should align humanitarian assistance practice more closely to the committee's interpretation of the International Covenant on Economic, Social and Cultural Rights.
- Member states should incorporate human rights principles into the Food Aid Convention, the global treaty governing food aid.

NUTRITION OF MOTHERS, INFANTS, AND PRESCHOOL CHILDREN

The global community should help national governments in their efforts to ensure the well-being of mothers, infants, and preschool children.

Timely initiation of breastfeeding, exclusive breastfeeding during the first six months of a child's life, and continued breastfeeding for the next six months and beyond dramatically reduce child deaths. Improved child survival has a direct bearing on a country's national income. Nevertheless, such community/family-based interventions do not receive the attention or the financial resources they need to ensure their universalization.

We recommend that:

- States should create a Minimum Essential Program (MEP) as a part of the progressive realization of the right to adequate food for infants. This would provide a clear-cut program on implementation of a minimum and essential service and support package for pregnant and lactating women. This program would provide all women access to accurate information on optimal feeding practices, skilled counseling, and practical support at birth and later. Formally employed women would receive six months of paid maternity leave, and low-income women employed outside the formal sector would receive financial support. National legislation would establish the MEP, and accountability mechanisms would be established to ensure that families receive the support to which they are entitled.
- The global community should create and finance a Global Fund for Infant Nutrition and Survival to support national plans to scale up key breastfeeding interventions to prevent infant deaths.
- States parties' reports under the Convention on the Rights of the Child should explicitly address infants' right to adequate food and nutrition.
- The United Nations Children's Fund (UNICEF) should take responsibility for developing global coordination plans.
- The International Baby Food Action Network (IBFAN) and the World Alliance for Breastfeeding Action (WABA) should be given a mandate for monitoring, evaluation, and capacity building for program implementation, given these international NGOs' recognized expertise in these areas.

Addressing certain infections could make a significant contribution to reducing malnutrition. Intestinal parasites infect some 2 billion people, mainly in developing countries, and contribute to malnutrition and anemia. Measles is seldom fatal in developed countries, but it is an important cause of mortality in malnourished populations. Malaria causes over 1 million deaths a year in Africa alone. Established public health measures could significantly reduce the impact of these three infections on health and nutrition, especially among children. Some developing countries already have implemented effective programs to address one or more of these health problems, thereby reducing malnutrition. However, global action is necessary to overcome inequities in access to health care and services. There is a need for well-designed global programs, based on the human rights approach, to combat these infections.

We recommend that:

- Concerned states from the South and the North, acting together, should bring a resolution to the World Health Assembly that calls on all countries to follow specified guidelines to deworm infected populations, eradicate measles through immunization efforts, and ensure good treatment and insecticide-treated bed nets for all at risk of malaria.
- Parallel with this WHA resolution, the World Health Organization should establish a unit to assist countries with control measures, and capabilities to provide technical expertise and funding, and to ensure monitoring and surveillance.
- WHO should hold high-level talks with UNICEF and the World Bank to elicit their support and active involvement.
- WHO should obtain pledges of assistance in this effort from major international NGOs currently involved in health and nutrition activities in developing countries, and also from foundations and the private sector.

NUTRITION OF SCHOOL-AGE CHILDREN

School feeding programs improve school attendance dramatically, help boost female enrollment (which is known to lead to intergenerational improvements in nutrition), protect children from hunger in the classroom, and have a strong impact on educational achievement.

We recommend the development of a global treaty on school feeding to better enable the mobilization of financial resources. This has the potential to foster political will and public participation that can make the crucial difference between success and failure. There is scope for international cooperation at different levels for a rights-based global school feeding program. Three key domains for cooperation are cost sharing, program design, and quality enhancement. Where national and local governments take the initiative to set up good programs, the international community should provide assistance in developing complementary school health programs.

ACCESS TO PLANT GENETIC RESOURCES
FOR FOOD AND AGRICULTURE

Farmers and plant breeders require access to plant genetic resources, as they form the building blocks of agricultural innovations upon which continued food supplies depend. The world needs to continuously increase crop productivity and to develop new varieties to face current and future biological, environmental, and sociopolitical stresses. Plant genetic resources are crucial for sustainable food security. They form the basis of farmers' livelihoods, and consumers in both rich and poor countries indirectly depend on farmers' and breeders' access to these resources. Conserving plant genetic diversity is also important for effective response to humanitarian emergencies, which can destroy local seed systems. However, both the products and processes of agricultural research are increasingly subject to patents and other forms of intellectual property rights (IPR) protection. Mechanisms must be developed for making plant genetic resources, seeds, crops, and technologies essential for food security easily available. The global community must maintain a fair, equitable, and reasonable balance between public and private interests and ensure public access to seeds in order to realize the human right to adequate food.

We recommend that:

- The governing body of the International Treaty on Plant Genetic Resources for Food and Agriculture (ITPGRFA) should become the global community's principal forum for ensuring public access to seeds as a means of realizing the human right to adequate food. Maintaining public access will require negotiations among states parties to coordinate and harmonize the various relevant international agreements, including the WTO's Agreement on Trade Related Aspects of Intellectual Property Rights (TRIPS) and the Convention on Biological Diversity, which establishes sovereign national rights over plant genetic resources. Discussion should be transparent and involve input from a wide array of nonstate stakeholders.
- States parties to the ITPGRFA should ensure that the treaty's Multilateral System, which ensures facilitated access to substantial amounts of germplasm, operates effectively.
- States parties to the treaty should effectively address the question of intellectual property rights and the Multilateral System's materials. One approach is to ensure that this material and any derived innovations remain free from IPR. Alternatively, in implementing the treaty's provision requiring payments to the Multilateral System when breeders commercialize derived innovations, the governing body could charge a substantially higher fee if breeders seek IPR. The resulting royalty revenue could

fund public gene bank maintenance and provide benefits to the farm communities that originally developed parent crop varieties. A variation on this option would prohibit IPR protection of derived varieties in developing countries.

- The global community should provide the ITPGRFA governing body with adequate resources to challenge IPR claims when necessary and to monitor commercialization and royalty payments.
- The treaty governing body should become a vehicle to promote cooperation among gene banks, firms, NGOs, farmers, and governments to utilize germplasm effectively to advance food security. The governing body could also promote collaboration and sharing of information resources, perhaps including trading of patents (patent swaps) between parties, to produce crops and varieties useful for food security.
- The governing body should develop models on how to effectively implement IPR and Farmers' Rights. It is important to find ways to resolve the tensions arising from various international agreements that are taking resources out of the public domain. Case studies of how various countries are attempting to implement the relevant international agreements, and the lessons learned, could be disseminated globally.

FOOD SOVEREIGNTY

As the world food system globalizes, many of the world's food producers are becoming ever more marginalized. Consumers' right to food cannot be realized at the expense of the right to an adequate standard of living of the world's small farmers and farm workers, regardless of the country in which they live.

Many civil society groups, including the global association of farmers' organizations, La Via Campesina, have rallied around the notion of "food sovereignty" as a means to ensure sustainable rural livelihoods. This concept centers on the idea that local small-farm agriculture should receive priority in national policies and that global trade agreements and aid policies must not undermine family farms in either developed or developing countries.

We recommend that:

- States parties to the ICESCR should ensure that their domestic agricultural policies, development cooperation programs, and international trade policies do not undermine smallholder farming in other countries.
- Intergovernmental organizations concerned with food, agriculture, trade, and macroeconomic policies should assess their programs, advice, and assistance conditionalities to ensure that they do not adversely affect rural livelihoods.

CONCLUSION

If the global community is ever going to seriously address the problems of malnutrition in all their forms, it will need to devise good rights-based plans. The so-called global strategies that have been formulated to date, offering little more than vague recommendations, are nowhere near what is needed. The recommendations in this chapter could serve as the building blocks of such a plan.

A serious strategy is a detailed plan of stepwise action under which designated actors using specific resources can be realistically expected to arrive at a concrete target within a specified time. It has a management body to run it and resources to carry it out. It monitors not only outcomes but also the associations between actions and outcomes. When the outcomes begin to veer off course, the managers should monitor that deviation and bump the effort back on track to ensure that the target will be reached.

It is not enough to point to national responsibilities and hope that national governments will do what needs to be done. The global community itself must make serious commitments and, together with all other actors, must work out each participant's particular roles in a clear way. The recommendations offered here suggest some promising paths.

Index

Page references in *italics* indicate a figure or table on the designated page.

About the Contributors

Author affiliations are provided here only for purposes of identification. In this book, the contributors speak for themselves not for their organizations.

Mike Brady is a specialist in monitoring the baby food industry against marketing standards adopted by the World Health Assembly and provides training to policy makers and nongovernmental organizations on the standards. He has been employed as campaigns and networking coordinator at Baby Milk Action, the UK member of the International Baby Food Action Network (IBFAN) for over ten years. See www.babymilkaction.org.

Marc J. Cohen is interim leader of the research program on policy processes in food security and nutrition at the International Food Policy Research Institute, and a Research Fellow in the Food Consumption and Nutrition Division. His research focuses on the role of legislation and legal systems in food security, global humanitarian aid policy, conflict and food security, community empowerment and food security, and the right to adequate food. He is also a professorial lecturer in international development at the School of Advanced International Studies, Johns Hopkins University. See www.ifpri.org.

Federica Donati is human rights officer at the Office of the High Commissioner for Human Rights. She currently supports the mandate of the United Nations special rapporteur on the right to food.

Arun Gupta, a pediatrician turned child health activist from India, works as national coordinator of the Breastfeeding Promotion Network of India (BPNI) and regional coordinator of International Baby Food Action Network

(IBFAN). He has a strong interest in infant nutrition and survival, human rights, and breastfeeding. His organizational websites are www.bpni.org, www.worldbreastfeedingtrends.org, and www.ibfan-asiapacific.org.

George Kent is professor of political science at the University of Hawai'i. He works on human rights, international relations, peace, development, and environmental issues, with a special focus on nutrition and children. His website is at www2.hawaii.edu/~kent.

Rolf Künnemann is the human rights director of FIAN International and coordinates FIAN's program on extraterritorial obligations. He has been involved in organizing FIAN in Asia, Europe, and Latin America and has been a resource person in a number of international expert seminars on economic, social, and cultural rights. See www.fian.org.

Michael C. Latham is graduate school professor of international nutrition at Cornell University. He is a medical doctor with degrees in public health and tropical medicine. He has worked extensively in nonindustrialized countries in Asia, Latin America, and particularly in Africa. His research publications cover a broad range, including nutrition and infection, tropical child health, and infant feeding. He can be contacted at MCL6@hawaii.edu.

Anitha Ramanna is a lecturer in the Department of Politics and Public Administration, University of Pune, India. Her research interests are in the areas of intellectual property rights and agriculture, farmers' rights, biodiversity issues in developing countries, and policy making on genetically modified crops.

Sandra Ratjen is an international jurist and the head of the UN desk at the FIAN International Secretariat. Her main fields of work are monitoring state policies related to the right to food, justiciability of the right to food, and extraterritorial obligations. See www.fian.org.

Margret Vidar is human rights advisor at the Right to Food Unit in the Food and Agriculture Organization of the United Nations. She works on follow-up to the Voluntary Guidelines to Support the Progressive Realization of the Right to Adequate Food in the Context of National Food Security, and human rights–based approaches to food security and implementation of the right to food in national policies and legislation. Website: www.fao.org/righttofood/en/index.html.

S. Vivek is a student in the Social Sciences program at Syracuse University in upstate New York. He is also closely associated with the Right to Food Campaign in India.

TODA
INSTITUTE
for Global Peace and Policy Research

TODA Institute Recently Published
Books on Global Peace and Policy

America and the World: The Double Bind, edited by Majid Tehranian and Kevin P. Clements

Crossing the Red Line, edited by Mehrangiz Kar

Fear of Persecution: Global Human Rights, International Law, and Human Well-Being, by James White and Anthony Marsella

Globalization and Identity: Cultural Diversity, Religion, and Citizenship, edited by Majid Tehranian and B. Jeannie Lum

Worlds on the Move: Globalization, Migration, and Cultural Security, edited by Jonathan Friedman and Shalini Randeria

Eurasia: A New Peace Agenda, edited by Michael Intriligator, Alexander Nikitin, and Majid Tehranian

Beyond Reconstruction in Afghanistan: Lessons from Development Experience, edited by John D. Montgomery and Dennis A. Rondinelli

Democratizing Global Media: One World, Many Struggles, edited by Robert Hackett and Yuezhi Zhao

The *Toda Institute for Global Peace and Policy Research* promotes peace initiatives at national, regional, and international levels by bringing peace researchers, policymakers, and community activists into communication and collaboration on selected projects in conflict resolution. The Institute encourages and proposes concrete strategies translating into action, focusing on four themes for international dialogue: (1) Human Security and Global Governance, (2) Human Rights and Global Ethics, (3) Social Justice and Global Economy, and (4) Cultural Identity and Global Citizenship.

For more information, please visit www.toda.org